P9-APJ-095

THE EXPERIMENTAL PSYCHOLOGY OF ORIGINAL THINKING

WILBERT S. RAY
Cognitive Operations Laboratory
Bethany College

THE EXPERIMENTAL PSYCHOLOGY OF ORIGINAL THINKING

The Macmillan Company, New York
Collier-Macmillan Limited, London

FIRST PRINTING

Library of Congress catalog card number: 66-25645

THE MACMILLAN COMPANY, NEW YORK
COLLIER-MACMILLAN CANADA, LTD., TORONTO, ONTARIO

Printed in the United States of America

To

Barbara Sells Burke
A friend of psychology

BARBARA IS A HEAD CASE!

Foreword

The Critical Issues in Psychology Series, paperback source books for the undergraduate in psychology, are designed to provide authoritative and provocative reviews of selected topics germane to a spectrum of courses. Each volume offers an original inquiry into major facets of the point at issue and presents as well a set of illuminating reports carefully chosen to represent salient positions of historical or current significance. It is expected that this combination will offer both instructor and student opportunity to read stimulating, even challenging, argument with primary sources at hand.

Recent years have seen a resurgence of research and theoretical interest in problem solving and thinking. Although psychology was early concerned with what were then called the "higher mental processes," these tended to be overlooked with the advent of behaviorism and its strictures against "mentalism." As behavioral science has broadened its base, however, these obviously critical functions of the human mind have recaptured the attention of many psychologists. The recent revival of interest in thinking has very largely centered on the problem of creativity, or originality, the topic of the present work.

The author, Wilbert S. Ray, was awarded his Ph.D. in 1930 from the University of Wisconsin. After a period of service as a clinical psychologist, he taught at a number of colleges and at present is professor of psychology at Bethany College. His interest in human problem solving is one of long standing, as indicated not only by his own research efforts but also by his appointment as a research psychologist for five years with the Personnel and Training Research Center of the U.S. Air Force.

MELVIN H. MARX, *General Editor*

Preface

Creativity and originality are today widely discussed as the hope for the future of man. Experimental psychologists, who do not hope to save man quite as quickly as does the popular press, work patiently on the elements which constitute and influence the behavior called *thinking*. The history of research on thinking goes back to the beginning of the century, but the total amount of accumulated work is small. However, work on problem solving and its most important component, the invention of new ideas, has burgeoned since World War II. There now seems to be enough laboratory-based material on creativity and originality available to permit the publication of a book in the field.

It is hoped that this experimentally based brief volume will stimulate student interest and research in the area of original thinking. Such study may be facilitated if courses using the book offer laboratory work in which the student can see the concepts in operation and perhaps contribute some original work of his own. Many of the experiments described herein are given with enough detail so that they may be repeated in the laboratory without reference to the original reports, and in other cases the original reports are themselves quoted.

While the study of creativity and originality is the concern of many professional groups, this book only attempts to present some representative research done in this field by experimental psychologists. I regret that space limitations have necessitated the omission of much valuable work within psychology, not to mention related disciplines such as education.

As is always true in a work such as this, the cooperation of many individuals and organizations is involved. I am grateful to the authors and publishers who have given permission to quote from their material, as well as to the United States Air Force, the Office of Naval Research, and the National Institutes of Health who have contributed in various ways. I wish to express my appreciation to Macmillan's series editor, Melvin H. Marx, for his valuable advice. Last but most important, thanks are due to my students and colleagues at Bethany College and at the University of Reading, England, who have in many other ways influenced this work.

WILBERT S. RAY

Bethany, West Virginia

Contents

FOREWORD, BY MELVIN H. MARX vii
PREFACE ix

PART ONE: Inquiry and Argument

I. INTRODUCTION 3

"Original" Thinking Defined 3
A Technical Description of Thinking 4
Experimental Tasks Used in This Area 8

II. ORIGINALITY: LABORATORY STUDIES 14

Trial and Error in Thinking 14
Campbell: Blind Variation and Selective Retention 15
Laboratory Experiments on Originality 17
Maltzman: Training for Originality 17
Mednick: Strength of Associations and Originality 22

III. ORIGINALITY: NON-LABORATORY WORK 27

Guilford's Factor-Analytic Work 27
Originality in Behavior Other than Thinking 29
Contributions from Non-Psychologists 35

IV. PRODUCTION OF HYPOTHESES 39

Original Thinking as Operant Behavior 40
Inhibitory Factors 42
Note to Teachers About Originality Practice 44
Two Heuristics 44
The Unconscious Mind as a Source of Original Ideas 45

V. SET 47

Experimental Illustrations of Set 49
Luchins' Einstellung *Work* 49
Tasks Other than Water Jars 52
Guetzkow's Susceptibility to and Recovery from Set 54
Variables Facilitating the Establishment of Set 55
Variables Preventing or Extinguishing Set 57
Learning Variables and Set 59
Number and Probability of Reinforcements 59
Spontaneous Recovery 61
Set as Learning 62

VI. FUNCTIONAL FIXEDNESS 64

Duncker's Report on Functional Fixedness 65
Duncker's Hypotheses about Functional Fixedness 71
Post-Duncker Work on Functional Fixedness 74

VII. METHODOLOGY 83

Experimental Tasks 84
Desirable Features 84
Undesirable Features 86
Procedures 88
The Method of Spoken Thought 88
Artificial Intelligence 89

PART TWO: The Selected Readings

[1] "The Reinforcing Effect of Two Spoken Sounds on the Frequency of Two Responses," *J. Greenspoon* 97

[2] "Blind Variation and Selective Retention in Creative Thought as in Other Knowledge Processes," *D. T. Campbell* 104

[3] "Experimental Studies in the Training of Originality," *I. Maltzman, S. Simon, D. Raskin, and L. Licht* 111

[4] "On the Training of Originality," *I. Maltzman* 114

[5] "The Associative Basis of the Creative Process," *S. A. Mednick* 122

[6] "Creativity and the Need for Novelty," *J. P. Houston and S. A. Mednick* 124

[7] "Reasoning in White Rats," *N. R. F. Maier* 132

[8] "The Mechanism of the Assembly of Behavior Segments in Novel Combinations Suitable for Problem Solution," *C. L. Hull* 137

[9] "How We Think: The Analysis of a Complete Act of Thought," *J. Dewey* 150

[10] "Thought and Choice in Chess," *A. D. de Groot* 158

[11] "Mathematical Creation," *H. Poincaré* 159

[12] "Experimental Psychology: Incubation," *R. S. Woodworth and H. Schlosberg* 170

[13] "Mechanization in Problem Solving: The Effect of *Einstellung*," *A. S. Luchins* 173

[14] "On Functional Fixedness of Real Solution Objects," *K. Duncker* 177

[15] "Mild Stress and Problem Solving," *W. S. Ray* 191

BIBLIOGRAPHY 198

INDEX 207

PART ONE

Inquiry and Argument

CHAPTER I

Introduction

"Original" Thinking Defined

THE WORDS *think* AND *thinking* ARE USED IN MANY different ways. *Think* may refer to some sort of decision process, usually incomplete, as when a man says, "I think I shall go." It may refer to a memory process as in, "I am thinking of how frustrated I was last night." Or, as Bartlett (1958, p. 72) points out, *think* may refer to a belief: "Well, I think he is a reliable person," but the same sentence with a different inflection may express doubt. Two of the most important sorts of thinking are *critical* thinking and *original* thinking. Critical thinking examines existing sets of ideas and conclusions, as in "His discussion neglects the fact that. . . ." Original thinking produces new ideas, and it is this production of new ideas that is the concern of the present book. It should be understood that *new* means new to the thinker, whether or not someone else has already conceived that idea. Good students think about the material they read in textbooks, and if a student draws a conclusion from the material on one page, then reads the conclusion on the next page, he is still to be credited with originality since he thought of the idea before he read it.

The main theme of this book is to attempt to answer the question, "Can people *learn* to produce new ideas, to be original?" The emphasis is on original thinking, and not on critical thinking. This does not imply that critical thinking is not important, but only that it is not part of this essay. Logic, with its laws of thought, deals with critical thinking, and has little to offer to this discussion. The laws of the syllogism are methods of examining reasoning to find possible errors in it, but they do not tell anyone how to write propositions. The principle of identity and the law of the excluded middle are assumptions, rules which logic has adopted, much as football has adopted rules about roving backs. The thinking comes in the decision as to whether the principle of identity applies to this or that material, and this is critical thinking. Mathematics also has rules and assumptions; for instance, rules for counting by tens and assumptions about parallel lines. But mathematics, like logic, fails to tell a person how to do any thinking about the assumptions, whether it be critical thinking or creative thinking.

The word *creativity* is used to refer to the production of new ideas, but both creativity and originality have been defined in several ways, and creativity has taken on the aura of a "glittering generality" in phrases such as "creative advertising," "creative news photography," "creative camping," "creative physical education." There is today even a toy which teaches children "creative spelling"! The word *originality* seems preferable for use here. It means much the same as *imagination,* as that term was used in older psychology texts, and much the same as *productive,* as opposed to *reproductive* (Selz, 1924; James, 1890), thinking.

A Technical Description of Thinking

Thinking is something people do (speculation as to whether or not other animals think is interesting, but not germane to this book). It is a sort of behavior, an activity. An idea, a concept, a cognition is an event; it is something which occurs. Cognitions do not have lives of their own, nor do they exist in books or in college professors' lectures. A cognition is a response produced in the reader or listener. In discussing this activity, this thinking, in a more careful way, we find that one particular view of problem solving offers a convenient place to start.

All problems have common features. In each case the individual knows what the present situation is and what he would like it to be. What he does not know is how to change it from this to that. As Duncker (1945) says, "A problem arises when a living creature has a goal but does not know how this goal is to be reached." He speaks of the given and the desired situations. Problems range from familiar and purely practical cases, such as that of a car which will not start, to the abstract and unfamiliar, such as an examination paper which gives the student two or three axioms or assumptions and asks him to prove a theorem.

Problem solving may be defined (Ray, 1956) for experimental purposes as the process of attempting to change a given situation into a known and desired new situation, the method of change being at the moment unknown to S (subject), and the attempt to find it involving at least some activity within S. It is this activity which is called thinking. The search for the method of change is problem solving, and the method, when discovered, is the problem solution.

Problem solving is reasoning, but there may be some reasoning which should not be called problem solving. If the reasoner starts, for example, with two logical or mathematical ideas and combines them to see whether he can draw any conclusions from them, this would not fit the present definition of problem solving since the reasoner does not have a specific, known goal toward which he is working.

Both problem solving and other kinds of reasoning are parts of the larger field of thinking. Thinking, however, also includes reverie, daydreams, and attempts to recall the knowledge needed for answering examination questions. Thinking may be defined as any internal manipulation of symbols and will be described shortly under a complex-sounding rubric, *representational mediation processes.* These manipulations of symbols may be thoughts, ideas, cognitions, concepts, or whatever one may wish to call them. Here they will be called *cognitions.*

Thinking and cognitions should be described in a careful and cautious way. The diagram of Figure 1 may be familiar in its present form, but if not, the reader may recognize it as an extension of another, the one that goes *S-O-R*. The S here stands for stimulus, and the *R* stands for response. A given stimulus acts on the organ-

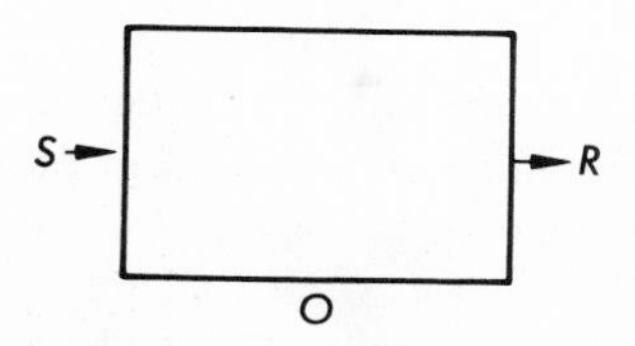

FIGURE 1. The empty organism.

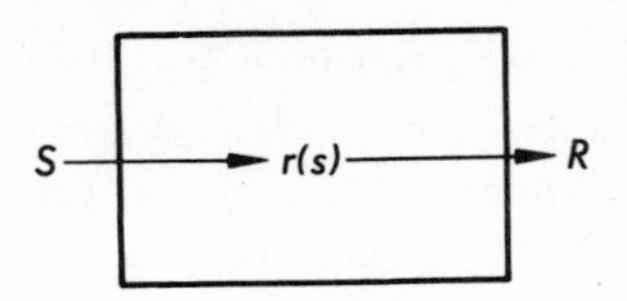

FIGURE 2. A mediation process in the organism.

ism (*O*), and a response appears. This is the simplest possible diagram of an activity studied in psychology. All readers of this book are psychologists in that they have noticed that a given stimulus will at one moment produce one response and at another moment a different response. For example, a doughnut at 11:00 A.M. is quite different from the identical doughnut at 1:00 P.M. Since the doughnut has not changed, and since the response to it has changed, an observer asks himself why. No training in psychology is necessary to bring forth the most probable hypothesis: the organism has had lunch and his hunger has disappeared. So it is assumed that things go on inside the empty box of the diagram. They may be called intervening variables.

The next diagram adds an intervening variable to Figure 1. The reference here is not to motivational variables like hunger, but to what Hull liked to call a "pure stimulus act." Figure 2 indicates no function as yet for the intervening variable. The particular sequence of letters used here should be read, "The external stimulus produces an internal response which, in turn, acts as a stimulus for an external response." An example of a response-produced cue would be found when a muscle, which has kinesthetic receptors, contracts and sends back to the central nervous system signals which, so to speak, tell the nervous system how far the limb has moved. It is *assumed* that something like this happens when the organism thinks; assumed that a thought is a response to some previous event, and at the same time a stimulus for a following event. If this assumption can be used to make predictions about the results of experiments, and if the predictions turn out to be correct, this comforts the experimenter and he feels that the assumption was justified.

The internal behavior indicated in the diagrams is called by Osgood (1953) a representational mediation process and by Kendler (1958) a response-produced cue. It was called a cognition above.

Figure 3 is a slightly more complex diagram which looks as if it might represent something which actually happens. Here there are

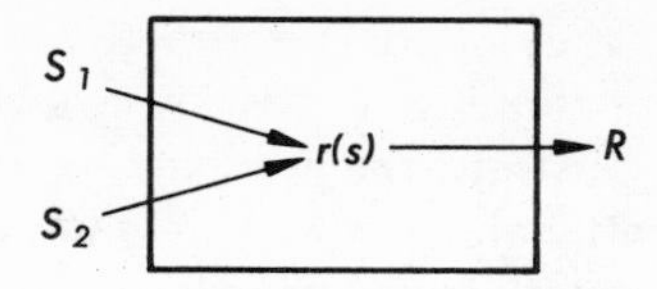

FIGURE 3. Either of two external stimuli arouse the same mediation process.

two external stimuli (simultaneous or successive) which produce the same internal response-stimulus event, which in turn gives rise to an external response. The organism may be classifying two items as similar. When the cognition or representational mediation process seems close to the external stimuli—as in this case—and is a categorizing or grouping response, it is usually designated as a *concept.* For example: two animals appear before a child, he responds to the similarities in them, and the external response *dog* appears. The child has formed a concept or already has a concept. It is convenient to name this concept with the word used and say he has a concept of a dog.

The concept in Figure 3 is the $r(s)$ event.

The fourth diagram (Figure 4) illustrates the way in which a cognition may be formed from two other cognitions or concepts

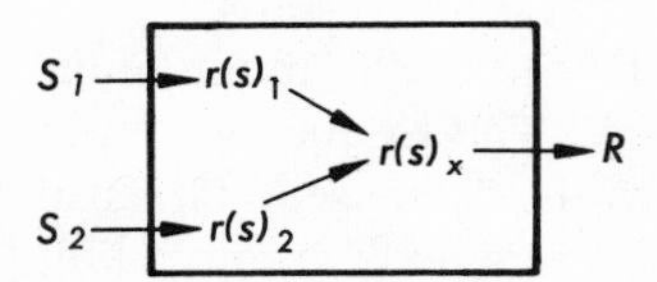

FIGURE 4. Two mediation processes combine into a new process.

rather than from two external events. It may be easily imagined that such a diagram would be very large and contain many, many $r(s)$ events if they represented the problem solving, for instance, of a girl trying to find a major field of study that would satisfy her own needs and at the same time satisfy the ideals her father held for her.

Remember that these statements are assumptions or hypotheses about what the organism does. Concepts or cognitions or representational mediation processes are acts, bits of behavior, processes, things going on. They use up oxygen, give off carbon dioxide, and are influenced by metabolic states. They cannot be seen, so they must be assumed, but modern psychology differs from more ancient philosophies (which talked of mind and body as different sorts of things), by assuming that mind is a function of the body just as much as is respiration, running, or kissing a girl. The last three of these four diagrams illustrate the reason the thinking behavior is symbolic or representational. An $r(s)$ somehow corresponds to, and is a symbol or representation of, an external stimulus, or of other symbolic processes.

Thinking is assumed herein to be internal behavior of the sort illustrated within the boxes in these diagrams. It is further assumed to be operant behavior.

If the reader has studied the field of learning he will remember that operant behavior is behavior which has stimuli that are internal rather than external—that is, the stimuli cannot be observed and controlled by the experimenter (E). The criterion of conditioning here is an increase in the rate or frequency of responses. The conditioning occurs if the operant behavior is reinforced, and in original thinking the reinforcement may take any of several forms: The new idea is put into use and the machine works, or someone congratulates the thinker. One of the prominent features of problem solving is that the solver himself can frequently recognize the correct solution when he reaches it, which is to say there is a self-reinforcement for the original thinking. This same thing occurs in human verbal behavior. Greenspoon [1] [1] had each subject (S) say nouns and reinforced each plural form with "mmm-hmm," murmuring "huh-uh" after all other words. The frequency of plural nouns increased, while use of other words decreased. Greenspoon's experiment is reprinted in Part Two of this book (see reading [1]).

It is the position taken here that original thinking is operant behavior the frequency of which can be increased by reinforcement.

Experimental Tasks Used in This Area

One way to define intelligence is by specifying the tests used to measure it. This is an "operational" definition, the best sort of definition for a person who knows nothing of the topic because he can look at the tests and find out the meanings of that highly technical term, *intelligence*. Similarly, the meanings of *thinking* and *originality* may be clarified by giving examples of experimental tasks

[1] Bracketed numbers refer to readings in Part Two.

which have been used in research in this field. Long and Welch (1941) used systematically varied tasks with children, of which the following is an example.

> *Picture problem.* This test consisted of photographs of six different kinds of vegetables. In each trial three of these were presented in pairs of two, three rows deep. Opposite each of the three rows were pictures of a girl; two of these presented the girl sick in bed; the third showed her jumping rope. . . . The experimenter explained to the subject that the little girl ate such and such and was either sick or well. The child was instructed to pick out the one vegetable that made the little girl sick.

The writers also say (p. 23), "In these problems the possible causes were presented in such a manner that Mill's Joint Method of Agreement and Difference could be employed in determining the correct antecedent." Of 15 children six to eight years old, some solved this problem successfully, others did not. It seems improbable that any of the children had ever heard of Mill's Joint Method of Agreement and Difference.

As children learn to talk they learn to name and thus to classify objects. When a child applies the word *Daddy* to some man other than his father, he is in the process of forming cognitions of Daddy and non-Daddy. The individual carries around with him somewhere, presumably in his brain, the basis of these concepts or cognitions, $r(s)_m$, in Figure 5 (m for memory). When a new stimu-

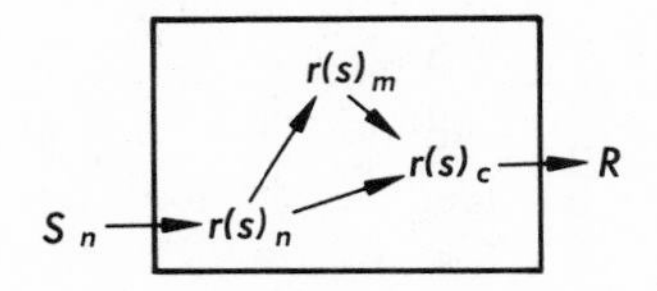

FIGURE 5. A stimulus arouses a memory process and interacts with it.

lus, S_n, comes along it produces an internal mediation process, $r(s)_n$. The two mediation processes are compared, $r(s)_c$, and an external response (for instance, Daddy or something representing non-Daddy) is produced.

Such responses can be brought under experimental control through the use of such tests as the Wisconsin Card Sorting Test (Figure 6).

> The University of Wisconsin Card Sorting Test . . . consisted of a pack of 4 *stimulus cards* and 64 *response cards* which were devised so that each card contained from one to four identical figures of a single

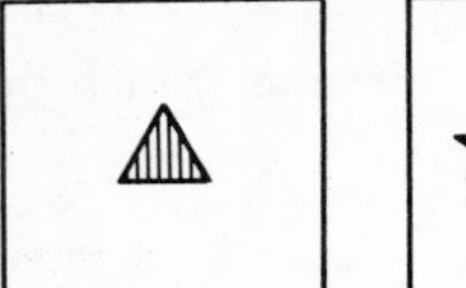

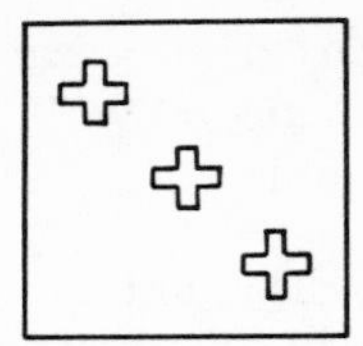
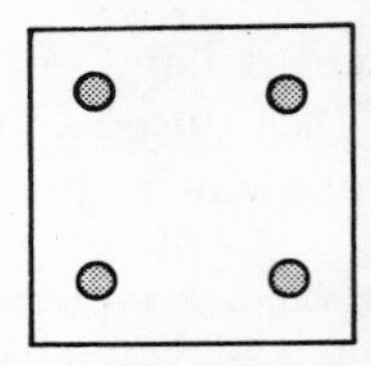

Figure 6. Sample cards as used in the Wisconsin Card Sorting Test. (Based on description in Grant and Berg, 1948.)

color. Four kinds of figures were used: stars, crosses, triangles, and circles. Four different colors were used: red, yellow, green, and blue. A single card might have four red stars, or two green circles, or any of the 64 possible combinations of colors, numbers, and forms. Each card could then be sorted or categorized according to the color, the number, or the form of the figures. The four stimulus cards were: *first,* one red triangle; *second,* two green stars; *third,* three yellow crosses; and *fourth,* four blue circles. (Grant and Berg, 1948.)

These cards present a limited number of possible hypotheses, and one cannot always tell from one trial what hypothesis S is using, although one can discover it with repeated trials, assuming that S does not change it while working. In using these cards, Ss display little originality, especially since there is a tendency among modern experimenters in the field of concept formation to call to S's attention the possible hypotheses before S starts to work. It will be noted that this concept-formation task is a learning task, and that here is a place where thinking and learning overlap.

It has been said that new ideas are not completely new, but are new combinations of old elements. One such possible new combination can be found in the free-association experiment adapted and used by Maltzman and his associates. Maltzman, Bogartz, and Breger (1958) say:

In terms of *S–R* theory the response that occurs to a given stimulus in the free association situation is the one which is dominant in the response hierarchy elicitable by that stimulus. It has the greatest amount of excitatory strength at the moment of stimulus presentation. Responses that are uncommon or original must be lower in the response hierarchy, possess a weaker excitatory potential. If, therefore, a situation could be arranged in which *S* is induced to give responses low in his hierarchy, there would be an increase in the originality of his responses. Training of this nature might then produce a disposition to give uncommon responses in other situations. The procedure employed in this study in an attempt to produce the desired effect is the simple one of repeatedly presenting the same stimulus words with instructions to give a different response each time. . . .

Procedure.—The Ss were treated in identical fashion on the initial presentation of the free association training list, and received the usual instructions to respond as quickly as possible with the first word that came to mind. After their first completion of the training list the two experimental groups were instructed to again respond as quickly as possible to each word, but to give a different response from the one used before. The training list was repeated five times in this fashion. . . . The experimental groups received the test list of new words after the last repetition of the training list while the control group received the test list after their first completion of the training list.

This is an example of an experimental task actually used in research on originality, which was defined as uncommonness. This sort of thing can also be done with the *first* set of responses to the free-association stimulus words. In a laboratory experiment accompanying a course in general psychology at Bethany College in 1964, 50 stimulus words were used. The frequencies of response words were counted by an IBM machine. One of the 80 students Ss produced 27 responses (out of 50) which were given by no other S. Two Ss each produced 22 such unique responses. One produced 19, one 17, and all produced at least two each. So perhaps originality, at least when defined as uncommonness or uniqueness of responses, is not so rare as one might think—and it will be noted here that there was no request for different responses as there was in Maltzman's work.

Another example of an experimental task used in research on originality comes from Mednick's (1962) *Remote Associations Test* (RAT):

A first problem concerns the type of material of which the stimulus item should be composed. If the test is to be appropriate for all fields of creative endeavor, the material must either be nonsensical so as to avoid bias favoring any specific means of creative expression, or it must be so common in society that familiarity could be assumed to be high across fields of interest. The problem involved in constructing the nonsense materials so as to avoid favoring any interest groups soon proved to be apparently insurmountable. This left us searching for materials with which most individuals in the culture could claim acquaintance; this, in turn, brought us to verbal materials. . . .

Several words from mutually distant associative clusters must be presented to the subject; his task must be to provide mediating links between them. Further (a factor of extreme importance), the mediating link must be strictly associative rather than being of a sort that follows elaborate rules of logic, concept formation, or problem solving. In their final (or at least present) form, the test items consist of sets of three words drawn from mutually remote associative clusters. One example might be:

Example 1:	rat	blue	cottage

The subject is required to find a fourth word which could serve as a specific kind of associative connective link between these disparate words. The answer to Example 1 is "cheese." "Cheese" is a word which is present in the word pairs "rat-cheese," "blue-cheese," and "cottage-cheese." The subject is presented with several examples so that he has an adequate opportunity to achieve the specific set necessary for the task.

Example 2:	railroad	girl	class
Example 3:	surprise	line	birthday
Example 4:	wheel	electric	high
Example 5:	out	dog	cat . . .

(None of these examples is a test item from any form of the actual test.) The two college level forms of the test (one coauthored by Sharon Halpern and the other by Martha T. Mednick) have 30 items each; the subject is allowed 40 minutes; his score is the number right. . . .

Answers to sample RAT items: 2. working; 3. party; 4. chair or wire; 5. house.[2]

Later chapters of this book discuss two phenomena that interfere with original thinking: functional fixedness and set. Consider an example of a task which may be used in an experiment on set. These problems seem to have been first described in the psychological literature by Terman (1906), and are used in the Stanford-Binet Intelligence Scale, where they are called ingenuity problems. The S is given a problem in which a mother sends her son to the river to bring back 4 pints of water. She gives him a 5-pint can and a 1-pint can. How does he get 4 pints; measuring, not guessing? S then gets a more complex problem: jars holding 21, 127, and 3 units must be used to get 100 units. Call the jars A, B, and C. The solution is to fill the 127-unit jar, then pour out enough to fill the 21-unit jar; then fill the 3, then the 3 again, leaving 100 in the original jar. This may be generalized to $B - A - C - C$. S solves several such problems, then is presented with a situation in which the containers hold 23, 49, and 3 units, from which he must get 20. If he uses the method he has been practicing instead of the shorter method, $A - C$, he is said to be set on the longer method.

[2] Reprinted by permission from S. A. Mednick, "The Associative Basis of the Creative Process," *Psychol. Rev.*, 1962, **69**, 220–232.

Maier's two-string problem (1930) has been widely used. Two strings hang from the ceiling and S is requested to tie them together. He finds that they are far enough apart that he cannot reach them both. Several solutions are possible—for example, to tie a weight to one end of the string, set it swinging, carry the other string to the center, and catch the swinging string when it comes close. Certain reservations about this problem are found in Chapter II and in Chapter VII.

Some of these tasks will be referred to below in greater detail.

Summary

This chapter has defined original thinking as the production of new ideas. It then gave a technical description of thinking in general in terms of mediation processes. Examples were given of experimental tasks used in research on thinking in general and on original thinking in particular.

CHAPTER II

Originality: Laboratory Studies

EBBINGHAUS (1908) SAID, AND MANY PEOPLE HAVE quoted him, that psychology has a long past but a short history. This is perhaps more true of originality and creativity than of other parts of psychology. Many authors and many books have dealt with thinking from a common-sense, rational viewpoint using individual testimony. Two of the most widely quoted of such treatments are Poincaré's [11] [1] description of the way in which he discovered a mathematical proof, and Ghiselin's "The Creative Process" (1952), which is a collection of statements from outstandingly creative scientists (including Poincaré), authors, and painters as to how they think they produced or invented their ideas, pictures, or poems. This rational type of contribution is not considered in this book, although materal is included which is not directly and immediately based on experimental results, such as that in this next section.

TRIAL AND ERROR IN THINKING

Is original thinking a trial-and-error process? Most people have undoubtedly had some experience, such as trying to select a topic on which to write a paper, during which several topics were considered, reasons for and against each were weighed, and one was finally

[1] Bracketed numbers refer to readings in Part Two.

selected. The various topics may be viewed as trials, and those rejected were, in this process, "errors." Saying that thinking proceeds on a trial-and-error basis simply means that ideas arise and that some are rejected while others are accepted. Common observation of one's own thinking makes this assumption seem so obvious that no one could deny it, and many theorists use this assumption without even stating it, as, for example, do Maltzman and Mednick, who refer to errors and therefore imply trial and error. *Gestalt* psychologists like the term *insight* as opposed to trial and error, but they also report their experimental subjects as making errors. Trial and error in thinking is an old assumption, going at least as far back as 1855 in Bain's "Senses and the Intellect."

In spite of the fact that trial and error in thinking seems obvious, two objections have been raised. One is that although some thinking may include error trials, other thinking produces the correct solution immediately. There are two counter-arguments here. First, if trials took place on a random basis, some first trials should be correct by chance. Second, it seems that, to quote Duncker (1945, p. 11), some ideas are "too fleeting, too provisional, too tentative" even to be considered, are suppressed immediately, and are forgotten within the moment. And if an individual has forgotten all about the first few trials, the one which he reports as first was obviously not first at all.

Another objection to accepting the existence of trial and error is an objection to unrestricted trial and error. Some theorists may adopt the hypothesis of unrestricted trial and error, but this assumption is not essential, and many psychologists assert that the relation of a specific thinking process to a particular topic means that the ideas which are used in the trials will be related to that topic. The girl who is thinking of Saturday's dance will seldom include the fact that Riemann invented a new geometry.

The reader will note that trial and error, blind or not, is a description, not an explanation, of thinking.

Campbell: Blind Variation and Selective Retention

A modern view of trial and error as the basic process in original thinking is provided by Campbell [2] who suggests trial and error as the basis for all acquisition of knowledge, as his title indicates: "Blind variation and selective retention in creative thought as in other knowledge processes." He has in previous papers (1956a,

1956b) described the manner in which blind trial and error may be regarded as basic to adaptation and to visual perception.

Campbell's viewpoint may be summarized thus: men think "creatively" by producing ideas or cognitions, some of which turn out to be correct or "useful," some of which do not. Through some second process men select the useful ideas, and through a third, retain them. ("A mechanism for introducing variation, a consistent selection process, and a mechanism for preserving and reproducing the selected variations," 1960, p. 381.) These second and third processes or mechanisms are ordinarily called *judgment* and *memory*.

It has been said that if twenty chimpanzees sat down at twenty typewriters, they and their descendants would eventually write all the books now found in the library of the British Museum. Of course, this might take some time, and the work of reading through all the junk to find the books might be more than the work of writing the books, but it is conceivable. Is the production of new knowledge by blind variation and selective retention as improbable as the production of a library by chimpanzees? Campbell says no and offers several arguments for his position.

1. Not all problems have been solved. The number of solutions awaiting the future as compared with the number solved in the past is anyone's guess.

2. The number of nonproductive thought trials (errors) by the total intellectual community must be tremendous.

3. Thinking ordinarily proceeds from the foundation of useful ideas, thus preventing the multitudinous trials which would have followed from the tremendous number of nonproductive trials.

4. There are many cases in which a man starts out to solve one problem, but discovers on the way that he has (serendipitously) solved some other problem.

5. Newell, Shaw, and Simon (1958) have persuaded a digital computer to attempt to prove the 60-odd theorems in the *Principia Mathematica* of Whitehead and Russell and concluded, that within any practicable time limit the job could not be done on a pure trial-and-error basis. Campbell points out, however, that where the machine starts at the beginning of the process, the man works from the two ends (which were called in Chapter I the given and the desired situations). If the given situation and the goal are seven stages apart, and there are four possibilities at each stage, there are 16,384 sets of seven trials each (16,384 routes) for the machine to

take, but by starting at both ends this number is reduced to 256 (omitting the matter of making the judgments referred to above). Two hundred fifty-six routes is still a lot of work, but not compared to 16,384, and certainly not if the goal is important.

The moral of these five points of Campbell's is that even blind variation does not go through all the unimaginably large number of trials which are possible, and, even so, there have been in the course of time an almost unimaginably large number of trials, most of them wasted because they have provided no knowledge for the rest of mankind.

Campbell's article, somewhat condensed, is in Part Two, reading [2].

This view of trial-and-error thinking has been described at some length because the viewpoint is important and seems to be accepted by all (or, perhaps, almost all) theorists in this field, whether or not they specifically use the term itself.

Laboratory Experiments on Originality

Many persons assume that original thinkers are born, not made. That is not the position of this book, nor is it the position taken in their research by the psychologists Maltzman and Mednick, who have reported their theories as to how originality arises and reported also the experiments to which their theories have led them. Their work presumes that people are "naturally" original (in the sense that original behavior is operant behavior), and that the quantity of originality can be increased.

Maltzman: Training for Originality

Maltzman [4] does not assume that trial and error is undirected, but rather assumes that the possible trials in a given situation are restricted in number. He defines originality as *uncommonness,* and his procedure is designed to get Ss to go to the farthest limit of their relatively small number of associations to each stimulus word, at which limits they differ from each other and thus give uncommon responses. These different responses are by definition original. Maltzman uses a standard experimental condition in which he reads to the S a word and requests the S to respond with the first word he thinks of, the usual free-association procedure. After 25 stimulus words have been used, Maltzman repeats them, asking for responses different from those given the first time. The list is repeated for a total of six presentations. Another (test) list is then given S to see whether he will give uncommon responses to these words. In the control group the Ss get one presentation of the training list, then one of the test list. Scores are frequencies with which particular response words are given by the Ss in the experiment. A score of one is earned by a word given only once among all the Ss, a score of two to a word given twice, and so forth. Thus the lower the S's score the more uncommon and original his responses. These are the sorts of scores reported in Tables 3 and 4.

The standard experimental condition is shown in Table 1.

TABLE 1

The Standard Experimental Condition *

	Training Condition	*Test Condition*
Experimental Group	A list of 25 words, repeated for a total of six presentations	Another list of 25 words, not repeated
Control Group	Same list of 25 words as above, not repeated	Same as above

* The stimulus words are *pencil, needle, rich, shut,* and so on.

TABLE 2

Stimulus Word	*Response Word*
TABLE	chair
	cloth
	wood
	leg
	food
	Mabel

δ This example of a habit-family hierarchy is adapted from Mednick (1962). See Figure 7.

Table 2 is an example of successive responses given to one stimulus by one S. The first time through the list he responded to *table* with *chair*, the second time with *cloth*, and so on. The association *table-chair* may be called a habit and Table 2 contains a family of habits. By definition the habit which appears first is strongest, so six habits are arranged in a hierarchy of habit strengths. This is an example of a *habit-family hierarchy.*

In a traditional learning experiment the S moves from one to the next habit in a hierarchy because the first habit is not reinforced and becomes extinguished. Maltzman (1955) pointed out that this phenomenon also occurs in problem solving. In the experiments under consideration, however, the substitution of one response for another is produced by the *E*'s instructions rather than by lack of reinforcement. To any stimulus word many Ss will give the same response word. The second time that stimulus comes around the responses (each different from the S's first response), will begin to differ from each other, and by the fifth repetition (the sixth presentation), uses of the same word by different Ss are much less frequent. It is these uncommon, unrepeated responses which Maltzman calls original and which he is trying to produce with his standard experimental condition. That is, he is trying to get each S to be different from the other Ss—to be original.

In one experiment (Maltzman, Bogartz, and Breger, 1958) the standard experimental condition was used with the additional condition that half the Ss in each treatment group were also specifically asked to be original on the test list. The results are given in

TABLE 3

Mean Originality Scores Produced by the Standard Experimental Condition Plus a Request for Originality *

	Originality Requested Before Test List	*Originality Not Requested Before Test*
Experimental Group	4.93	20.94
Control Group	7.61	23.98

* The lower scores are the more original responses. (Modified from Maltzman, Bogartz, and Breger (1958), Table 2.)

Table 3. In both rows of Table 3 the experimental group has a lower score than does the control group, and in both columns the request for original responses produced lower scores than occurred in the absence of that request. The test with the instruction to be original produced much more originality than did the training list, but, nevertheless, the training list did produce originality in both subgroups.

In the first experiment which used the standard experimental condition, the difference between the experimental and the control groups did not reach a satisfactory significance level, but in a second experiment it did. Also, in the second experiment an additional group of Ss responded to six lists of 25 words each instead of responding six times to the same list of 25 words, and this produced as much originality as did the standard five repetitions. Figures from this experiment are given in Table 4. There is little difference between groups on the pretest, but on the test the two experimental groups differ from the control group.

TABLE 4

Mean Originality Scores with Various Trainings Inserted Between Pretest and Test *

Type of Training Between Pretest and Test	*Pretest*	*Test*
None (control condition)	91.69	76.38
Five repetitions of Pretest	86.39	54.49
125 new stimulus words	97.06	53.40

* The Pretest and the Test are different lists of words, which prevents direct comparisons across the rows. Lower scores are the more original scores. (Modified from Maltzman, Simon, Raskin, and Licht (1960), Tables 1 and 2.)

In a third experiment Ss were asked to read responses which had come from a previous experiment, instead of producing their own, and this did not produce originality. The standard experimental condition, also used in this third experiment, did produce originality. Repetition of Guilford's Unusual Uses Test (Guilford, Wilson, Christensen and Lewis, 1951) instead of the ordinary training list did not produce originality on the standard test list.

At another time, a procedure was used which was designed to decrease originality; the decrease appeared with the Unusual Uses Test as a test list, but not with the standard test list.

A final experiment found originality persisting over a period of two days, although the amount had decreased as compared with a one-hour period.

Gallup (1962) repeated Maltzman's standard experimental procedure and found no increase in originality at all, an example of the discrepancies discussed below.

Rosenbaum, Arenson, and Panman (1964) report an experiment based on Maltzman's work, although with two variations: instructions to be original were given with the training rather than with the test list, and a factorial experimental design was used. The results: the groups receiving the instructions, "Try to be as original as possible," were more original than the other groups on the first trial of the training list. Over the five repetitions of the training list the groups became more original, but the advantage of the instructions disappeared. On the test list both instructions and training increased originality, but there was no interaction of instructions with training. Following the test list all Ss took the Unusual Uses Test. The results here were not as clear as on the test list, and it is suggested that this test is perhaps not suitable for this sort of application. Maltzman (1960) also finds differences between the unusual uses type of test and the free-association materials.

There is here, then, a standard experimental procedure (repetitions of the stimuli with requests for different responses) which sometimes seems to produce originality and sometimes does not. We can perhaps conclude that it seems that originality as defined by Maltzman can be produced in this fashion, but that there is not yet enough evidence to allow exact specification of the conditions under which the phenomenon will appear. Maltzman's own conclusion is, "The study reported here . . . lends some support to the hypothesis that originality can be learned in the same fashion as other forms of operant behavior" (1960, p. 16).

Another series of experiments is reported in Maltzman, Belloni, and Fishbein (1964). The authors point out that their laboratory's previous experiments had dealt with originality in situations where many original responses could be produced, but that these new experiments dealt with problems where usually only one response was possible. One method of facilitating that response, used several times in this series, was to supply the S with the solution in an indirect fashion through word-association techniques. For example, in using Mednick's (1962) RAT, one problem calls for *house* as a solution. (This test is discussed in Chapter 1). These experimenters assumed, with Storms (1958), that an association from *A* to *B* would also work from *B* to *A*. So, if *house* produced *home* in an association test, *home* should also produce *house.* If this is correct the word *house* can be aroused among S's mediation processes by giving him *home* before he receives the problem, and this should facilitate his responding with *house.* The reader will agree that this is a very neat bit of theory, but it had one difficulty—it did not work.

In addition to the above, which was used in various ways, other prompting techniques were attempted. Two experimental tasks were used: Maier's (1930) two-string problem, and Mednick's (1962) RAT. Of the two-string problem Maltzman, Belloni and Fishbein say, "Criticism of the two-string problem has repeatedly occurred (Duncan, 1959; Ray, 1955). It had been hoped, however, that the group form might prove a more adequate performance situation. These hopes were not realized, and as a consequence we discontinued our research with the two-string problem." The writers of this report conclude,

> Results from the present series of experiments indicate that performance on the problems employed which have only one correct solution cannot be facilitated by the originality-training procedures successfully employed with tasks having no one correct solution. Whether variations of the present training procedure and more extensive periods of training would yield nonspecific positive transfer to problems possessing only one correct solution are questions requiring further experimental study. (Maltzman, *et al.*, 1964.)

Reports such as this one of unsuccessful attempts to produce phenomena belong in literature, however, for the assistance they may give other experimenters in avoiding, or in modifying, procedures previously used in this trial-and-error process that is scientific research.

Quotations from Maltzman's reports are given in Part Two, readings [3] and [4].

Mednick: Strength of Associations and Originality

Mednick's work and Maltzman's work complement each other very neatly. Both men refer to associations and both use unique or uncommon responses as indicators of originality. Maltzman prefers the word *originality* and Mednick uses *creativity,* but they are referring to practically the same features of behavior. This book uses *originality* to refer to any new ideas, but Maltzman and Mednick use their preferred terms to mean not only new, but uncommon ideas, further qualifying their definitions to consider whether ideas are "useful" and "relevant."

Specifically, Mednick defines the creative thinking process as "the forming of associative elements into new combinations which either meet specified requirements or are in some way useful" (1962, p. 221), and refers throughout his paper to the highly creative person giving and liking remote or improbable or uncommon associations.

Mednick offers several hypotheses about sets of associations and methods of manipulating them:

1. The associations to any one stimulus may be arranged in either of two ways, with a flat or with a steep slope. These are illustrated in Figure 7. *Chair* is the closest associate, which means that it appears first and is the strongest. *Mabel* is the most remote associate and the weakest. But note that the strength of, for instance, the *food* associate is greater for the flat than for the steep slope.

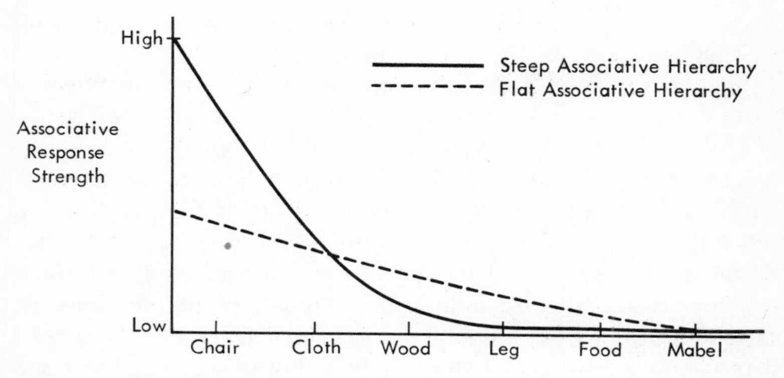

FIGURE 7. Associative hierarchies around the word *table*. (Reproduced by permission of the American Psychological Association and Sarnoff A. Mednick from S. A. Mednick. The Associative Basis of the Creative Process, *Psychol. Rev.*, 1962, **69**, 220–232.)

Such slopes may occur with different stimulus words within the same person, and some persons may have many more of one type than the other. Steep slopes imply that the associative responses appear more rapidly, and are more probably of the common type than with the flat slopes. The man with flat slopes will have more uncommon associations and will be more creative than the man whose slopes are mostly steep. Mednick further assumes that steep slopes are accompanied by a smaller number of associations.

Maltzman, Belloni, and Fishbein (1964, Fig. 2), however, with their procedure, including Mednick's RAT, found no differences between the word-association hierarchies of Ss of high originality and Ss of low originality.

2. The use of given materials in certain manners will produce the effect of a steep slope in making other uses less easily found. This is the same as saying that set and functional fixedness produce steep slopes. Mednick further presumes that a man may have many closely interconnected ideas in his own field of specialization, and may have them so firmly fixed into a system that they are not available for use in new combinations. This would suggest that originality in any particular area might be more probable with people who have not been working long in that field, and might explain why the productive people in some fields are the young ones. Gordon (1961) and Rignano (1923) have also remarked on this possibility.

3. The total number of associations which one has to a given stimulus will influence his ability to produce combinations which meet specified criteria.

4. Since many combinations of any set of elements are possible, the question arises as to why any specific one is produced rather than some other, and the hypothesis is offered that when the problem solver knows the goal he is trying to reach (see the definition of problem solving in Chapter I) the elements of the goal become additional stimuli. The two sets of stimuli, from the present situation and from the goal, act together to produce and select associative elements and thus to influence combinations of the elements. This is identical with Campbell's statement earlier in this chapter that problems are solved by working from both ends. The same sort of thing has been said by others. Duncker, for instance, says that in addition to analysis of the situation, "a genuine thinking process is characterized by the *analysis of the goal, of what is demanded,* by the question: '*What do I really want?*' and perhaps by the supplementary question: '*What can I dispense with?*' " (1945, p. 23.)

5. Massed work should produce more and better problem solutions than distributed work for two reasons. First, ideas which occur fifteen minutes apart are more likely to be put together than if one occurred today and one tomorrow. Second, the individual ordinarily starts with the more obvious and conventional possibilities, and it takes time to get past these; which suggests that the individual starts afresh after each of the rest periods in distributed practice. Maltz-

man would perhaps speak here of hierarchies, of the extinction of the more obvious responses, and of spontaneous recovery from the extinction.

On the basis of his definition and of such considerations as those just discussed, Mednick has constructed a test for selecting creative individuals, the Remote Association Test (RAT). This test was used as an example in Chapter I. The test correlated negatively with college grades, but there is a suggestion that it might have some correlation with the grades given by some teachers.

Three tests of Mednick's theory are quoted in Part Two, reading [5], and a more complex experiment in Part Two, reading [6].

The graph in Houston and Mednick's [6] Figure 1 is odd in that the two groups are as far apart at the start of the experiment as at the end—but in the opposite direction. Houston and Mednick expected this: "Pilot studies indicated that the high creative Ss tended to choose the nonnoun before any experimental manipulations were introduced." Bernard R. Singer of the psychology faculty of the University of Reading (England) has suggested to this writer that this may be due to the high RAT scorer's preference for more abstract words (and *abstract* and *concrete* are at least analogous to *uncommon* and *common*), which would be a preference for adjectives rather than nouns, and would thus lead Ss to choose these nonnouns before the conditioning began.

It might be interesting to repeat the experiment with the remote-association reinforcement given for the nonnouns, to see whether the lines on the graph then diverged instead of converging and crossing.

One should be careful in experiments like this to avoid the *mmm-hmm* effect found by Greenspoon [1] (see also Chapter I). More specifically, the *E*, in addition to reading words to S, might unconsciously give some sign of approval of nouns for one set of Ss. This possibility could be avoided by having the *E* be uninformed as to which Ss were in which experimental group.

Summary

This chapter began with a discussion of the possibility of treating thinking as a trial-and-error process.

Experiments from two laboratories (Maltzman's and Mednick's) have suggested that original thinking may be produced and manipulated. Maltzman's work has produced other experiments which have not always agreed with these results, but his own results have not always been consistent, anyway. Such inconclusive results are included in a book such as this to convince the reader that work in this field has only started, and that there is a great deal to be done. But at least it seems possible to perform experiments here, in what is possibly the most complex area of human behavior.

CHAPTER III

Originality: Non-Laboratory Work

Guilford's Factor-Analytic Work

A type of investigation of originality different from that discussed in the previous chapter is that of J. P. Guilford and his associates at the University of Southern California. Guilford's work is concerned with various measurements of intellectual abilities with the aims of distinguishing one sort from another and investigating the components of each sort. One of these abilities is originality (which he calls *creativity*), and it is this one which is of interest here.

On the basis of years of work Guilford has produced a "Structure of Intellect" (1956, 1966). The structure assumes that intellectual abilities are divided into five large classes: one memory class and four thinking classes. The thinking abilities are grouped into cognition, evaluation, convergent production, and divergent production. Guilford says of them, "The cognitive abilities have to do with the discovery of new information or the recognition (rediscovery) of old information. The productive abilities have to do with the use of information to effect certain outcomes. The evaluative abilities have to do with decisions as to the goodness, accuracy, suitability, or other forms of desirability or undesirability of information or of products" (1957, p. 3). The productive abilities are divided into convergent and divergent: "a distinction between thinking that converges upon one right answer and thinking that goes off in different directions." The divergent thinking is most like the sort of thing we are calling originality.

Within the class of divergent abilities, Guilford suggests several factors: word fluency, associational fluency, ideational fluency, spontaneous flexibility, and so on. Since factors are defined, in the end, by the tests involved, a brief look at several of the tests is in order.

Brick Uses Test. S is asked to list as many uses as possible for a common brick. Score is number of times the class of use is changed. Sample answers: "Weight down a pile of newspapers." "Build a wall." "Separate the shelves of a bookcase." "Replace a piece broken off a chair leg." "Hold up a window."

Unusual Uses Test. S must list other uses for a common object for which a standard use is given. For instance, a newspaper is ordinarily used for reading. What else might it be used for? Sample answers: "To start a fire." "To wrap garbage." "To swat flies." "To stuff packing boxes." "To cut out words to make up a kidnap note."

Object naming. S is required to name items belonging to the same class, as, for example, the mineral class. Sample answers: iron, uranium, granite, copper.

Insight problems. S must work problems requiring insight. Sample: A man went out to hunt a bear one day. He left his camp and hiked due south for ten miles, then due west for ten miles. At this point he killed a bear. He then dragged the bear back to his camp, a distance of exactly ten miles. What was the color of the bear? Why? Answer: White, polar bear; only at the North Pole could these directions have been possible. There are twelve such items in this test.

Guilford's factor-analytic work contains four levels of concepts. The basic one is made up of the tests themselves. These provide an operational definition of an ability, an *ability* being whatever it takes to score on the test under discussion.

On the next level of complexity several tests are combined as being different tests of an ability which is somewhat more general than the abilities needed for the individual tests. This more general ability is called a *factor*. The tests which identify the factor are, in turn, identified by their intercorrelations and by a method of combining correlations which is known as *factor analysis*.

On the two higher levels the factors are put together into classes, and the classes into a larger structure. As we get further from the data and the statistics, the classifications become more and more a matter of a set of categories and interrelations which are the products of cognitive operations by the scientist.

This book is not, of course, concerned with the whole of intellect, and this chapter examines only that part of Guilford's structure which is called *divergent production.* This gives three names for originality: *originality, creativity, divergent production.*

It may be noted that several of Guilford's tests have been used by other investigators. Unusual Uses was used by Maltzman and by Mednick (Chapter II). Brick Uses is popular, having been used, for example, by Maltzman, Mednick, and Osborn. This is one direct example of immediate interaction between Guilford's measurement techniques and the experimental laboratory work of others. The factor-analytic work both gives and receives hypotheses from the experimental work, but so far there has not been a great deal of such interchange. It is to be hoped that the amount may grow as the quantity of available information and hypotheses from each source increases, and as the psychologists in each field learn to look to each other for help.

It is interesting to note that Guilford says (1956, p. 280) that one factor, "spontaneous flexibility," is perhaps a matter of "reactive inhibition," or "refractory phase," or "satiation." "It seems to be a self-initiated tendency to avoid repeating oneself." It may be noted that Maltzman talks of this sort of thing in connection with habit-family hierarchies in his 1955 article, and tries to initiate by instructions the tendency to avoid repetition in the experiments on originality which have already been quoted.

Originality in Behavior Other than Thinking

The previous chapter and this chapter have discussed original or creative thinking. There are also other sorts of "new" behavior—again meaning new to the animal, not new to the world. Basically, new behavior in adults must almost always be either new combinations of stimulus and response (or of stimuli and responses), or new combinations of two or more existing responses. Thus, any learned behavior is new on its first appearance. A rat is put into a box, and a shock is applied to his feet. The resultant heightened activity includes jumping over a barrier, which gets him to a no-shock area. The jumping over the barrier is certainly new behavior. Another rat learns to push a lever to get food. The first push of the lever is new. After the rat learns to push the lever, the experimenter may gradually move it out through a slot in the box. The rat will follow the lever and puts his foot out through the slot to push it. The lever can even be moved around the corner of the box out of the rat's sight without the rat's giving up his dinner-producing activity. This again is new behavior, even though the rat's environment is directly engaged in producing it. This procedure is technically called *shaping behavior*.

In a similar fashion, alternation behavior, exploratory or curiosity behavior, the mass activity found in the human infant, and many or all operants—all are examples of new behaviors. Hull [8] [1] suggests that fractional anticipatory goal reactions account for new assemblies of behavior segments. It has been suggested that the use of language in ordinary conversation is largely original behavior. This topic obviously requires a book to itself, but at least a few suggestions may be offered as to how some of these new behaviors may arise.

1. Combinations of two pre-existing responses may be diagrammed thus, using the same symbols used in Chapter I, but omitting the box used there to distinguish the animal from the environment.

$$\text{Pre-existing: } S_1 \rightarrow R_1 \qquad \text{and} \qquad S_2 \rightarrow R_2$$

If S_1 and S_2 appear together for the first time, and if the *R*s are not incompatible, a new diagram may appear.

$$S_1 + S_2 \rightarrow R_{12}$$

the new response being a combination of the two previous single responses. If, for instance, a dancer puts together a well-known jump and a habitual head motion, we have a new dance step.

2. In a second simple case, a mediation process is in action when a new stimulus comes along, and the two combine in some such way as in the previous example.

$$S_1 + r(s) \rightarrow R_{12}$$

This situation was used by Judson, Cofer, and Gelfand (1956) and by Gelfand (1958). They had *S* learn a set of words which were relevant to a specific problem, then had him work on the problem. The list of words affected the succeeding problem solving. The

[1] Bracketed numbers refer to readings in Part Two.

paradigm also applies to experiments on set where the *S*'s activities in the immediate past influence his performance on a new problem.

3. The case of a habit-family hierarchy may be put into a diagram like this:

$$S \rightarrow R_1 \ (R_2, R_3, R_n).$$

This may be read: The stimulus aroused R_1, but if R_1 were to disappear it would arouse R_2, then R_3, and so on up to R_n. If the first response were extinguished the diagram would read,

$$S \rightarrow R_2 \ (R_3, R_n).$$

For example, take this case:

$$S_1 \rightarrow r(s)_1 \rightarrow R_1 \ (R_2).$$

Condition a new stimulus (S_c) to R_1. Now if the $S_1 \rightarrow \quad \rightarrow R_1$ chain is extinguished, will the S_c produce the R_2? If so, it may be concluded that S_c was conditioned to the mediation process, $r(s)_1$, and that the mediation process was conditioned to R_2; that is, that it was conditioned to the whole hierarchy of responses. Perhaps something like this occurred:

$$S_c \rightarrow r(s)_1 \rightarrow R_2.$$

It must also be true that the extinction of the chain in this example actually occurred between $r(s)_1$ and R_1.

Whatever conclusions are drawn, there would be here a new *S-R* act, the S_c producing the R_2, with which it had not previously appeared.

In this example a new stimulus was added. Consider adding a new response, which will make a more complex case.

4. Another situation might be one in which either of two stimuli arouses the same internal response and through it the same external response:

$$S_1 \rightarrow r(s)_1 \rightarrow R_1 \qquad \text{and} \qquad S_2 \rightarrow r(s)_1 \rightarrow R_1.$$

Condition one of the stimuli to a new response,

$$S_1 \rightarrow r(s)_y \rightarrow R_y.$$

Now, if $S_1 \rightarrow r(s)_1 \rightarrow R_1$ still persists in a subthreshold way, along with the new response, there will be a cross-conditioning so that S_1 arouses or tends to arouse two mediation processes, each with its external response. There will also be another cross-conditioning so that each mediation process tends to arouse the other external response. There should then be, among other connections:

$$r(s)_1 \rightarrow R_y \qquad \text{and} \qquad r(s)_y \rightarrow R_1.$$

Now the question is, will the stimulus which was not involved in the new conditioning (S_2) arouse the new response, R_y? If so, the action may have been like this,

$$S_2 \rightarrow r(s)_1 \rightarrow R_y$$

which would be a new stimulus-response connection, that is, a new act.

Note that this last item resembles the last item of Example 3.

The diagrams of this last set resemble those used by Hull (1939) and Osgood (1953) to explain mediated generalization. Whether or not this is really an example of generalization, and whether every case of stimulus or response generalization is new or original behavior is left to the reader.

5. As a complex example of this stimulus-response, or conditioning, type of explanation of new behavior, consider Hull's [8] hypothetical explanation of the assembly of behavior segments into new combinations, and Osgood's (1953) simplification of it. The explanation applies to a possible way in which two previously learned habits may appear together as one new behavior, but on a basis other than trial and error.

The central concept in Hull's theory of novel combinations is the fractional antedating (or anticipatory) goal reaction. He assumes that, by processes of conditioning and secondary conditioning, the final response to a goal object (for example, eating it) is somehow represented in miniature (fractional) responses which move back up the chain of acts to the stimulus which starts off the chain. Hull calls such responses *pure-stimulus acts,* and they are what have also been called mediation processes. They are symbolic processes although they symbolize or represent other responses, whereas some symbolic processes may stand for other stimuli.

Figure 8 shows a set of four tables with connecting pathways. A hungry rat is taught to go to table *F* for food, from either table *C* or table *B*. After this, he learns while thirsty to go from *C* to either *B* or *W* for water. These last two habits (*C* to *B* and *C* to *W*) are equally strong. Note that *C* is a common starting point for three

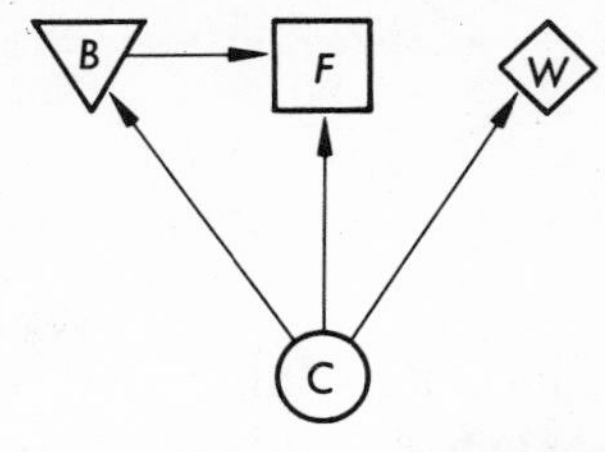

FIGURE 8. Slight modification of Maier's (1929) experimental arrangement, as simplified by Hull (1935).

paths, and that *B* is both a starting point (when the rat is hungry) and a goal point (when the rat is thirsty).

The test for the rat's ability to "reason" comes when he is put on table *C*, hungry, and with the path to *F* blocked. Will he, without trial and error, go to *B* and thence to *F*? If so, he will "solve the problem by combining the two separate experiences" (Maier [11]), which both Maier and this text would call reasoning. Maier reports that, in fact, rats do this. Hull attempts to explain it on the basis of conditioning, but such an explanation does not deny the fact, or the appropriateness, of the word *reasoning*. Osgood (1953, pp. 616–618) expands and improves Hull's explanation.

The fractional anticipatory goal response which started from the response to the food on table *F* we will call $r(s)_F$. When the animal learns the *B*-to-*F* habit, *B* should come to arouse $r(s)_F$, and the $r(s)_F$ will precede arrival at table *F*. The hunger stimulus will also arouse $r(s)_F$ (see Figure 9). Later the animal learns the *C*-to-*B*

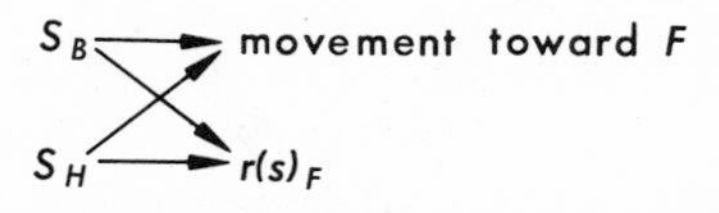

FIGURE 9. The situation at *B* after the *B*-to-*F* habit has been learned while the animal was hungry.

habit, and when he arrives at *B* the stimulus properties of *B* will arouse the $r(s)_F$; so that response should creep back up this chain and become also arousable by *C*. Then the sight of *C* will arouse movement toward *B* and will also arouse the $r(s)_F$, and the two should become crossconditioned so that $r(s)_F$ will tend to arouse the movement toward *B* (Figure 10). Because the *C*-to-*B* habit is learned under thirst conditions, the hunger stimulus will be absent during this last learning.

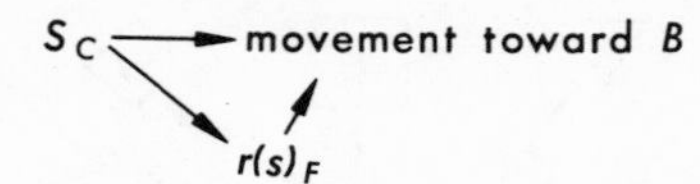

FIGURE 10. The situation at *C* after the *C*-to-*B* habit has been learned while the animal was thirsty.

It was assumed that the paths *C*-to-*B* and *C*-to-*W* are equally well learned (Figure 11). When the *hungry* rat is put on table *C* and the direct route to *F* is blocked, the $r(s)_F$ aroused by the hunger

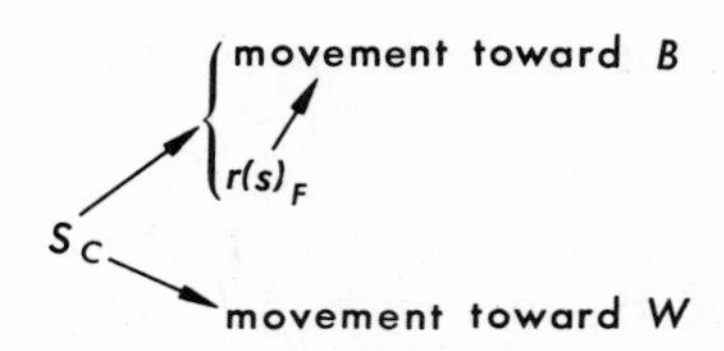

FIGURE 11. The situation at *C* showing the equally strong tendencies to move toward *B* and toward *W*.

stimulus will be added to that aroused by the table itself; the *C*-to-*B* tendency will be a little stronger than the *C*-to-*W* tendency, and the rat should choose the path toward *B* (Figure 12). Once he arrives at *B*, of course, there is no difficulty explaining why he proceeds from *B* to *F*.

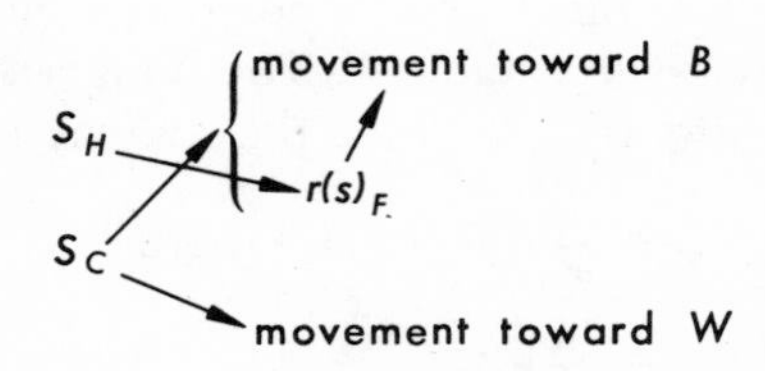

FIGURE 12. The diagram of Figure 11 with the hunger stimulus (S_H) added.

As Osgood points out, the explanation demands that the food paths be learned before the water paths. If the water paths are learned first, there is no reason to predict that the rat will solve the problem. (See Part Two, readings [7] and [8] and Osgood (1953).)

6. Verbal associations and verbal mediations offer many opportunities for the appearance of new behavior. Suppose an S learns an association, as, for instance, to say *green* when he hears the word *chair*. Then he learns to say *rapid* when he hears *green*. Now there are two short chains.

chair-green   green-rapid

Now teach S to substitute for *rapid* the pushing of a lever. Will he push the lever when he hears *chair?* If so, he has a new stimulus-response act which we may call an original act. Jenkins (1963) reports several such experiments and presents a great deal of information on underlying verbal mediational theory.

This gives six instances of stimulus-response or conditioning ways of looking at the origin of new behavior. On the use of this system of explanatory principles Hull (1935, p. 288), says that the working hypothesis here is that "the *principles of action* discovered in conditioned reaction experiments are also operative in the higher behavioral processes. The compound adjective in the expression, 'conditioned-reflex principles,' accordingly refers to the locus of *discovery* of the principles rather than to their locus of *operation*." Aside from any light which such principles may throw on originality, it is desirable to use this sort of hypothesis here to remind the reader that reasoning, thinking, and problem solving do not make up a section of psychology which stands off by itself, apart from the remainder of the field, but that, in fact, the principles of action are closely allied to other principles, procedures, and theories. In fact, it is quite easy to argue that original thinking is a type of learning.

Contributions from Non-Psychologists

Political scientists postulate something called a power vacuum, which seems to mean that if the most powerful nation in a particular geographical area loses its power, some outside nation will come in and take over control. The same sort of thing happens in psychology. If there is a topic which the psychologists will not, or do not, discuss, someone else will discuss it. There are instances, for example, where a department of psychology plays down abnormal behavior, but the department of education at the same institution considers it at length in several courses. In another school the department of psychology refuses to give a course in the psychology of advertising, but the school of business administration does give one, with no prerequisite of general psychology, and with a non-psychologist as the instructor. This might be designated as the psychology vacuum effect.

This seems to have happened with regard to original behavior.

The reader will, perhaps, have noted that the work of Campbell, Maltzman, Mednick, and Guilford is full of suggestions as to the nature of originality and how it may be produced in the laboratory, but the authors have not given many hints as to how an individual makes himself or his colleagues more original in daily life. However, in this vacuum have arisen two systems of practical methodologies for producing original thinking: Osborn's (1957) "brainstorming" and Gordon's (1961) synectics. The systems are interesting, although there is still some argument as to their usefulness. But if adoption by industrial, commercial, and United States military organizations are evidence, they are very useful.

Osborn's brainstorming is a relatively simple procedure. Five to ten people are needed, one of them to be the recorder. A topic is proposed, usually in the form of a question, the group gives answers, and the recorder (who is not to give any answers) writes them on a blackboard. The theory is that there will be a social facilitation effect, that people will be stimulated to think of more answers not only by the specific answers their fellows provide, but by the very fact that the others are giving answers. There are two rules which are given to the participants: "Never criticize," and "Quantity, not quality." Criticism of ideas would have two undesirable results: it would keep people from making suggestions that they feared the others might not like (which means it would prevent uncommon, unique, and remote associations), and it would take time from the desired type of behavior. The quantity rule has the same intent of trying to get out all the ideas possible, and implies the hypothesis that the greater the total number of ideas, the greater the number of useful ideas. Evaluation or judgment of the ideas is done at a separate time, perhaps even by a separate set of people. The blackboard is desirable because it gives opportunities for refreshing one's memory as to what has already been said. Of course, it also implies that the recorder can write rapidly and sufficiently clearly, and can in some cases condense an idea into two or three words.

The procedure is not complex, and could be tried in the classroom. Practice will probably improve the group's performance and will almost certainly improve the recorder's. It must be remembered, however, that the technique is suitable for some questions, but not for others. Brainstorming may be useful for inventing a new name for a breakfast food or suggesting ways for a club to make money, but one cannot hope to use it for serious or useful suggestions on broad social topics such as the problem of teen-age drug addiction or the prevention of nuclear war.

Experiments by Taylor, Berry, and Bloch (1957) lead them to conclude that individuals can produce more solutions working alone than working in brainstorming groups. Ss were assigned to brainstorm in sets of four. Each group of four working together was matched by four working in solitude. The group of four produced, on the average, 37.5 suggestions, whereas the mean number the individuals produced was 19.6. The four individual workers produced among them 77.4 ideas, but, of course, many ideas were repeated, something that would seldom happen in the group situation. Taylor proceeds by calling his set of four individual workers a *nominal group*, and counting the number of different ideas this group suggested. The results say that four persons working alone produced 68.1 ideas per problem, while four persons working together produced 37.5, a statistically reliable difference.

If Taylor is right, the question may still arise, "Even though people can produce more ideas alone, will they in fact do so?" Taylor reports that his group participants were enthusiastic about the brainstorming procedure, but makes no such report about the solitary workers. And it seems less probable that people will think about a topic when alone than when in a room with others all thinking about the same topic at the same time. If this is so, then brainstorming may produce more actual work than does individual work. The other method, synectics, also requires people to work at their thinking in groups.

Gordon (1961) defines synectics as the joining together of different and apparently irrelevant elements (as has been suggested by many workers in this field). Synectics is said to be "The mental activity in problem-stating, problem-solving situations where artistic or technical inventions are the results" (p. 33). The synectic process involves making the strange familiar, and making the familiar strange. This latter is accomplished by four kinds of analogy. Direct analogy is comparison of parallel facts, knowledge, or technology. Symbolic analogy is condensation of the possible solution into an image, often poetic, often wordless, as when a participant suggested that a collapsible jack was similar to the Indian rope trick. Fantasy analogy is a matter of saying to oneself something like, "I know it works this way, but what if it worked that way?" The most original of the kinds of analogy Gordon and his co-workers have discovered is personal analogy in which a chemist "may personally identify with the molecules in action. . . . He becomes one of the molecules. He permits himself to be pushed and pulled by the molecular forces." Other examples are given in which the participants in the synectic process tried to feel like can openers or like cans being opened.

Brainstorming has become widely popular and seems to be a successful method of getting ideas in at least some cases. Synectics may seem a trifle bizarre—how can one feel like a can being opened?—but it too may prove useful as time goes on. However, both authors as well as their co-workers have developed new strategies and techniques for extending the range of individual invention of ideas, as in Gordon's "making the strange familiar, and making the familiar strange." The question arises whether it might not be better to allow each thinker to develop his own techniques, hoping for new ones at frequent intervals. Different problems may require different strategies of attack, and the same problem may profit from one strategy today and another tomorrow. Experiments on set have demonstrated that a person can adopt a method of solving problems which may prevent his noticing the existence of other and better methods (Chapter V). Originality may be desirable in the methods of finding original answers.

CHAPTER IV

Production of Hypotheses

FROM THEIR FIRST UNDERGRADUATE COURSES IN EXPERIMENTAL psychology to the time they choose topics for Ph.D. dissertations, students experience perhaps their greatest difficulty in the matter of finding experiments for themselves. This chapter is devoted to a discussion of the production of hypotheses for theses or dissertations, but it is limited only to inventing the hypotheses and not to questions as to whether the hypotheses are worthwhile.

The difficulty is illustrated in this quotation from Cohen and Nagel (1934, p. 245) which includes a quotation from an early seventeenth-century book, Francis Bacon's *Novum Organum:*

> The search for order among facts is a difficult task. Few succeed in it. But it has always been the hope of some thinkers that easily learned rules might be found according to which anyone undertaking such a task may be assured that success will crown his efforts. And some writers on scientific method have proudly believed they had actually found such rules. Francis Bacon was one of them. "Our method of discovering the Sciences," he wrote, "is such as to leave little to the sharpness and strength of men's wits, but to bring all wits and intellects nearly to a level. For as in drawing a straight line or describing an accurate circle by the unassisted hand, much depends on its steadiness and practice, but if a rule or a pair of compasses be applied, little or nothing depends upon them, so exactly it is with our method." The methods which Bacon recommended for discovering the causes of things are popularly believed to express the nature of scientific method. They were elaborated by John Stuart Mill and formulated by him as the *methods of experimental inquiry*.

Original Thinking as Operant Behavior

The position taken here is that original thinking, including the production of research hypotheses, is operant behavior, and that its frequency can be increased by reinforcement. The reinforcement in ordinary original thinking, which has been called the loneliest work in the world, is self-reinforcement; when a man gets an idea he can and does say to himself, "There, that's a good idea," or something like that.

The reader learned in general psychology or in the psychology of learning that operant behavior is behavior which needs no immediate external stimulus to elicit it, and that its frequency or rate can be increased by reinforcing it whenever it appears. There are no experiments showing that originality can be thus amplified, but there are laboratory demonstrations of the fact that language behavior (which is at least much like thinking) can be affected. Chapter I referred to a study by Greenspoon [1] [1] in which the S's use of certain parts of speech was increased by the *E*'s saying "mmm-hmm" and other Ss' use of the same type of words was inhibited by "huh-uh."

The recommendation is, then, that the student deliberately sit down and practice the production of hypotheses, the expectation being that the appearance of an original idea will provide a self-reinforcement, with a resulting increase in the rate of production of original ideas. More specifically, the student could well start with two or three hypotheses and try to produce more hypotheses from them. Potentially useful detailed suggestions for this procedure will be given after a few remarks on the identification of hypotheses.

A hypothesis is an attempt to explain observations, although sometimes it is offered before the observations are collected. "The relation of meaningfulness to clustering" is not a hypothesis, but "meaningfulness promotes clustering" is, as is "meaningfulness does not promote clustering." Statements of fact, such as descriptions of experimental results, are not hypotheses, although they may become so if stated generally and applied to the results of experiments yet to be executed. Further, one must be sure his hypotheses are not value judgments (since *true* and *false* do not apply to value judg-

[1] Bracketed numbers refer to readings in Part Two.

ments), nor definitions. Anyone may define anything in any way he wishes, and the definitions may be clear, vague, or many other things, but cannot be true or false.

A hypothesis has been described as a statement which is capable of being true or false, although Popper (1961, pp. 40–41) wants to put the emphasis on *false:*

> The criterion of demarcation inherent in inductive logic—that is, the positivistic dogma of meaning—is equivalent to the requirement that all the statements of empirical science (or all "meaningful" statements) must be capable of being finally decided, with respect to their truth *and* falsity; we shall say that they must be *"conclusively decidable."* This means that their form must be such that *to verify them and to falsify them* must both be logically possible. . . .
>
> Now in my view there is no such thing as induction. Thus inference to theories, from singular statements which are "verified by experience" (whatever that may mean) is logically inadmissible. Theories are, therefore, *never* empirically verifiable. If we wish to avoid the positivist's mistake of eliminating, by our criterion of demarcation, the theoretical systems of natural science, then we must choose a criterion which allows us to admit to the domain of empirical science even statements which cannot be verified.
>
> But I shall certainly admit a system as empirical or scientific only if it is capable of being *tested* by experience. These considerations suggest that it is not the *verifiability* but the *falsifiability* of a system that is to be taken as a criterion of demarcation. . . . My proposal is based upon an *asymmetry* between verifiability and falsifiability; an asymmetry which results from the logical form of universal statements. For these are never derivable from singular statements. Consequently it is possible . . . to argue from the truth of singular statements to the falsity of universal statements. (See also Cohen and Nagel, 1934, pp. 8–10.)

And, of course, the proposition that science is probabilistic means that, practically, we can never *prove* that any statement is undoubtedly correct or undoubtedly incorrect. No statement can actually be proved true or false.

Professional journals provide a convenient, and nearly inexhaustible, source of hypotheses. There may be advantages to the reader in practicing the working out of hypotheses. One might start by reading an experiment report, writing out all the hypotheses found in it, and then writing new hypotheses from them. The following excerpt from Rosenbaum, *et al.* (1964) is included as a practice exercise. Write out all the hypotheses in it.

> A series of studies by Maltzman and his associates . . . has consistently demonstrated that a training procedure designed to elicit uncom-

mon responses will affect performance on subsequent tasks by facilitating original responses. The basic training procedure involves successive presentations of a single list of stimulus words to which the Ss are instructed to give different associations on each presentation. A control group receives only one presentation of the stimulus words. The results indicate that the training procedure facilitates the elicitation of uncommon responses to a test list of new stimulus words. The training procedure also facilitates original responses on a clearly unrelated task of suggesting different uses for a common object.

When all the hypotheses found in the above selection have been written out, perhaps two points about them should be considered. First, if hypotheses are to be combined into new ones, it might be desirable that they be as short and simple as possible. Can any of the written statements be broken down into two or three shorter statements? Second, it might be desirable to try to write out, for this once, all the hypotheses which the selection implies rather than states. When any statistical statement is made, it implies all the mathematical and statistical statements that lie behind it. These are hardly necessary at this time.

From simple statements of hypotheses, more may be derived. Remember that for present purposes the interest is in quantity, not quality. Do not hesitate to write down hypotheses which are far away from the original set. It will be remembered that both Maltzman and Mednick attempted to induce Ss to give remote, novel associations. One may be unsuccessful the first time he tries this, but, if so, perhaps he should try again the next day, thus taking advantage of the principles of distribution of practice.

Since there are large individual differences in creativity, it may be instructive to compare these hypotheses with those of another person. More information may also be obtained by the study of books of logic and the reading of Chapters XI and XIII in Cohen and Nagel (1934) containing information on hypothesis production. With further attempts at finding and developing hypotheses, the student will find that the production of hypotheses is an activity involving self-reinforcement, practice being the heart of the matter.

Inhibitory Factors

If original thinking is operant behavior, valued by the world, and presumably reinforced by the world, then why is it so difficult to find originality, especially in school and college work? The answer apparently is that ever since the first grade the student has been told that he should think, but he is reinforced only when his thinking produces the right answer, which will not always happen if thinking is a trial-and-error process. Ray (1962) has offered three hypotheses which might take care of such a situation:

1. Originality is often a re-combination of elements into new patterns, which implies that the elements must be present. Therefore a basis of knowledge in a field is necessary to permit original thinking in that field.
2. Thinking is a process, an activity, and it can be increased in amount, and perhaps in quality, by practice.
3. Originality in thinking should be reinforced, with evaluation of the product of the thinking to occur at a different time and on a different occasion. This means that "bad" ideas (when bad ideas can be identified at all) should be reinforced as well as "good" ideas.

Another kind of difficulty is that people frequently become set on one explanation, and are unable to reconsider the ideas involved in it. Ideas within some one field may be so firmly cemented into sets that they cannot be broken out and examined individually. Or, on the other hand, they may be so separated in the individual's thinking that it never occurs to him that they could be combined. Rignano (1923, p. 279) says this same sort of thing:

> Imagination . . . itself is more free and more daring when it is not restrained and frequently stopped by the knowledge of opinions and principles, which impose themselves as dogmas and from which the thinker may believe there is no escape.

Mednick (1962) also:

> The greater the number of instances in which an individual has solved problems with given materials in a certain manner, the less is the likelihood of his attaining a creative solution using these materials. . . . Thus, if a newcomer to a field has the requisite information, he is more likely to achieve a creative solution than a long-time worker in the field.

And Gordon (1961, pp. 94–96):

> The expert is often the man least able to create a new idea. . . . [He] tends to discuss the problem in the language of his own technology. This language can surround the problem with an impenetrable jacket so that nothing can be added or modified.

Highly trained people naturally tend to think in terms of the dogma of their own technology and it frightens them to twist their conventions out of phase.

Note to Teachers about Originality Practice

Practice in original thinking or hypothesis production can well be used as a class exercise. A summary of classroom procedures includes:

1. Give the class a new question to answer (for example, show them an adjustable vertical-horizontal illusion card and ask what changes would increase the absolute size of the illusion), or a set of data from which to draw conclusions, or a small set of hypotheses to work from. The amount of time needed will depend on the type of material used, but should, at the beginning, be short—ten minutes or so.
2. Have the class practice simultaneously, with each student writing down his own ideas. This tends to insure that every student participates.
3. Then have the members of the class read aloud their products, with no comment of any sort from anyone.

If the students have thesis topics or seminar reports or individual experiments looming on the horizon, this fact will motivate the work and persuade the student to save the sheets on which he has written his ideas.

Two Heuristics

The material of this chapter up to this point has dealt with only relatively simple originality in the invention of single hypotheses. There are, of course, many reasoning processes which are much more complex and include the invention of hypotheses and sets of interrelated hypotheses, the drawing of conclusions, and so on. It seems desirable to quote two general descriptions of complex reasoning for their possible heuristic value to the reader. The first, Dewey's [9] Analysis of an Act of Thought, is an old, rational, and well-known description.

Another analysis of the way in which a man thinks, new and empirical, is that of de Groot [10].

De Groot's statement, like Dewey's, is a description of thought rather than direct advice on how to think. De Groot seems to be saying that in complex thought processes a man considers various problems, subproblems, and sub-subproblems, but not in any particular order. He also says that originality in the sense of finding new ways of looking at problems seems to occur at the ends of pauses in the work.

It will be noted that both Dewey and de Groot are talking in *general* terms of the process of thinking. Various *specific* hints, gimmicks, and techniques can be offered, and the reader is referred to Chapter III for remarks on such procedures.

The Unconscious Mind as a Source of Original Ideas

There is a very popular hypothesis which says that the unconscious mind is a fine source of original ideas: that one way to solve a problem is to forget it for a while, during which time the unconscious mind will work on the problem and present a solution, usually when the individual is not expecting it. In other words, the hypothesis is that while part of a man's mediation processes are busy with something else, other processes are solving the problem. The most frequently quoted evidence for this assumption is a statement from a French mathematician, Henri Poincaré [11].

The concept of unconscious thinking is widely accepted, another famous statement being that of Wallas (1926), who incorporates it into the second of his four stages of thought: preparation, incubation, illumination, verification.

Now the Unconscious is a psychological concept which is widely known and, presumably, widely accepted both by psychologists and by laymen, largely because of Freud's emphasis on it. It is, however, a complex concept which cannot be operationally defined and which leads to no experiments. The law of parsimony warns the thinker to avoid the complex and to try to substitute simpler assumptions.

What are the objective facts which this proposition about unconscious thinking is presumed to explain? Basically, that a man works on a problem unsuccessfully, there is a period of rest from the work, and the problem is solved after this period of rest. Additionally, but apparently not essentially, the solution appears as the first trial after the rest period, in what has already been described as the trial-and-error process of thinking. A further feature of the phenomenon, the appearance of the solution when the thinker was not working on the problem (frequently reported as coming "while I was shaving") may probably be disregarded as anecdotalism. The trouble with this "data" is, of course, that it does not include the millions of times men shave without solving problems.

That not all psychologists accept the unconscious as an explanation is illustrated in a quotation from Woodworth and Schlosberg [12], who suggest four hypotheses as possible alternates to the unconscious-mind-at-work hypothesis. (Their last one refers to the disappearance of sets over a period of time, which will be discussed in Chapter V.) Two more alternatives may be offered.

First, a solution on returning to a problem is, after all, one more trial in a trial-and-error process, and it must often be true that a man stops work just short of that one more trial.

Second, it has been suggested that any increase in stress interferes with problem solving (Ray, 1965a). If, for example, discouragement, frustration, or even intense concentration are stressful, and if these stresses disappear before the thinker returns to his problem, their absence might take away the inhibition which had previously prevented the finding of the solution.

These, then, are alternative hypotheses, more testable than those relating to the work of the unconscious mind, and experimentally minded psychologists will prefer them until there is some experimental evidence for the hypothesis that the unconscious mind deals with problems. In a framework of experimental psychology, this is a question of the effect of distribution of practice on problem solving and original thinking—a question on which there is not much laboratory evidence.

CHAPTER V

Set

THE FIRST LABORATORY INVESTIGATION OF THINKING was carried out at the University of Würzburg, close to the beginning of the current century. The most frequently used procedure was to say to the subject something like, "Think of the whole of which I shall give you a part: arm." The thinker, the S, was to give the response word and then to introspect on the process, looking to see, for instance, whether it was entirely sensory material. No discussion of the results of these experiments is included here, but modern interpretations of them appear in Boring (1950), Humphrey (1951), van de Geer (1957), and de Groot (1965). The work is mentioned here because the *task* or *Aufgabe* (Watt, 1905) ("Think of the whole of which I shall give you a part") produced in the S a *determining tendency* (Ach, 1905) which influenced the thinking that started when the stimulus word (*arm*) appeared. Here is an example of a situation in which a pre-existing condition had an effect on the thinking when the thinking occurred. This pre-existing condition, this determining tendency, is a *set,* and this chapter is devoted to set as it influences thinking and problem solving. Set, as well as the functional fixedness discussed in the next chapter, is the opposite of originality because it exists on occasions in which S does *not* think of a new way to do things. Set refers to the methods of solution used, and functional fixedness refers to objects used in problem solving.

Sets are common and not unknown to the layman. A very temporary set is introduced by the race starter's "Get ready, get set, go." Someone is set to buy a particular brand of tooth powder and never considers any other. A student gets into the habit of starting books by reading the first chapter, and it is difficult for a professor to convince him that sometimes he should start with the last chapter. If a man is set for toast every morning he is disturbed when there is none.

The concept of set is very popular in experimental psychology, even though the term means many things (English and English, 1958; Gibson, 1941). Set here refers to an increase in the probability of use of a specific method of solving problems, this use produced by the use of that same method with preceding problems, or, sometimes, produced by instructions from *E*. In most of the experiments, the preceding problems occurred in the immediate past.

Let us consider a bit of theory in order to clarify this definition of set. In Chapter I problem solving was defined as the process of changing a given situation to a specified, different situation. The given situation has been described (Ray, 1956) as producing a cognition (or cognitions) in the problem solver (see Figure 13), the assumption being that he does not operate with switches, wrenches,

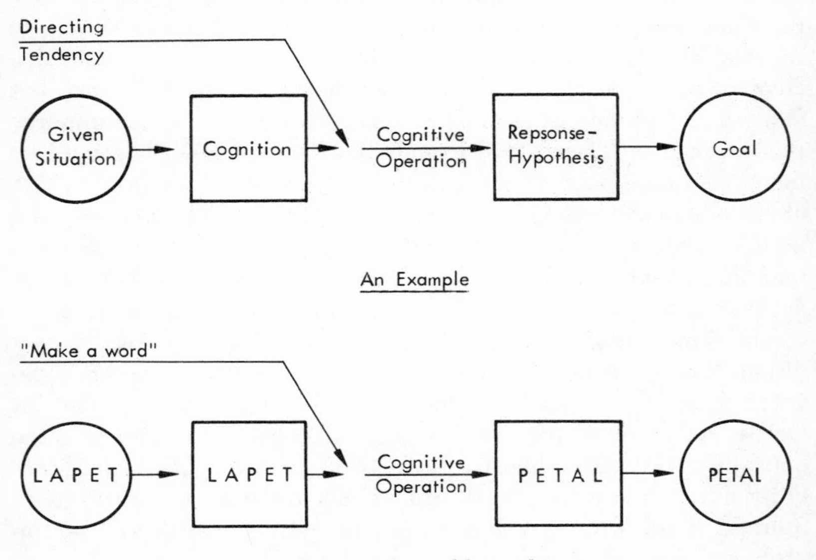

FIGURE 13. Diagram of a problem-solving process.

or numbers on a piece of paper, but with the inner, cognitive processes (mediation processes) which represent them. The specified different situation, or goal, is produced by *response hypotheses*. This phrase is derived from the fact that any observable action or overt response by S can be assumed to be the result of some hypothesis, and this hypothesis can only be identified by his responses, whether verbal, manual, or otherwise (Krechevsky, 1932). The processes of getting from the cognitions to the response hypothesis will be called *cognitive operations*. These are the thinking, reasoning, problem-solving processes which are the center of interest of research in this area. One further assumption must be made: that the whole process is guided by a directing tendency that tells S where he wants to go, helps him perceive the problem materials in this or that way, and, in the case of set, gives him response hypotheses to use. The directing tendency in experiments on set is produced either by *E*'s instructions or *E*'s arrangements to give S successive problems which demand the same response hypotheses.

The four suggested sections of the general problem-solving process will often appear in this order: directing tendency, cognition, cognitive operation, response hypothesis.

It can now be suggested that the behavior exhibiting that characteristic which we call set is behavior which includes all of these processes except the cognitive operations; more simply, we may say that the solver uses response hypotheses without any accompanying cognitive operations. For example, under a certain directing tendency, S carries out arithmetic procedures on given numbers, but *he does not stop to think about what he is doing*. A specific response hypothesis which will be mentioned shortly is B – A – 2C.

For ease of reference we may call this response hypothesis a *method* of solving.

Experimental Illustrations of Set

Luchins' *Einstellung* Work

The best-known and most often quoted work on set is that of Luchins (who, like Duncker and Maier, was a student of Wertheimer's), the first report of which was "Mechanization in Problem Solving: The Effect of *Einstellung*" [13].[1] *Einstellung* is a German

[1] Bracketed numbers refer to readings in Part Two.

word which is today translated as set, and its use emphasizes the fact that this work is a development of the research of the German psychologists at Würzburg, mentioned above. (For Luchins' own description of his method, see reading [13].

One of the difficulties in research in the field of problem solving is that the experimental tasks we ask our Ss to solve are not reliable, standardized problems. In an attempt to improve the Luchins problems Bugelski and Huff (1962) have developed another list. One of the advantages claimed for the list is that the arithmetic, which unnecessarily confuses some Ss in the Luchins problems, is easier. It is also reported that the set is acquired more quickly with these tasks than with the older ones. These new problems are given in Table 5. The arrangement of the tasks is as in the Luchins list except

TABLE 5

Bugelski and Huff's *Einstellung* Problems *

Given			
A	*B*	*C*	*To Get*
43	89	2	42
25	59	2	30
32	69	3	31
52	78	3	20
43	93	4	42
31	61	4	22
17	37	3	14
41	86	4	37
47	68	4	51
27	59	5	22
13	35	3	16

* From B. R. Bugelski and E. M. Huff, "A Note on Increasing the Efficiency of Luchins' Mental Sets," *Amer. J. Psychol.*, 1962, **75**, 665–667. Reproduced by permission.

that instead of one sample and five set-producing problems, there are here six set-producers. There are many other problems and arrangements of problems available: for instance, in van de Geer (1957) and in Cowen (1952).

Table 6 gives results from one of Luchins' early experiments. All Ss solved all the problems in this experiment, whether by the longer (set) method or the shorter (direct) method. The figures in Table

TABLE 6

Percentages of Set Solutions in the Test Problems *

Group	*N*	*The Two Problems Before the Extinction Problem*	*The Two Problems After the Extinction Problem*
Control	57	0%	0%
Set	79	81%	63%
"Don't be blind"	86	55%	30%

* Modified from Luchins (1942), Table I.

6 are the percentages of times that Ss used the set method in the test Problems 7, 8, 10, and 11. No one in the control group ever used the set method. The group that had been trained in the set method by using it on Problems 2 to 6 used it also on the first two critical problems in 81 per cent of the cases. (That is, 79 Ss each solved two problems, and of the total of 158 solutions, 81 per cent were by the long method.) After the extinction problem the number fell to 63 per cent. No figures are given as to how many Ss solved the extinction problem nor as to how many of those solving or failing to solve the extinction problem continued to use the set solution on the last two criticals.

Another condition was introduced by asking some Ss to write on their papers after Problem 6, "Don't be blind." This cut down the number of set solutions both before and after the extinction problem.

The Luchins (1942) monograph contains reports of over 200 experiments on *Einstellung*, examining conditions which increase and decrease the effect. See also Luchins and Luchins (1950).

J. P. van de Geer (1957) reports a complex experiment with this same sort of problem. After two examples he uses two unsolvable problems, then seven set-producing problems, two extinction problems, eight critical problems, and two more extinction problems. The preliminary unsolvable problems are omitted in some conditions, as are the two extinction problems toward the middle of the series. The Ss were Dutch schoolchildren in Leiden, eleven or twelve years old. Some of his many conclusions are

1. The unsolvable problems increase motivation and thus produce more set, as Cowen (1952) also found. The effect appears especially

when the Ss are also requested to work rapidly. (A request for working rapidly also introduces an element of stress. See Ray [15].)

2. A large number of training problems (five or seven) produces more set than do one or three.

3. Extinction problems reduce the set effect.

4. Extinction problems reduce set more when there are also unsolvable problems and with five or seven training problems.

5. Girls take on set more easily than boys and have more difficulty in overcoming it, but this may be due to the fact that the tasks were arithmetic, a type of work in which girls are generally thought to be less interested than are boys.

6. The appearance of set has no relation to intelligence level. (But note the restricted range of intelligence levels with only eleven and twelve year old Ss.) Van de Geer concludes that this agrees with the hypothesis that differences in amount of set reflect differences in amount of motivation, and the amount of motivation may reflect personality variables.

Tasks Other than Water Jars

Rees and Israel (1935) produced sets in methods of solving anagrams. Their training anagrams were all solved by one method; their test anagrams each had two solutions, one of which was arrived at by the same method as in the training problem. S tended to use the method of solution in which he had been trained. In one experiment the letters of the anagram were always arranged in one order: for example, 5 4 1 2 3 (the numbers being the positions of the letters in the word). Thus *n e l i n* turns into *linen.* After 15 "order" anagrams, S gets 15 two-solution anagrams; in the "trained" group, 95 per cent of the words produced were order solutions, while in the control group only 47 per cent used this solution. Six of the ten Ss were unable to describe the uniform arrangement of the letters in the anagrams, that is, they apparently did not realize there was such an order. In another experiment Rees and Israel used words concerning nature (*rains, grass, stems*) for training, and the experimental group tended to find such words in the test anagrams, most Ss again unable to describe the method of solution.

In still another experiment each training anagram was both a nature *and* an order anagram, and the Ss were 85 per cent successful in finding solutions. But when the test anagrams had either nature *or* order solutions, the percentages of success were 35 and 53 respectively.

Some of the Rees-Israel experimental conditions were repeated by Maltzman and Morrisett (1953a), using various conditions of single and compound classes of anagrams in training and in testing. They confirmed the older experiment in finding order anagrams easier to solve than nature anagrams, and, in general, compound classes easier than single. They also reported (1953b) that adding instructions ("look for words referring to flowers . . . ") made the set solutions easier to find, that is, increased the strength of the set.

An interesting theory about this anagram task resulted from Safren's (1962) extending to anagram solution a hypothesis put forward by Deese (1959) in connection with immediate recall. After one anagram has been produced, that word will arouse other words in S's memory. So the next solution word will be the product of the letters of the present anagram with possible assistance from the associations aroused by the previous word. If the second word comes from the same category (for example, plants) as the first word, the probability of the second solution word being in the group of aroused associations will be higher than if the two anagrams are from different categories. Solution words from the same category, then, should be easier for S to find than solution words from different categories, and plant training, for example, should facilitate plant responses in the test. Safren points out the similarity of this hypothesis to one put forward by Maltzman and Morrisett (1952). Safren's data support her hypothesis and support as well the additional hypothesis that giving S a label for the category should produce the same effect—that of getting ready a number of associations.

Another significant feature of Safren's work is that her categories were constructed on the basis of previous work with similar Ss rather than on the basis of an individual *E*'s rational judgment.

The reader will note that there is here an instance of a mediation process; arousal of associated words, and selection of words from that pool.

Sets in a concept-formation task have been built up and broken down by Grant and Berg (1948). *S* is handed a pack of cards that have various combinations of number, color, and shape; the cards show, for example, one green triangle or three blue circles. (See Chapter I.) S is to find by trial and error the "correct" criterion (number, color, or shape) by which to sort the cards. After he has sorted, say, eight successive cards correctly by shape, *E* changes the criterion to color or number, but without telling S that he has done so. Thus, after S has heard eight successive *yes*es, he now gets *no* for doing the same thing. Two questions arise: how long will S take to overcome the set for what he has been doing, and, having overcome it, how long will it take him to find the new method?

Guetzkow's Susceptibility to and Recovery from Set

One study has that very desirable aspect which some experiments carry: it has been repeated, modified, and discussed by other experimenters. Guetzkow (1951) suggested that set is really a complex process that can be broken down into two parts: susceptivity or susceptibility to set, and overcoming set—taking on a set and giving it up. Working with water-jar problems, he gave his Ss five long-method problems (B − A − 2C), then two two-method problems, then a short-method problem. The test for establishment of a set is whether or not the long method is used on the two critical problems. People who use it here are said to be *susceptive* or *susceptible* to set. Then comes the question of the solution of the final, short-method problem. It is said that anyone who used the long method on the critical problems must *recover from* or *overcome* his set in order to solve the final problem. It may be supposed that a control group could have solved this last problem easily (see, for example, the results of the control group in Table 6), and thus we can conclude that failures here were due to the persistence of the set rather than to the intrinsic difficulty of the problem.

Counting only those Ss who solved all five of the training problems, Guetzkow found that 77 per cent of the men showed the set by using the long method on the critical problems, and 73 per cent of the women did so. There is no statistically reliable difference between these two figures, so it is concluded that men and women are equally susceptible to the set. But in the final problem, 59 per cent of the men and only 42 per cent of the women were able to overcome their sets and solve the problem. The difference is statistically reliable. The conclusion, then, is that men and women do not differ in susceptibility to, but do differ in recovery from, sets. So Guetzkow's suggestion that set has at least two parts, susceptibility and recovery, seems like a reasonable, rational analysis, and the experimental data support the assumption that these two sorts of behavior are actually distinct and operationally separable.

Guetzkow points out that after a person overcomes a set, the question arises as to whether he can solve the problem presented. That is, the set may lead to failure, or the intrinsic difficulty of the problem may lead to failure. Note that in the Wisconsin Card Sorting Test (Grant and Berg, 1948) susceptibility, recovery, and the finding of new solutions can be measured separately, although this cannot be done with water-jar problems, at least not as they have been used.

Van de Geer (1957) repeats and extends Guetzkow's work. He assumes that differences between groups of Ss cannot appear when there is no set or when the set is so strong that no one can avoid it; differences can appear only with intermediate degrees of strength of set. He further assumes, on the basis of evidence discussed above, that larger numbers of training problems will increase the strength of set. He then compares susceptibility to set in girls and boys when there are two training problems and when there are six. His data indicate that the six problems do produce more set as measured by long-method solutions of critical problems, and that while there is no difference between boys and girls with two problems, there is a difference with the stronger set produced by six. Thus van de Geer finds a sex difference in susceptibility to set, whereas Guetzkow does not.

It will be noted that discrepancies in data such as this one offer a fine field for investigation. Examination of the two experiments shows them different in the number of training problems (six in van de Geer's experiment, five in Guetzkow's); in the age of the Ss (eleven-year-olds and twelve-year-olds versus college students); and in nationality of the Ss, with accompanying differences in culture (Dutch and American).

Such discrepancies also appear in the reports on functional fixedness in Chapter VI, and another appears in Guetzkow's (1951) failure to confirm Maier's finding that *E* influences *S* by telling him to surmount his set.

Variables Facilitating the Establishment of Set

Set may be produced by direct instructions from the experimenter, as was done in the Würzburg procedure, but it is usually produced in the laboratory by giving *S* a series of problems which all require the same response hypothesis sequence, as in the experiments described in this chapter. Larger numbers of these training problems increase the amount of set, as reported by van de Geer (1957), Guetzkow (1951), Gardner and Runquist (1958), and others.

Increased stress or motivation will increase the amount or strength of set. At the start of some of his experiments van de Geer gave the Ss two insoluble problems and then requested some of them to hurry. The combination of the two conditions increased the amount of set. (Ray [15] reports that these two conditions—frustration due to failure and set for speed—interfere also with problem solving in a non-set task.) Strength and frequency of set behavior are also regarded as personality variables. When it is said that a man has a rigid personality it is implied that he acts as if he had a great many sets which act frequently and over a long period of time. Rigidity as such is not discussed in this book, but a review of literature on the subject is found in Chown (1959).

Effects of massed and distributed practice on the formation of set were compared by Kendler, Greenberg, and Richman (1952). They used the types of problems used by Luchins, but had S actually pour beans from one container to another. In the spaced condition a three-minute period after each problem was filled with rating cartoons for humor. The massed practice produced more set. These men have an interesting theory suggested by their results. In most learning experiments the advantage is with distributed practice, but massed practice produces more extinction than does spaced work. The suggestion here is that the learning of set is a matter of extinguishing wrong responses; S does not learn to start with B, but does learn not to start with A or C, either. Set disappears during the rest periods because the inhibition of the incorrect responses disappears, with the result that the massed practice produces the greater amount of set.

Gardner and Runquist (1958) gave Ss 6, 11, or 21 water-jar training problems, then one short-method extinction problem. They found that the greater the number of training problems, the more time it took S to overcome his set and solve the extinction problem. They also predicted that the extinction problem would erase the differences in strength of set among the three groups, and, when they gave one further problem of the long-method type (the training type), they found that the differences in time of solving the problem had disappeared.

The same conclusion about the number of training problems comes from Youtz (1948). He used 5, 10, 20, or 40 long-method training problems, then 10 single-solution test problems. Gardner and Runquist say that the largest amounts of training produced the longest solution times on Youtz's first test problem, but that this difference had disappeared by the second test problem, which supports their assumption that one extinction problem brought all the groups back to the same level of strength of set. Van de Geer (1957) also found a difference between boys and girls on the first extinction problem, but not on the second. However, he also found a difference extending through two extinction problems into the next (critical) problem when the motivation was high enough and there was a larger number of set-producing problems: that is, under the most favorable conditions for producing set.

Set can be established, or established more easily and thoroughly, by several conditions: instructions, the use of a specific method of solution, massed practice, the structure of the problem, and certain motivational conditions. The larger the number of training problems using one specific method, the stronger the set; which corresponds to the increase in habit strength produced by an increasing number of reinforcements. Indeed, since the S ordinarily recognizes a solution as correct after he has found it, we may say that there is here a self-reinforcement. If so, the increase of the number of problems *is* increasing the number of reinforcements. There may be the germ of an experiment here. What would be the effect of an increasing number of problems if the S could not tell whether each solution was or was not correct?

The next section of the chapter deals with situations which prevent or extinguish set, and it will be seen that many of the experiments quoted could have been mentioned either here or in this next section —which is to say, facilitation and inhibition are not always as different as they may seem.

Variables Preventing or Extinguishing Set

Set may be facilitated by instructions, practice, massed practice, stress, and certain problem structures; of course, the opposite conditions will prevent or extinguish the establishment of set. Furthermore, there is evidence that one extinction problem may wipe out the set, although strong sets may persist through more than one. What other conditions may inhibit set?

Luchins [13] decreased the amount of set by saying to his Ss, "Don't be blind." Maier (1933) got the same effect by warning his Ss to avoid "habitual and persisting activity," but Guetzkow (1951) failed to confirm these results. (Guetzkow suggests that his own Ss may have recovered from the set but been unable to solve the problem, which was Duncker's X-ray problem.) The THINK signs which one sees hanging on many office walls are attempts to use this technique to prevent sets.

Luchins and Luchins (1950) carried out several experiments that tested the possibility that three variables might prevent or destroy set: they started with a given amount of fluid in a water-jar problem and kept track of the amount remaining after each problem; they added an extra, unnecessary container; and they had S actually pour the fluid from one container to another. None of these arrangements prevented set, but the first one cut down the amount. Only 33 of the 139 sixth-grade pupils tested completely obeyed the instructions to keep track of the amount of fluid remaining, but these 33 showed only 35 per cent set solutions of the first two critical problems whereas those who did not obey the instructions showed 81 per cent set solutions.

Note that the two groups reported here are not equivalent groups. Perhaps whatever made the 33 children follow instructions also prevented set solutions on the criticals.

It may be remarked that keeping track of the amount of remaining fluid is an activity that is not the actual solving of water-jar problems, which makes this a sort of spaced practice. Kendler, Greenberg, and Richman (1952) reported that spaced practice cut down amount of set. Of course, the act of pouring from one container to another is also spacing.

Benedetti (1956) repeated the procedure of increasing the number of jars, and reported that with his conditions this did lower the amount of set.

Training S with several problems that demand the same method of solution produces a tendency to use that method when it is not essential, and the greater the number of training problems the greater this tendency. Will it also be true that using *different* methods in the training will prevent the set, as in Harlow's (1949) experiments in which training monkeys and children with different solutions made it easier for them to find different solutions? Experimenters say *yes,* as might be expected.

Schroder and Rotter (1952) report a concept-formation experiment in which they used cards somewhat similar to those of the Wisconsin Card Sorting Test. The Schroder-Rotter cards differ from each other in three dimensions: color, the shape of an inside form, and the shape of an outside form. Each S is presented with one of four conditions: (a) five problems using one dimension; (b) seven problems using that same dimension; (c) seven problems using two dimensions separately so that S gets training in shifting from one to another, the two solutions being arranged in this order: *x, y, y, x, x, x, x;* (d) problems the same as the last, except that the solution shifts four times instead of two: *x, y, x, y, x, x, x.* The test series was the same for all four treatment groups. The first four test problems demanded the dimension not previously used in any training, and the next five were arranged in a series which shifted progressively from this third dimension back to the one which had been used exclusively during training in the first two groups and which is indicated by *x* in the last two groups.

Now to simplify the above: some Ss got the ordinary set training, whereas other groups got training in which two response hypothesis systems were mixed. When they must shift to a problem with a new solution, which Ss will shift most easily? On the first trial of the test series the time of solution showed that the shifts were quicker for the groups trained on shifting; the more such training, the easier the shift. The shift required later in the series, from the new back to the *x* solution, showed the same result. Therefore, training with different methods inhibited set. It also appeared that seven training problems produced more set than did five.

Three methods of measuring the dependent variable in water-jar set experiments have been mentioned: two criticals, one extinction, two criticals; several criticals; several criticals with a gradual shift from one to another method of solution.

Learning Variables and Set

Number and Probability of Reinforcements

Another example of mixed training is reported by Adamson (1959). The training condition for one group of Ss was six "order" anagrams, the order being 2, 3, 4, 1. The other group had the same six anagrams mixed at random with six more, each of these having an order different from the first six and different from each other. Adamson calls these groups, respectively, 100 per cent and 50 per cent reinforcement. On the test series, which had anagrams with still different orders, the 100 per cent group was reliably faster than the 50 per cent group. That is, the partial reinforcement group showed more set, and the set showed more resistance to extinction. Learning studies usually report that partial reinforcement produces resistance to extinction, but it may be pointed out that in those experiments the animal is reinforced for a response and, later, not reinforced for that same response. As was said above, if S produces a word from an anagram, he recognizes that he has a word, and this may be called self-reinforcement. This self-reinforcement occurs in all anagram experiments (and in other places; for instance, in water-jar problems). It is the reinforcement in the 100 per cent group of this experiment. In the 50 per cent group, the S was reinforced 50 per cent of the time for making the set-producing response, but he was also reinforced the other 50 per cent of the time for making other responses. This, plus the rather unusual arrangement of six training problems in one group and twelve in the other, make these results difficult to interpret. However, this does look like the mixed-problem training that Schroder and Rotter used, and Adamson's results are exactly the opposite of theirs.

Buss (1952) reports another experiment with complete and partial reinforcement. He had S learn to say *vec* (an arbitrarily chosen nonsense syllable) to tall blocks, and *not vec* to short blocks. Some Ss were shown only tall blocks and the *vec* was always reinforced; others saw only tall blocks and *vec* was reinforced 50 per cent of the time. Then the response was reversed without telling S (as in the Grant-Berg and the Schroder-Rotter experiments). Now the 100 per cent reinforcement treatment showed more set, in apparent contradiction to Adamson's results. Note that this work used the traditional arrangement—100 per cent reinforcement for a response compared with some reinforcements and some silences to the same response. There was no self-reinforcement in the latter set-up.

To increase the confusion in the available data still further, consider an experiment in which Grant and Berg (1948) used different numbers of reinforcements and different numbers of shifts from one solution method to another. They used the Wisconsin Card Sorting

Test described in Chapter I and in this chapter, and had Ss find six successive solutions; that is, they had the Ss shift five times. Different groups of Ss had different numbers of reinforcements—from 3 to 10—on each solution before the shift. They found that the larger numbers of reinforcements produced easier shifting, but only after practice at shifting. The larger numbers of reinforcements gave results significantly different from those with the smaller numbers, but only on the fourth and fifth shifts. The statisticians would say that there was an interaction between number of reinforcements and number of shifts. This result contradicts those quoted in the previous section of this chapter in which larger numbers of reinforcements increased amount of set.

The reader has here another opportunity to consider various sets of data (Schroder and Rotter, 1952; Adamson, 1959; Buss, 1952; Grant and Berg, 1948) which seem to disagree with one another, and to try to relate them. Because this book makes no pretense to being a complete report of all available data and hypotheses, other experiments can probably be found which will support one or more of these sets of data, and still others which contradict them.

Spontaneous Recovery

The possibility of spontaneous recovery of set after extinction was investigated by Runquist and Sexton (1961) in an experiment which developed from that of Gardner and Runquist (1958). They built up a set (water jars again), gave S one extinction problem, and then gave him a long-method test problem immediately or after an interval of 10 minutes, 30 minutes, or 48 hours. Control groups were tested without having had the extinction problem. The extinction and spontaneous recovery group did better as the interval lengthened and the control group did worse. The set would, of course, enable the control group to work faster than the group in which the set had been extinguished.

Tresselt and Leeds (1953) report evidence that the set produced by water-jar problems persists at least for seven days (their longest period) and that it may even increase in strength during that amount of time. Such an increase is contrary to the effect found in the Runquist-Sexton control group.

Frick and Guilford (1957) used Luchins' five set-producing problems followed by five critical problems. They report that the Ss who solved all five of the training problems shifted to the short method on the first test problem in 66 per cent of the cases; those who solved only four training problems shifted in 30 per cent; and those who solved three test problems shifted in 19 per cent. Thus, the more training problems solved, the less set. On this basis they conclude that the test problems produced no set at all. Here, however, as in the case of the Luchins-Luchins (1950) experiment previously discussed, the three groups of Ss are not equivalent groups; one group is made up of the most skillful solvers of this particular problem, and so on. Furthermore, it might be assumed here that failing to solve a problem is frustrating, and that frustration produced set, as it did in experiments reported by Ray [15] and others. This would explain the above results; the more failures (the more stress), the more set.

In summary, set may be prevented, extinguished, or generally inhibited by a warning against it, by the mere fact of the S being male, by incubation (see Chapter IV), or by an extinction problem or two (but possibly this is only a temporary effect). Asking the subject to keep track of the amount of remaining fluid in water-jar problems may prevent set, as may having extra and unnecessary jars. Spaced practice seems to inhibit set.

It seems reasonable also to assume that training with two or more methods of solution as opposed to one method would prevent or decrease set, and Schroder and Rotter say that it does. Adamson gives the opposite conclusion, but he trained his Ss with one method and compared it to one method mixed in with six others. The evidence on partial reinforcement is not clear.

Training with more than one method of solving becomes originality training.

It might be added here that several investigators have reported that set seems to have no relation to intelligence level: (Guetzkow, 1951; Luchins, 1942; van de Geer, 1957).

Set as Learning

Set and functional fixedness (Chapter VI) are undoubtedly learned forms of behavior, and many of the experiments on these two phenomena have involved the same independent variables used in other parts of the field of learning: massed and spaced practice, partial and complete reinforcement, various numbers of reinforcements, extinction and spontaneous recovery, and so on. Further, many of the theoretical constructs of learning are used here: habit-family hierarchies, mediated generalization, trial and error, expectancies. Set and functional fixedness can be regarded as transfer of training, positive or negative, as the case may be.

As one example of this, Ray (1965c) gave Ss one, two, four, six, or eight water-jar training problems. He looked to see how long the effects of the set persisted in a group of thirty two-solution problems. More than half of the total number of Ss used the set method throughout the thirty test problems, so he counted the number who did this in each treatment condition. His results show that the persistence of the set response is a positive growth function of the number of reinforcements.

Some psychologists, for example, Leeper (1951), treat the whole field of problem solving and thinking as part of the general field of learning. Underwood (1949) says on this point, "The question which must be ultimately answered is whether or not the basic principles which explain learning may be used also to explain thinking." He later (1952) refers to the need for "more definite answers to questions concerning the amount of overlapping of basic processes responsible for the wide variety of behavior changes from those called conditioning through those called thinking." This question does not command much space in this book. A more immediate question is whether the phenomena, hypotheses, and techniques developed in the general field of learning are useful in the investigation of thinking. To this question, of course, there can be no answer but *yes.*

CHAPTER VI

Functional Fixedness

THE LAST CHAPTER AND THIS ONE DISCUSS CONDITIONS that prevent originality and inhibit problem solving in general: set and functional fixedness. Both chapters deal with behavioral effects on immediately subsequent problem-solving processes. There is a much larger body of experimentation on these inhibitions than on the facilitation side of the problem.

One question here is whether matters can be so arranged that a man will use a particular method of solving problems and will then continue to use it when some other method might be more efficient or might even be essential. This is the phenomenon of *set:* the man is set in his ways of solving the problems. Another question refers to the objects that he uses in solving problems. If an object is used for one purpose, will this prevent, or at least interfere with, its use in another way? This is *functional fixedness:* the function is fixed to the object, and it is then more difficult to use the object for some other function. Set and functional fixedness are really very much alike, the difference being that set refers to methods of solving the problem, and functional fixedness refers to the object manipulated in the solving of the problem. (Woodworth and Schlosberg (1954) refer to the phenomenon as *functional fixity*, and Scheerer and Huling (1960) say it is part of a broader set of processes which they call *cognitive embeddedness.*)

Duncker's Report on Functional Fixedness

The first experiments on functional fixedness were described by Duncker in his monograph, "On Problem Solving" (1945), which is now a classic in this field. He says there is no more fundamental difference among problems than the matter of the ease with which parts of the problem can be rearranged into new combinations. He refers to this matter as the *disposability* of the elements, elements being the parts of the problem and the materials to be used. He uses the term *heterogeneous functional fixedness* to refer to the situation in which an object serves first in a function different from that demanded in subsequent problem solving, and he asks, "What determines whether, and to what degree, heterogeneous function fixedness of an object hinders the finding of this object?" [14] [1] He then goes on to suggest that whatever is discovered about objects will apply to thought material in general. (*Thought material* might refer, for example, to the parts of a mathematical puzzle in which there is no object present for S to manipulate. The experiments which have been reported, however, make use of objects, not concepts.

Duncker (1945, p. 99) later discusses "homogeneous fixedness," which is not really fixedness, but is instead positive transfer of training. On this topic he says, "For transfer to be possible, F_1 and F_2 need not be just the same function. If one considers the functions concretely enough, they are always different. Hook for the whisk broom is not the same as hook for the shoehorn. But what matters is merely that the two functions be based on the same general function in the same way, ultimately on the same properties (dispositions) of the crucial object." Positive transfer will be considered in more detail below.

Duncker reports experiments involving eight problems named after the main object used in each: the gimlet, pliers, box, weight, paperclip, cork, book, and yardstick problems. Since the box problem is used in several experiments, it may be selected as a model for a description of functional fixedness and the manner in which it is produced. His general design is the same for all the problems.

Given: On a table, among many other objects, lie a few tacks;

[1] Bracketed numbers refer to readings in Part Two.

three little pasteboard boxes (more or less the size of match boxes), apparently not identical in size, shape, color, position; and three candles. In one experimental situation, the candles are placed in one box, the tacks in another, and the matches in the third. Required: Put the candles side by side on the door of the room at eye height ("for use in visual experiments").

The solution of the problem is to fasten the boxes to the door with the tacks so they become platforms for the candles. In the control condition the boxes are empty, but in the experimental condition they are filled with the tacks, candles, and matches. They are, then, used as containers. The container function becomes fixed to the boxes, and they are less likely to be perceived as available for use in the platform function.

Duncker reports (see Table 7) that in the control condition all seven *Ss* solved the problem, but that only three of the seven *Ss* in the experimental condition solved it. The lower proportion of success is attributed to the pre-utilization of the boxes for containers. The pre-utilization produced the functional fixedness, and the functional fixedness inhibited the problem solving.

The results of five such experiments, using the first five problems named above, are shown in Table 7. Duncker reports no statistical

TABLE 7

Number of *Ss* Succeeding or Failing in Five Problems *

	Experimental Group		*Control Group*	
Problem	*Success*	*Failure*	*Success*	*Failure*
Gimlet	10	4	10	0
Box	3	4	7	0
Pliers	4	5	15	0
Weight	9	3	12	0
Paperclip	4	3	6	1

* Modified from Duncker (1945), Table 1.

evaluation of the reliability of the results, but comparison of the numbers of failures in the control conditions of the five experiments with the numbers of failures in the experimental conditions makes the difference between the conditions seem convincing without statistical support.

The reader will note the very elegant matching of the difficulty level of these problems to the abilities of the Ss. The problems are just hard enough that, although almost all Ss can solve them in the control condition, many Ss fail in the experimental condition. If the difficulty level were too high, all Ss in both treatments would fail, and if it were too low, they would all succeed. Universal failure or universal success would prevent any effect of the experimental variable from appearing. In one problem (the cork problem), the difficulty level was so high that practically no one succeeded in either condition, which prevented any difference between the two treatments.

In experiments quoted later (Adamson, Glucksberg) the matching of difficulty level with subjects' ability is not good; assuming that the problems were presented in the same way we must assume that the German Ss were quite different from the Americans. Duncker, however, reports nothing about the source of his supply of Ss.

Duncker, having convinced himself of the reality of the functional fixedness effect, now goes on to look for explanations of it. This is done by seeking conditions under which it will occur and variables which will affect it. He first uses the cork problem. The S is requested to draw a triangle in ink on a card, to fasten the card to a stick, and to fix the stick horizontally across a doorway. The stick is two centimeters shorter than the width of the doorway. The problem can be solved by using a cork as a wedge between the end of the stick and the side of the doorway. The cork is in use as a stopper in a bottle containing the ink necessary for drawing the triangle. The stopper function presumably inhibits the wedge function.

The usual control is not used in this experiment. Instead, the cork is a stopper for an empty bottle, and the triangle is drawn in pencil. The cork in the bottle of ink may be described as having a *central* function, since S must actually do something with it, while the cork in the empty bottle has a *peripheral* function. The prediction is that the peripheral function will cause less fixedness than does the central function. Duncker reports, however, that the peripheral function did not make the problem easier, but actually made it harder. His Table 2 [14] shows that one of seven Ss solved the problem after the central function, and not one of seven solved it after the peripheral function of the cork. He remarks that even though the extra difficulty produced by the peripheral function has been confirmed in "similar experiments undertaken in a seminar," the available data is not impressive in showing that the peripheral function produced greater difficulty. Here is an experiment which should be repeated, especially since the hypothesis about centrality and peripherality seems so appealing. The hypothesis is, however, used again in problems dealing with specificity of goal.

A similar experiment used the box problem. The central function was use as containers for the candles; the peripheral, use for containing neutral material such as buttons. Three of seven Ss solved the problem after seeing the boxes in their central function, and one of seven after the peripheral use of the boxes—again an unimpressive set of data for concluding that the peripheral function made the problem more difficult.

The prediction was that the peripheral function would show less fixedness effect (would make the problem easier), than did the central function, but the data lacks support for this hypothesis. Another hypothesis is offered to explain this result: the "contact" which S had with the box in taking the candles from it (or in thinking about taking out the candles?) facilitated its use in the succeeding problem. This contact effect would act in a direction opposed to that of functional fixedness, and the contact occurs only in the central function. An experimental way of separating the contact and the fixedness influences awaits the attention of some future investigator.

The central-peripheral variable, then, produces no effect, at least as far as present evidence goes. The next question Duncker takes up is the effect of having the first function of the object be in a situation which is psychologically distinct from the problem situation, although all the work is done in one time period and in the same physical set-up. Using the object for a purpose completely separate from the problem is contrasted with using it for a purpose that is part of the problem. A picture is projected on a screen, and the S is to raise it, which can be done by putting a book under the front of the projector. The book is a table of logarithms which has been used in one treatment to calculate the angle through which the lens should be raised. In the other condition the book is used to solve a separate logarithmic problem, and the angle question is not mentioned. The prediction is that use of the book for calculating the angle of the projector should produce functional fixedness, but using it for the psychologically separate arithmetic problem should not. Similar predictions were made for the pliers and yardstick problems. The results for the three problems are shown in Table 8. The

TABLE 8

Number of Erroneous Solutions Preceding Success *

	Control, No Pre-Utilization	*Both Functions in Same Problem*	*Psychologically Distinct Problems*
Total number of errors; 9 Ss, 3 problems each.	35	58	32

* Adapted from Duncker (1945), Table 7.

table shows that when the object is used in the problem, with no preliminary use for anything else (the control condition), the nine Ss produced 35 error trials before reaching the correct solutions. There were two further conditions. When the problem was preceded by a function in which the object was used for some purpose related to the main problem (for example, calculating the angle of the projector), it tended to become fixed to that solution, was less easily used for the necessary main-problem function, and thus made the main problem harder, as measured by the number of errors (58) preceding solution. However, when the preliminary use was separate and distinct from the main problem, this fixedness was not present, and the number of errors was about the same as in the control condition. This confirmed the hypothesis that functional fixedness occurs only when the first function is in a situation closely related to the problem.

Duncker asked his Ss to "think aloud" during their work, and the errors reported above are apparently vocal statements made by the Ss before success. This makes a rather poor dependent variable, as Duncker himself says. "Even the best-intentioned protocol is only a very scanty record of what actually happens. . . . Many . . . phases do not appear in the protocol because . . . they are too fleeting, too provisional, too tentative, occasionally also too 'foolish,' to cross the threshold of the spoken word" (1945, p. 11).

The third and last of the hypotheses which lead to experiment says that the goal to be reached may require more or less specifically the function which the object is to fill. The less specific or significant the indication the more likely it is that S will have to examine each possible object in a search for its possible functions. This, says Duncker, is the real cause of functional fixedness. The pre-utilization or first use of the object hides that function, and the more functions there are among which to search, the less likely it is to be found.

In testing this hypothesis, the goal in the box problem is made more specific by saying to S, "Use for the solution the tacks and something which can easily be fastened to the door with tacks." (Notice this removes the tacks from the set of objects to be considered, narrowing the search area. This is in addition to specifying the function which the box must serve.) In the other experimental condition the tacks are removed from the table, and S is told to ask for anything he may need.

The independent variable makes use of the central and peripheral functions described above (and, since the main prediction is confirmed, lends support to the hypothesis about central and peripheral functions). Only one candle is used. There are two boxes on the table, one used in the central function of holding the candle, the other with the peripheral function of holding buttons. If the candle holder takes on the container function, then the button box should be selected for the platform. Thus, use of the button box implies functional fixedness of the candle box.

Combining the statements of the last two paragraphs results in the suggestion that the less specific goal (the condition with no tacks visible) should increase fixedness, and therefore S should choose the button box for the platform in the main problem. This is what happens, as Table 9 shows.

TABLE 9

Number of Choices of the Two Boxes *

	Less Specific Goal, No Tacks, etc.	*More Specific Goal, "Use the tacks . . ."*
Candle box	7	10
Button box	7	1
Both at once		1

* Adapted from Duncker (1945), Table 10.

With the less specific goal the Ss chose the button box 50 per cent of the time, but with the more specific indication, 13 per cent of the time; there was more functional fixedness with the less specific goal. Duncker says that this principle has great significance for his theory of "solution through resonance."

The reported evidence shown in Table 9 supports the prediction about specificity or significance of the goal as well as the one about central and peripheral uses of the object. It would be more impressive if the *E* had said, "Use for the solution something which can easily be fastened to the door" and had left the tacks on the table instead of saying "Use for the solution the tacks and something which can easily be fastened to the door with the tacks."

Duncker's Hypotheses about Functional Fixedness

Four of Duncker's hypotheses have been encountered up to this point:

1. Use of an object for one function may inhibit its use for a different function. This will occur only when S has to examine the object for its functions in seeking the second function. (But compare, Hypothesis 4 below.)

Most of the other hypotheses represent attempts to specify conditions which will facilitate or inhibit functional fixedness, and are therefore subsidaries of the first hypothesis.

2. Functional fixedness will be increased if the object is used in such a way that S has to handle it (as in taking a cork out of a bottle) rather than merely observe its presence: the central-peripheral hypothesis.

3. Functional fixedness will be decreased if the first function is in a situation separate and distinct from the problem situation: the separate-problem hypothesis.

4. As the S knows more specifically what he is to do in the problem situation the functional fixedness decreases. (In connection with the experiment which tests this hypothesis, one might say that giving S a hint about the solution function decreases functional fixedness.) This is true because the more specific goal cuts down the amount of search for the possible functions of the objects. (And consider Hypothesis 6.) This may be called the specificity-of-the-goal hypothesis.

In addition to the above hypotheses, all of which have led to experiments, Duncker offers these:

5. Functional fixedness will be affected if the goal offers perceptual hints about the object to be used.

The direction of the effect will depend on the specific hint and on the available objects. The suggestion of a hammer will help or hinder, depending on the presence or absence of a hammer.

6. The action of functional fixedness is the prevention of the finding of functions when considering objects.

Considering the function and then looking for an object to fill it should, then, be more successful. (See Hypothesis 4.) This is one way in which starting backwards from the goal makes a problem easier. (See Chapter I.)

7. If the first function persists during the search for the new one, functional fixedness will increase. The hypothesis and experiment concerning the first function as part of, or separate from, the main problem (see Hypothesis 3), may be regarded as a special case of this hypothesis.

In the box problem, the candles ordinarily remain in the box (the function persists) while S is searching for the platform object, but in the cork problem he has finished using the cork before he starts to look for a wedge.

8. If the first use is a frequent function of the object, this will make it harder to perceive it in a new function, increasing the functional fixedness.

9. If the second function is a frequent function of the object, and the first infrequent, this will make it easier for S to find the second function, inhibiting the functional fixedness.

In connection with Hypotheses 8 and 9, see the report on van de Geer's work in the next section of this chapter.

10. The more different functions the object has, the easier to use it in still another, new way, decreasing functional fixedness. Flavell, Cooper, and Loiselle (1958) report an experiment which substantiates this hypothesis.

11. Functional fixedness will decrease if the second function is one which can be filled by several different objects (many heavy objects will serve as hammers).

12. A necessity for a physical change in the object (as in bending the paperclip into a hook) will increase functional fixedness.

Duncker points out that this is at least similar to, and perhaps identical with, a necessity for changing the *Gestalt* in which the object is presented. A cork as part of an ink container is different from a lone cork on the table.

13. If the object whose function is being considered is present perceptually rather than in the S's cognitive processes, this will facilitate functional fixedness. This would mean, for example, *E*'s having the tacks on the table as contrasted with telling S to ask for anything he needs.

14. By the process called *stimulus generalization* (including *semantic generalization*) the fixedness may spread to objects similar to the one which carries the first function. Glucksberg (1964) reports an experiment in which semantic generalization facilitated functional fixedness.

15. If the object is not very appropriate for the second function, this will increase the fixedness.

For instance, a round cork does not make a very good wedge. Duncker points out the similarity of this hypothesis to Hypothesis 5. Compare it also with Hypothesis 9.

16. Functional fixedness will be reduced if the first function leaves the object in a position suitable for the second function.

For instance, if the gimlet is used to bore a hole, it is right there to hang a cord from.

17. A special difficulty in finding a new function arises when the new one is the opposite, or obverse, of the first function; for instance, a hammer and anvil have "opposite" functions. This might be the case when the box holds the candles and then the candles have to fill the box (perhaps to keep it from blowing away).

18. Functional fixedness is the result of the object's function becoming embedded in a functional whole in such a way that it is no longer visible as a separate item.

The pliers' function as a holder of nails may be lost in its function as a puller of nails. As perceptual analogies: a bright spot on the wall is lost to view when the whole wall is brightly illuminated; the sound of a consonant is lost when a word is heard.

19. The *relief* of the functions or uses of an object may change. Relief here is used in the same sense as in a relief map. Some parts are higher than others. Some functions stand out and others recede until they are completely gone as far as the S is concerned. The function produces a relief in the object, and producing a new function for that object would mean changing the relative reliefs of different functions. Analogously, one may at one time notice the

general smoothness of the ocean, and at another notice how high the crests are above the troughs. See van de Geer in the next section.

A good deal of attention has been devoted here to Duncker's work for various reasons. He was the first man to advance the concept of functional fixedness and has done the most extensive work on it. He is often quoted, but the references omit most of his experiments and seldom mention the large set of hypotheses which he advanced. Further, his translator emphasized literal rather than free translation, making the 1945 English edition very difficult to read. We venture to hope that the present summary is easily comprehended, and without too much distortion. (See Part Two, reading [14].)

Post-Duncker Work on Functional Fixedness

The earliest post-Duncker experiment on functional fixedness is that of Birch and Rabinowitz (1951). They raised several objections to Duncker's experimental conditions (many of which Duncker had himself mentioned), but this experiment deals with only one of those objections: the question as to whether the objects used for the problem solving were "appropriate" (see Hypothesis 15 in preceding section). In order to take care of this question they use two objects that are assumed, on the basis of the control-group results, to be equally appropriate: a relay and an electrical switch. Half the Ss are given the switch for the first function and are presented with a choice of the two objects for the second. The other half are given the relay for the first, then are given the choice. The question is whether the S will choose for the second function whatever he did not use the first time.

The first function is the use of the object in completing the wiring of an electrical circuit; the second is as a pendulum in Maier's two-string task. A control group of six engineering students "with a wide variety of electrical experience" did not do the preliminary wiring.

In the control group, half of the Ss chose each object for the pendulum weight. In the experimental group, 17 out of 19 Ss chose for the pendulum the object which they had not previously used. There is here, then, a verification of the fundamental hypothesis, which says that there is such a phenomenon as functional fixedness. (Note, however, that the Ss in the control group are not from the same population as those in the treatment groups.)

It will be noted that the pre-utilization of the objects was in a situation separate from the problem situation, as in one of Duncker's experiments described earlier in this chapter (with the hypothesis repeated in Hypothesis 3 in preceding section). However, as Adamson and Taylor (1954) have said, Duncker's experiment found no fixedness in this separate-problem situation, while the Birch-Rabinowitz work directly contradicted that result. No satisfactory explanation of this discrepancy is apparent unless it lies in the fact that the two experiments used different problems, and, of course, different Ss. Forster, Vinacke, and Digman (1955) had a group of Ss work at seven problems and found that the persons successful at one problem were not at all the ones successful at the next. Adamson (1952) makes a similar report. He used 28 Ss in the experimental group on each of three problems: box, gimlet, and paperclip. He also reported that the individuals who showed functional fixedness in one problem did not necessarily show it in the next. Individual differences among the Ss may be more important here than one might think from the lack of consideration of the topic in the reports of experimenters.

Duncker's experiments used only a small number of Ss in conditions not always clearly specified, so Adamson (1952) repeated the basic demonstration of the existence of functional fixedness, using three of Duncker's problems.

Adamson used 29 Ss in his experimental group, 28 in the control group. Each S went through the problems in this order: the box, the gimlet, and the paperclip. The results substantiate the existence of functional fixedness, giving results significant at the .01 level or better in each problem.

In the box problem 41 per cent of the Ss solved the problem; in the gimlet problem, 90 per cent; and in the paperclip problem, 100 per cent. The elegance of Duncker's having problems of the correct difficulty level for his Ss was pointed out above. This is not true here; the problems are too easy. Of course, it is also true that when Ss all go through the three problems in the same sequence, and the percentages of success are, successively, 41, 90, and 100, one begins to think that there may be a practice effect involved. It does seem possible, however, that Adamson's Ss were better problem solvers than were Duncker's. As was said previously, the Ss who solved one problem were not always those who solved the next.

Adamson has confirmed the Duncker (1945) and the Birch-Rabinowitz (1951) reports of the reality of functional fixedness. Adamson and Taylor (1954) now go on, using the Birch-Rabinowitz experimental design and tasks, to investigate whether the functional fixedness is permanent or whether it affects only immediately subsequent behavior.

They used five groups of Ss, and had them try the F_2 problem after intervals of a minute, a half-hour, an hour, a day, and a week. The amount of functional fixedness did not decrease for the first half hour, but then fell off and was completely gone by the end of the week. They suggest that the loss is not a function of time, and indeed, it is widely accepted that nothing could be a function of time alone. Their hypothesis concerning this decrement is in terms of retroactive inhibition, which is often offered as an explanation of forgetting.

The Adamson-Taylor article also contains a report of an experiment on the relation of functional fixedness to set and to susceptivity to set.

Van de Geer (1957) points out that Duncker, Adamson, and Birch and Rabinowitz all used their critical objects in ordinary ways for the first function and in unusual ways for the second. He reports an experiment in which this situation is reversed. In his experimental condition the object is used in the unusual manner first, then in the more usual way; in the control condition the usual function is first.

One problem consists of a block made of two sections, and S has to find out how to separate the two parts. S had to think of the correct solution before being allowed to touch the block. The parts of the block are fastened together with a long machine screw. This does not really enter into the problem—at least there is no report that any S failed to solve the problem or that anyone had trouble with the screw. The important feature of the screw is that either of two critical objects can be used to loosen it. It has a hexagonal head and a slot across the head, so it can be turned with a wrench or with a screwdriver. The function of the block problem is only to provide S with a choice of the critical objects: screwdriver and wrench.

Table 10 shows the results of the experiment. In the condition with the unusual use first (the two-string task), there was no particular change from the first to the second problem, but in the other condition Ss tended to use the screwdriver if they had previously

TABLE 10

Number of Changes of Tool from the First to Second Problem *

	Number of Ss using Same Tool in Both Problems	*Number of Ss Using Different Tool in the Second Problem*
Block, then string, condition	4	15
String, then block, condition	9	12

* Adapted from van de Geer (1947), Table 1. Chi square shows a difference significant at .05 in the upper condition and no significant difference in the lower condition.

used the wrench and to use the wrench if they had used the screwdriver. Therefore, the use of the tool first in an ordinary function made it unavailable for later use in a new function, and this applied to both tools; but if the first function was an unusual one, functional fixedness did not appear.

This result agrees with Duncker's prediction that if the first function is a frequent function of the object, it will be harder for S to perceive the object in a new function (see Hypothesis 8, preceding section). *Frequent* here is the same as *usual.*

However, here is a case in which the two functions of the object are in separate situations: the block problem and the two-string problem. Duncker predicted that there would be no functional fixedness here (see Hypothesis 3, preceding section). Van de Geer's experiment, like the Birch-Rabinowitz experiment (on which it was modelled), finds functional fixedness in these circumstances, so this one of Duncker's hypotheses has now been denied twice, although Duncker's experiment sustained it. Again, however, one may wonder about the extent to which the discrepancy is due to differences in the problems.

It is here suggested that *problems* may well differ in ways such that they produce different processes in Ss.

Glucksberg, using students at New York University as subjects, reported an experiment (1962) in which functional fixedness is one part of the work. He used Duncker's box problem (which Glucksberg calls the candle problem). The mean time to success for the fixedness group was 9.25 minutes, and for the control group was 4.33 minutes, the difference being significant at the .001 level. The number of successes was high in all groups, and the differences between groups on this measure were therefore too small to be significant.

One program of research on functional fixedness (Ray, 1965b; Duvall, 1965) began by attempting to construct a new task that would contain several objects of known preference ratings in a non-problem-solving situation. Duncker as well as Birch and Rabinowitz had pointed out that some objects are more suitable for certain functions than are others, as, for instance, it seems improbable that one could functionally fix a hammer so thoroughly that any S would, a moment later, prefer a padlock for driving a nail. If two objects are equally preferred, it should be possible for S to use either in the first function, choosing the other object for the second function. On the other hand, if one object is preferred for a function, and the object is used for that function when it is the second function in a functional-fixedness experiment, then the law of parsimony demands that the second-function use be attributed to preference rather than to any functional fixedness.

It was further assumed that functional fixedness should appear whether or not the second function was in a problem-solving situation.

Six objects were used to set up the preference hierarchy: a padlock, a 12-inch ruler, a corner brace, a glass ash tray, a door knob with the spindle removed, and a screwdriver, each to be used to drive a nail (Ray, 1965b). The results are shown in Table 11.

TABLE 11

Preliminary Object-Preference Study

	Median Rankings		
	Girls (Ages 13 to 17)	*Boys (Ages 13 to 17)*	*Men (Ages 23 to 57)*
Screwdriver	1.5	2.1	2.9
Padlock	2.0	2.1	1.1
Door knob	1.8	1.7	1.4
Ash tray	3.9	3.9	3.4
Corner brace	3.4	3.9	4.0
Ruler	5.1	5.4	5.3

On the basis of these preliminary results, it was concluded that either the padlock-door knob cluster or the ash tray-corner brace cluster could be used in an interchangeable-object experimental design, with whatever object was used for the first function becoming functionally fixed and the other object of the pair being used for the second function. Further, one object from the most-preferred cluster used with one object from the second-preferred cluster should produce results in which the most-preferred object could not be functionally fixed.

Duncker's weight problem was used in the three experiments implied in the preceding paragraph, with the first function being that of a pendulum, and the second being that of a hammer, the latter a repetition of the function used in the preliminary preference study. There was no real problem here as S was only requested to drive a nail by using any of the objects on the table. As an additional check on the preliminary results, each experiment included a control condition for preference as a hammer, with no preliminary use as a pendulum.

The results of the experiments are shown in Table 12. The padlock and the ashtray were unequally preferred in the preliminary study, and unequally preferred in this experiment, and, as predicted, it was impossible to set up any functional fixedness. The door knob and the padlock were equally preferred in the preliminary study, but unequally preferred here. The padlock is preferred in the preference determination and preferred also in the two functional fixedness treatments. On the hypothesis just used for padlock and ash tray, no functional fixedness can be expected, and none is found. This check on preference for the hammer function gave results quite different from those of the preliminary study, casting doubt on the reliability of the findings of that study.

The ash tray and corner brace were equally preferred, as predicted from the preliminary study. But the functional-fixedness treatment produced *positive* transfer of training instead of the negative transfer that is functional fixedness.

The results of this last experiment were astonishing and puzzling, but they led to a situation which is relatively rare in psychological research: a repetition of the experiment by another experimeter in another location using the written description as his guide. Glucksberg (1964c) did this with high-school-age subjects from the region of Princeton, N.J. He confirmed the finding of positive transfer in the ash tray and corner brace experiment.

Since the results of Ray's experiment contradicted all previous

TABLE 12

Frequency of Use of Available Objects for the Second Function
Total N = 108

Available Objects	*First Function (Pendulum) Attached To*	*No. of Ss Using Each Object for Second (Hammer) Function*	*Chi Square*	*P*
Padlock	Padlock	9	.60	
Ash tray		3		
Padlock		9	.60	
Ash tray	Ash tray	3		
Padlock		10		
Ash tray		2		
Door knob	Door knob	3	.00	
Padlock		9		
Door knob		5	1.77	.20–.10
Padlock	Padlock	7		
Door knob		3		
Padlock		9		
Ash tray	Ash tray	8	1.34	.30–.20
Corner brace		4		
Ash tray		2	5.34	.02
Corner brace	Corner brace	10		
Ash tray		6		
Corner brace		6		
Fixed object		18	6.00	.02
Non-fixed object		6		

Note: "Fixed" object is the one used in the first function; "Non-fixed" object is the other one of the pair.

reports in this field, it was decided that some previous experiment should be repeated to see whether the results were replicated (Duvall, 1965). The Birch-Rabinowitz (1951) experiment was chosen. These investigators had had Ss use an electrical switch to complete a circuit, then gave the Ss a choice of the switch or a relay for use as a pendulum weight in Maier's two-string task. Another group of Ss used the relay in the circuit, then made the choice. A control group showed no preference for either object as a pendulum weight.

The Duvall experiment, in addition to duplicating the Birch-Rabinowitz set-up, also reversed the functions. That is, in addition to the two treatment conditions just described, there were two more conditions, in which S did the two string problem first, then did the circuit wiring. Still another pair of control conditions tested S's preference for the two objects on the two string task and on the circuit with no previous use of either.

The first finding was that the two objects were not equally preferred as they had been in the Birch-Rabinowitz work; the switch was preferred over the relay at about a 2 to 1 ratio in both two-string and circuit-wiring controls. In two of the experimental conditions the switch was correspondingly preferred, which is not evidence for functional fixedness. In a third condition the switch was used first in the circuit, and then the relay was used (by 12 of the 16 Ss) on the succeeding two-string problems indicating functional fixedness.

However, in another condition the positive transfer again appeared. The switch was preferred over the relay in the circuit-wiring control condition by a ratio of 10 to 6 Ss. When the switch was forced on S for use as the pendulum weight in the two-string task and S was then given a choice for use in the wiring, the switch was preferred by a ratio of 14 to 1. A ratio of 14 to 1 is reliably different from 10 to 6.

The reversal of functions in this experiment is a design used by van de Geer (1957). He pointed out that previous experiments (including that of Birch and Rabinowitz) had used the experimental objects first in their usual functions and then found the fixedness in a later, unusual function. He then used a reversed-functions experiment in which F_1 was followed by F_2 for one set of Ss, and F_2 was followed by F_1 for a different set (Table 10). His hypothesis was confirmed by his results: the use of the unusual function first prevented functional fixedness.

These results do not deny van de Geer's prediction that putting the unusual function first will prevent functional fixedness, and they go beyond that and find positive transfer.

It was suggested by Duncker (1945, p. 99) that "homogeneous fixedness" (positive transfer), is due to the use of the same property of the object in the two functions. It has been very kindly suggested to the present writer by Goodnow (1965) that in Ray's (1965b) experiment the pendulum and hammer functions are both uses of the same property of the objects: weight. However, Duvall (1965) found positive transfer when a switch was used as a weight, then as an electrical component, which are certainly not uses of the same property. Further, Duncker used the weight property in his weight problem (Table 7), which included the same pendulum and hammer functions as in the Ray experiment (1965b), and he reports something which looks like functional fixedness (although his chi square significance level as calculated by this writer gives a significance level of between 5 and 10 per cent). The present evidence, then, does not confirm the hypothesis that uses of the same property will produce positive rather than negative transfer of training.

Another possible explanation of positive transfer lies in the usualness or familiarity of the object for the required function, and in its position as first or second in the experimental design. Van de Geer's results, on the other hand, do not support this hypothesis.

Functional fixedness, to conclude, is in the same position as other phenomena discussed in this book; the conditions that facilitate or inhibit it are not clear.

CHAPTER VII

Methodology

THE DIFFICULTY OF EXPERIMENTAL RESEARCH IN ORIGINAL thinking, and in problem solving in general, is increased by a lack of enough community experience to provide tasks and procedures which are reliable and valid, whose content is understood, and which are standardized but at the same time can be altered within known limits. The more traditional fields of learning have Skinner boxes, mazes, nonsense syllables and paired-associate procedures, operant conditioning, and methods of measuring retention or habit strength. Such resources for experimenters are provided by a long history of experimentation and by research designed for investigating the features of the tasks and procedures. Such history and research are both in short supply in the area of problem solving.

A list of desirable criteria of problem-solving tasks has been offered by Ray (1955) and amplified by Andreas (1960). Descriptions of tasks are given in several places, for instance in Woodworth (1938), Krech and Crutchfield (1958), and the Ray article. The tasks which have been mentioned in this book are listed with page references in the index. The author proposes to repeat in this chapter the list of criteria with modifications, and to make some further remarks on research methods in this area.

EXPERIMENTAL TASKS

Desirable Features

There is no doubt that the two most important criteria of desirable experimental tasks are reliability and validity. *Validity* here refers to whether the task is a problem-solving task or is one whose products may be assumed to indicate that S must have gone through the process called original thinking. (Note that this is not statistical, experimental-design validity discussed by, for example, William Ray (1960).) Such validity is called *face validity,* which means in this case that the experimenter assumes that the task requires thinking and, further, assumes that other persons will agree with him, as they usually do. One difficulty arises here, however: that of whether the problem is so simple that one questions whether it really causes any thinking in S.

Reliability in the area of original thinking, on the other hand, is in a deplorable condition. There are actual measured statistical determinations of reliability in a few cases, as in Guilford's (Guilford, Wilson, Christensen, and Lewis, 1951) Unusual Uses Test, or in Peterson's (1932) report on the reliability of a set of 20 problems dealing with moments of levers. Usually, however, reliability is not measured but is, rather, intuitively assumed to be present if a task is used repeatedly, always producing the same sort of results. Some tasks seem to do this, as in the cases of some anagram tasks or in water-jar problems. But the reader will remember that there have been several reports in previous chapters of experiments which have been repeated with results different from those first achieved. An experiment was reported in Chapter VI in which the reliability of the results, and thus of the tasks, was demonstrated by another experimenter's repeating the experiment, producing the same positive transfer shown in the original experiment. However, Duvall (1965) reports that a third use of the task produced negative transfer. The original experiment and Duvall's replication of it were carried out in the same laboratory with identical pieces of apparatus, same procedure, and one of the original set of test administrators. If such conditions as these at one time produce positive and at another time negative transfer, research in this field is indeed in a sorry state.

Three further desirable features of problem-solving tasks remain to be mentioned. One is a score continuum in which the possible dependent variable scores may cover a range of several points rather than be confined to a two-point continuum of pass or fail. Such continua are most easily produced in situations where S must give repeated responses, as in sorting cards in the Wisconsin Card Sorting Test (Chapter I), or solve a series of problems all much alike, as in the Unusual Uses Test or the Remote Associates Test.

The fourth of the criteria is a matter of having as much as possible of S's work be overt rather than hidden within him. An elegant example of overt work is provided by tasks such as the Wisconsin Card Sorting Test, where *S* has three possible hypotheses (color, form, or number) and *E* may surmise which hypothesis is in use by watching S sort three or four successive cards. Another example is provided by a game called Making the Last Draw (Ray, 1955) in which S and *E* alternate draws from a pile of several objects, each taking one or two as he wishes. *S* gets the first trial, and is required to learn how to ensure his own drawing of the last item. With an odd number of objects, S must start by drawing one object. He can develop and use his starting hypothesis without knowing what else to do in order to be successful (the problem solution includes more than one hypothesis); and *E* can see whether he does it repeatedly. Ss frequently do this without being able to verbalize the action and without realizing that they are doing it. (These examples illustrate the response hypothesis assumption discussed in Chapter V.)

A final desirable characteristic of a task may be called its congruity. This refers to its suitability for (a) the subject population available and (b) the experimental hypothesis under test. Obviously the difficulty level must be such that not all of the Ss succeed nor all fail. It should, indeed, be such that *E*, using the score continuum mentioned previously, can differentiate the results of one treatment from those of another. And the difficulty level must not call for special knowledge on the part of the Ss, unless *E* is willing to supply that knowledge as did Moore and Anderson (1954) with their symbolic logic problems. Mednick (1962) says of this special knowledge difficulty,

> A first problem concerns the type of material of which the stimulus item should be composed. If the test is to be appropriate for all fields of creative endeavor, the material must either be nonsensical so as to avoid bias favoring any specific means of creative expression, or it must be so

common in society that familiarity could be assumed to be high across fields of interest. The problems involved in constructing the nonsense materials so as to avoid favoring any interest groups soon proved to be apparently insurmountable. This left us searching for materials with which most individuals in the culture could claim acquaintance; this, in turn, brought us to verbal materials.

Another consideration which may be classed as congruity refers to the content of the task. Szekely's (1950) Inclined Plane Task includes a ramp with a pulley at the top. In a modification of this task, a string running over the pulley is attached at one end to a toy truck, and at the other end to a sort of barge which floats in a tank of water. S is asked to move the truck down the plane (by pouring water into the tank), and then to move it up the plane (by laying a heavy object on the barge). A nice simple two-problem apparatus. Actual use of the equipment, however, produces eight or ten solutions: for example, pulling the truck up the incline by moving the tank of water away from the ramp. The moral of this example is that *E* should always make preliminary trials of a task, no matter what the literature says about it—at least the literature in its present state of the art.

Undesirable Features

Some of the points just made may be amplified, and other concepts introduced, by pointing out some undesirable characteristics of tasks. One big difficulty with some tasks—for instance, with that perennial favorite, the Maier two-string task—is that they are cumbersome and awkward. Until someone publishes a formula which will obviate the need for doing so, this task must be adjusted by trial and error to the room in which it is to be used. The strings must be hung from the ceiling (which is sometimes impossible with the high ceilings found in many old college buildings), several feet apart, and with enough space around them that they will not swing against the walls on any side. The distance between them has to be adjusted by trail and error, as does the length of the string, with due regard to the possible long legs of the S who is six feet, six inches tall.

In connection with the two-string task, Maltzman, Belloni, and Fishbein (1964), after using it in three experiments, say:

Our inability to reproduce the results reported by Judson *et al.* (1956) indicated the inadequacy of the two-string problem as a dependable problem-solving task. Variability in our results from one experiment to the next also corresponded to the difficulty Judson *et al.* found in reproducing the results of their first experiment in a reliable fashion. . . . Criticism of the two-string problem has repeatedly occurred (Duncan, 1959; Ray, 1955). It had been hoped, however, that the group form might prove a more adequate performance situation. These hopes were not realized, and as a consequence we discontinued our research with the two-string problem.

Some of these tasks can be made less unwieldy by miniaturization. The Cognitive Operations Laboratory at Bethany College has, for instance, offered S a box a foot high with two strings hanging from the "ceiling." A doll's chair stands in one corner of the box, and other full-size objects, such as a meterstick, a ball of cord, and so on, are laid on the table beside the box. The S is requested to imagine solutions and give them to *E*. Other workers (Guetzkow, 1951; Judson *et al.*, 1956; and Maltzman *et al.*, 1964) have used "group" forms of this problem, giving S a picture of the room with the objects in it, and asking him to imagine and write down his solutions. Just how similar these tasks are to the hanging of strings in a room is a question remaining to be answered.

Glucksberg (1964b) has simplified the set-up of Duncker's box problem by asking S to fix the candle platforms to a "wall" which is a piece of board set up on a table.

Maier's hat-rack problem could certainly be put into a box, say three feet high, with boards and a clamp of the appropriate size, allowing actual manipulation of the apparatus rather than imaginary manipulations.

It is interesting to note that investigators of problem solving may exhibit undesirable sets in their use of tasks as dependent variables. For example, the two-string problem has several possible solutions, but many successive experimenters have given S credit for success only if he used the pendulum solution. One reason for this seems to be that some previous *E* gave credit for this solution only, the procedure being repeated without *E*'s stopping to think about it—in fact, without any cognitive operations by *E* on the matter. One fine measure of originality is, obviously, the number of solutions which S can find to each problem, and this demands credit for all solutions.

Another, and even better example of set in experiment design appears with repetitions of Luchins' (1942) procedure with water-jar problems. After the training problems Luchins used two two-method problems, then one short-method (extinction) problem, then two more two-method test problems. This arrangement showed what Luchins wanted to demonstrate, but it is not apparent why succeeding experimenters have repeated it when they wanted a measure of the strength of set. The obvious measure of strength of set here is resistance to extinction, which should be measured in a long series of two-method problems whose object is to see how long it takes S to change from the long to the short method of solution.

Procedures

The Method of Spoken Thought

In 1917 Professor Edouard Claparède recommended a new method for the investigation of thinking processes:

> Nous avons employé un procédé nouveau destiné à parer aux défauts de la méthode habituelle d'introspection, et que nous avons appelé "méthode de la réflexion parlée." Le sujet, auquel on donne un problème plus ou moins difficile à résoudre, est prié de penser à haute voix, de raconter au fur et à mesure ce qui se déroule dans sa conscience, ses hésitations, ses doutes, les idées qui lui viennent à l'esprit, etc. Cette méthode s'est montrée féconde. Elle évite les inconvénients de la "rétrospection," et ceux du "dédoublement." (Claparède, 1917.)

This method is still in use by, for instance, Scheerer and Huling (1960) and de Groot (1965). Duncker (1945, p. 11) also used it although he himself points out deficiencies in the procedure:

> A protocol is relatively reliable only for what it positively contains, but not for that which it omits. For even the best-intentioned protocol is only a very scanty record of what actually happens. The reasons for this insufficiency of protocols which are based on spoken thoughts must interest us also as characteristic of a solution-process as such. Mediating phases which lead at once to their concrete final realization, and thus are not separated from the solution by clear phase-boundaries, will often not be explicitly mentioned. They blend too thoroughly with their final solutions. On the other hand, mediating phases which must persist as temporary tasks until they find their final application to the situation have a better chance of being explicitly formulated. Furthermore, many superordinate phases do not appear in the protocol, because the situation does not appear to the S promising enough for them. Therefore they are at once suppressed. In other words, they are too fleeting, too provisional, too tentative, occasionally also too "foolish," to cross the threshold of the spoken word.

Even Duncker's statement that the protocol is "relatively reliable only for what it positively contains" is open to doubt, because it assumes that S is able to give correct spoken descriptions of his cognitive processes. Anyone who has watched Ss solve a fairly complex problem and repeatedly produce the solution and has then asked S to describe his response hypothesis knows that some Ss can do this correctly, some cannot do it at all, and some give descriptions of their methods which are obviously incorrect and sometimes ridiculous. If the reader wishes to demonstrate this to himself, Making the Last Draw (described earlier in this chapter) is a fine problem with which to start. Ss' inability to describe what they are doing has been reported by, for example, Rees and Israel (Chapter V).

If the information secured by asking S to proceed aloud is incomplete or even erroneous, then it obviously cannot be used as data, although it is often of value in making suggestions about items which an experimenter may then test experimentally. It is at this point that tasks which produce overt behavior by S become helpful.

This warning against dependence on the method of spoken thought must not be considered a prohibition of all experimentation in which the S's responses are verbal, whether written or oral. Mednick's Remote Associates Test, for example, requires S to produce verbal responses. Maltzman's Standard Experimental Procedure also is a verbal task with verbal responses. Free-association tasks, anagrams, arithmetic tasks, and dozens of others are purely verbal, both on the stimulus and on the response side. The warning is not against verbal behavior, but against S's verbal descriptions of his cognitive operations or response hypotheses. This warning should, however, be extended to include individuals' descriptions of their own thinking—descriptions which are so often quoted as evidence in this field, as, for instance, Poincaré's description; Patrick's studies of poets, artists, painters, in which she asked them to describe their thought processes; and Ghiselin's (1952) collection of statements about how people thought they were thinking. These publications make fascinating reading, but they do not provide data.

Artificial Intelligence

Machines which learn, think, or simulate human perceiving have long interested man, from the days of chess-playing automata (Poe,

1936; eleventh edition of the Encyclopaedia Britannica under *automation and conjuring*); through conditioned-response learners (Baernstein and Hull, 1931; Hoffman, 1962); to more complex learners such as Ashby's (1960) Homeostat, an adaptive machine which seeks a goal; Walter's (1953) turtle which shows several complex phenomena; Berkeley's (1949) Simon, which compares and makes decisions; Uttley's (1959) conditional probability learner, and many others. The most recent and most sophisticated "intelligent machine" is the Logic Theorist of Newell, Shaw, and Simon (1962).

By far the most complex of the artificial intelligence machines which man has invented is the digital computer, which has fascinated the man in the street as well as psychologists, telephone theorists, communications theorists, neurologists, logicians, mathematicians, and many others. One of its more dramatic manifestations is the prediction of election results hours before the results are available. Newspapers carry frequent stories of computer music and poetry. More practical purposes are the translation of Russian into English, the retrieval of library information, the inventory control of the Air Materiel Command. De Solla Price (1965) reports a study of the network of scientific papers based on citations of one paper by others. He includes a graph of the percentages of papers published from 1862 through 1961 which were cited in 1961, showing, as might be expected, that later papers are quoted more often than earlier papers and showing dips in the years of both world wars. This could never have been done by hand. This "intelligent" behavior by computers is in addition to their original purposes such as solving complex mathematical equations for engineers, controlling the re-entry point of space vehicles, working out analyses of variance problems for statisticians. Guilford's structure of intellect (Chapter III) demands, as a first step, simple correlations between each pair of forty or fifty tests, with 300 to 500 scores on each test. The time necessary to calculate these simple correlations by hand, plus the time necessary for the more complex factor analyses, would make such work impracticable.

The simulation of human problem solving is the most complex process that can be requested of a computer. The best-known attempt at this problem solving has been done by the Logic Theorist of Newell, Shaw, and Simon (1958). The Logic Theorist is a set of routines or "programs" to be put into a computer. Newell, Shaw, and Simon start by treating problem solving as information processing.

They then assume that the sensory processes by which information is inserted and the motor processes by which the solution is returned to the outer world are trivial. The heart of the matter, they reason, lies in the processing of the information inside of the machine, whether the machine is a computer or a human brain. The theory postulates

1. A set of specific items in a memory, with various relations (such as *larger than*) among the items.
2. A number of primitive processes for handling memory items and relations. (A simple example is the symbolic logic rule which says that *A* and *A* equal *A;* Jones today and Jones tomorrow are still Jones. The computer can then substitute one *A* for the two *A*s.)
3. A set of rules for combining these primitive processes into programs, for instance, sequences of processes, or the comparison of processes or sequences to discover whether they are identical.

These authors then point out that their theory assumes that there are similarities among programs, similarities within an individual when he solves mathematical and chess problems, and similarities between individuals when they solve mathematical or chess problems. A computer can compare programs for similarities.

The Logic Theorist makes at least two general contributions to the psychology of thinking: it shows that the complex processes of problem solving can be compounded out of elementary processes, and shows that such elementary processes can solve difficult problems, thus taking away the "mystery" component of people's attitudes toward problem solving.

A set of experiments with the Logic Theorist in the computer demonstrates certain similarities to human problem solving. Axioms and simple theorems from *Principia Mathematica* of Whitehead and Russell (1925), plus the program called the Logic Theorist, are put into the memory of the computer, and the computer is requested to prove and remember the proofs of the first 52 theorems of that work. The Theorist was 73 per cent successful. In a second experiment the memories of the proofs were obliterated and the Theorist given a complex theorem which it could not prove although it had done so in the first experiment when it remembered the preceding theorems. In a third experiment, the Theorist was given one theorem necessary to the proof of the complex theorem of the second experiment and was asked to prove the complex one. It did so, but with a good deal more effort than had been necessary in the first experiment when the complex theorem had been part of a preceding, remembered, series.

The Logic Theorist is a *model* of intelligent human behavior, as are the other examples of artificial intelligence, with the exception of Maelzel's chess player, which was a fraud (as are all stage magicians' automata). All these examples have been of machines except for the Theorist which is a collection of procedures which can be carried out by a digital computer or by a man, although the man needs much more time than does the computer.

In a discussion of the electronic digital computer as an analogue or model, Simon and Newell (1963) start by denying that a computer cannot do any "thinking" beyond simple arithmetic, and that it must be instructed in detail what arithmetic to do. They then point out that the problem which is of immediate concern is not whether we can teach a computer to, for example, play chess, but whether we can teach the computer to learn to play chess. (Note the similarity here to teaching the computer to solve symbolic logic problems by letting it work up through them rather than by starting with one high up in the difficulty scale.) The authors translate "learn to play chess" into "construct for itself new subprograms."

One may ask, "How intelligent is artificial intelligence?" but let it be remembered that this is a man-in-the-street question, not one in which model builders and computer people are especially interested. Bernstein and Rubin, who *are* computer people, say (1965), "We shall adopt a working definition of intelligence in computers. . . . We should like to be able to give a problem to a computer without specifying the method of solution." If a computer can develop its own subprograms it can perhaps develop its own complete program, which would fulfill Bernstein and Rubin's criterion. Certainly the electronic digital computer can solve mathematical problems, but can it learn to play chess without being given rules for the development of gambits? Such a question may be actually unanswerable, but there is one act which would certainly earn for the computer the title of a real thinking machine: the act of the machine's suggesting experiments to be carried out on human subjects. Or perhaps the people who work with computers can, on the basis of their work, suggest experiments to be carried out on human subjects.

Simon and Newell say, "We assert with considerable conviction that there is nothing a digital computer can do that a human being, given time, patience, and plenty of paper, cannot do also." On the other hand, human beings can do many things in the intellectual field that computers cannot do. To paraphrase the last sentence of Herrick's *Brains of Rats and Men* (1926),

> Men are bigger and better than computers.

It is also probable that whereas computers do their problem solving systematically, original thinking is anything but systematic.

PART TWO

The Selected Readings

Important Sources Included in Whole or in Part

[1] J. Greenspoon, "The Reinforcing Effect of Two Spoken Sounds on the Frequency of Two Responses"
[2] D. T. Campbell, "Blind Variation and Selective Retention in Creative Thought as in Other Knowledge Processes"
[3] I. Maltzman, S. Simon, D. Raskin, and L. Licht, "Experimental Studies in the Training of Originality"
[4] I. Maltzman, "On the Training of Originality"
[5] S. A. Mednick, "The Associative Basis of the Creative Process"
[6] J. P. Houston and S. A. Mednick, "Creativity and the Need for Novelty"
[7] N. R. F. Maier, "Reasoning in White Rats"
[8] C. L. Hull, "The Mechanism of the Assembly of Behavior Segments in Novel Combinations Suitable for Problem Solution"
[9] J. Dewey, "How We Think: The Analysis of a Complete Act of Thought"
[10] A. D. de Groot, "Thought and Choice in Chess"
[11] H. Poincaré, "Mathematical Creation"
[12] R. S. Woodworth and H. Schlosberg, "Experimental Psychology: Incubation"
[13] A. S. Luchins, "Mechanization in Problem Solving: The Effect of *Einstellung*"
[14] K. Duncker, "On Functional Fixedness of Real Solution Objects"
[15] W. S. Ray, "Mild Stress and Problem Solving"

[1]

The Reinforcing Effect of Two Spoken Sounds on the Frequency of Two Responses [1]

JOEL GREENSPOON

The reinforcing effects of various stimuli presented immediately following a response have been investigated largely with infra-human Ss. In the context of experiments using the operant conditioning paradigm, the accepted definition of the reinforcing stimulus is a stimulus introduced following a response that increases the probability of occurrence of that response. Despite this research utilizing infra-human Ss, there has been relatively little effort to identify reinforcing stimuli for human Ss. Many investigators have conditioned humans, but they have used only a few reinforcing stimuli. Thorndike demonstrated the effectiveness of "right" and "wrong" in increasing the frequency of different responses (1935). Hurlock (1925) demonstrated that praise and reproof significantly affected performance in the classroom situation. . . . Most of the research involving reinforcing stimuli with human Ss has, however, been designed to test problems other than the identification of reinforcing stimuli for human Ss. The primary purpose of this research was to investigate the effect of the introduction and omission of two spoken sounds following a pre-determined response on the frequency of occurrence of that response.

[1] Accepted for publication October 1, 1954. This article is based upon a dissertation submitted to the Department of Psychology of Indiana University in partial fulfillment of the requirements for the Ph.D. degree. This research was supported in part by a grant from the Graduate School of Indiana University. Appreciation is expressed to Dr. C. J. Burke for his aid in the statistical analyses and to Dr. T. A. Sebeok for his aid in the phonetic analysis of the contingent stimuli.

SOURCE: Joel Greenspoon, "The Reinforcing Effect of Two Spoken Sounds on the Frequency of Two Responses," *The American Journal of Psychology*, 1955, **68**, 409–416. Reprinted by permission of *The American Journal of Psychology*.

PROCEDURE

The experiment was simple in design. *S* was asked to say words, and as he went along, some of the words were followed by a spoken sound from *E*. Conditioning and, later, extinction were both obtained.

The experiment was conducted in a small room, 7 × 7 × 7 ft., with sound-insulated walls, and lighted by one 75-w. ceiling bulb. The room contained a small table and two chairs. *S* sat in one chair placed beside the table and was unable to see *E* who sat behind him in the other chair. A small red light was placed on table where it could be seen by *S*. He could also see a microphone that was attached to a Peirce Wire Recorder. The recorder sat on a small stand out of sight during the experiment, but it was visible to *S* when he entered the experimental room. A stop watch was used to record time.

Seventy-five undergraduate students in elementary psychology and speech classes at Indiana University were randomly assigned to five different groups of 15 *Ss* each. Each *S* was tested individually.

The two contingent stimuli were "mmm-hmm" and "huh-uh." [2]

Two responses were defined for use in the experiment. One response included any plural noun. The second response included all verbal responses except plural nouns and is called non-plural responses. The defining characteristic of the plural and non-plural responses was based on common grammatical usage.

The experimental session was 50 min. in length. *S* first entered the experimental room and seated himself. A brief, casual conversation, to acclimate *S* to *E* and to the experimental room, preceded the following instructions:

"What I want you to do is to say all the words that you can think of. Say them individually. Do not use any sentences or phrases. Do not count. Please continue until I say stop. Go ahead."

No additional instructions were given during the remainder of the experimental session. *S* received no information about the correctness of his response or the significance of the contingent stimulus that was introduced.

For Groups I and II the contingent stimulus was introduced following each plural response during the first 25 min. For Group I the contingent stimulus was "mmm-hmm" and for Group II it was "huh-uh." For Groups III and IV the contingent stimulus was introduced following each non-plural response during the first 25 min. For Group III the contingent stimulus was "mmm-hmm" and for Group IV it was "huh-uh." *Ss* in all groups continued to respond for an additional 25 min. during which the contingent stimulus was omitted. One control group was used, in which no contingent stimulus was introduced during the entire 50 min. session.

[2] The two stimuli used in this experiment, "mmm-hmm" and "huh-uh," are called contingent stimuli rather than reinforcing stimuli since one of the purposes of the experiment was to determine whether or not these two stimuli were reinforcing stimuli.

At the end of the 50 min. of responding each S was asked the following questions: (1) What do you think it was all about? (2) Did you notice any change in the kind of words you were saying? (3) What do you think the purpose of the "mmm-hmm" (or "huh-uh") was? (4) How long do you think you were saying words?

Results

The first step in the treatment of the data was to eliminate those Ss who were able to verbalize the relationship between the contingent stimulus and the response which it followed. One S in Group I and nine Ss in Group II reported that they noted the relationship of the contingent stimulus and the response it followed. The elimination of these 10 Ss reduced to 65 the number for whom the data were further analyzed.

The second step in the analysis was to determine the ordinal position of the first plural response. The control group and the two experimental groups in which the plural response was the measured response were compared. The mean ordinal position of the first plural response of Groups I and II and the control group is presented in Table 1. The three

TABLE 1

Mean Ordinal Position of First Plural Response of Control Group and Experimental Groups in Which Contingent Stimulus Was Introduced Following Each Plural Response

Control Group (*No Stimulus*)	*Group I* ("*Mmm-hmm*")	*Group II* ("*Huh-uh*")
21.13	23.71	20.83

values did not differ significantly as an F of 0.0626 with 2 and 32 degrees of freedom was obtained. The groups of Ss were probably selected from the same population with respect to the readiness to give the first plural response. No corresponding analysis was made for Groups III and IV.

The total 50 min. of responding was divided into ten 5-min. periods for purpose of the additional analyses. The data of the control group and the experimental groups in which the contingent stimulus was introduced following each plural response are presented first. Both periods, during which the contingent stimulus was introduced and omitted, are included. . . .

The mean number of plural responses for each 5-min. period by Groups I and II and the control group is presented in Table 2, with

TABLE 2

Mean Number and Standard Deviation of Plural Responses for Successive 5-Min. Periods for Control Group and for Experimental Groups in Which Contingent Stimulus Was Introduced Following Each Plural Response (Stimulus omitted last five periods of experimental groups)

5-Min. Periods	*Control Group (No Stimulus)*		*Group I ("Mmm-hmm")*		*Group II ("Huh-uh")*	
	Mean	*SD*	*Mean*	*SD*	*Mean*	*SD*
1	15.47	11.60	25.50	22.80	11.33	5.62
2	11.20	9.22	22.07*	13.53	7.17	5.50
3	11.00	6.83	22.43*	16.90	2.83*	2.68
4	10.53	7.74	19.07*	13.19	4.83	3.85
5	8.40	8.93	20.86†	11.36	3.83	3.19
6	8.13	5.77	16.21*	12.18	7.33	6.90
7	8.27	6.50	11.64	9.24	4.83	5.46
8	10.87	10.30	10.50	8.68	3.00	4.40
9	6.67	6.48	11.43	10.11	7.33	6.13
10	8.33	7.94	9.50	7.38	4.83	5.88

* Mean difference between experimental and control groups significant between the 5 per cent and 1 per cent level of confidence.

† Mean difference between experimental and control groups significant beyond 1 per cent level of confidence.

the corresponding standard deviations. The generalized analysis of variance was applied separately to the plural responses during the periods when the contingent stimulus followed each plural response and when it was omitted.[3]

The between-group-variance for the periods 1–5 when the contingent stimulus was introduced for the experimental groups was significant beyond the 1 per cent level of confidence. The between-group-variance was significant between the 5 per cent and 1 per cent

[3] The generalized analysis of variance was developed by C. J. Burke of Indiana University. It can be applied to those cases in which there is correlation between measurements within the various groups. The test is designed to evaluate variance and co-variance simultaneously. The measurements in successive periods of the groups used in this experiment are presumably correlated since they are made on the same Ss. If the result is significant, then *t*-test can be used to find the locus of the differences. The results of this analysis are presented in terms of the confidence level from conversion tables developed by Burke. The information necessary to compute the statistic was obtained through personal communication.

levels of confidence during the remaining periods when the contingent stimulus was omitted.

The *t*-test was applied to determine the locus of the differences in the mean number of plural responses between the experimental groups and the control group; every 5-min. period was examined separately. The results of this analysis show that Group I had a significantly greater mean number of plural responses than the control group for the last four periods in which the contingent stimulus was introduced and for the first period in which the contingent stimulus was omitted. Group II had a significantly smaller mean number of plural responses than the control group in one period in which the contingent stimulus "huh-uh" was introduced and in none of the periods in which the stimulus was omitted.

Substantially the same analysis was made of the data for Groups III and IV, in which non-plural rather than plural responses were followed by the contingent stimulus. . . .

The mean number of non-plural responses with corresponding standard deviations for each 5-min. period for the two experimental groups and the control group is presented in Table 3. The general-

TABLE 3

Mean Number and Standard Deviation of Non-Plural Responses for Successive 5-Min. Periods of Control Group and Experimental Groups in Which Contingent Stimulus Was Introduced Following Each Non-Plural Response
(Stimulus omitted last five periods of experimental groups)

5-Min. Periods	*Control Group (No Stimulus)*		*Group III ("Mmm-hmm")*		*Group IV ("Huh-uh")*	
	Mean	*SD*	*Mean*	*SD*	*Mean*	*SD*
1	102.67	34.50	93.93	39.33	95.07	40.50
2	79.40	28.01	84.33	34.99	87.60	37.46
3	75.40	26.49	82.13	36.59	87.00	36.75
4	72.27	26.79	80.80	35.46	84.60	35.38
5	73.60	29.96	79.33	35.46	90.47	41.10
6	70.47	28.11	75.93	34.23	80.20	26.53
7	72.47	26.53	74.73	33.53	76.07	33.47
8	67.73	24.70	70.27	30.67	77.60	32.70
9	70.87	25.03	71.60	33.16	71.20	29.70
10	68.93	28.05	72.87	35.11	68.87	24.47

ized analysis of variance indicated that the difference among the groups when the contingent stimulus was introduced was significant beyond the 5 per cent level of confidence. The difference was not statistically significant during the periods when the contingent stimulus was omitted. The analysis by means of the *t*-test showed none of the mean differences to be statistically significant.

Discussion

The results obtained from the introduction of "mmm-hmm" were consistent for both of the responses, plural and non-plural. Since, according to the initial definition of the reinforcing stimulus, any stimulus introduced following a response that increases the probability of occurrence of that response is a reinforcing stimulus, we may conclude that "mmm-hmm" is a reinforcing stimulus. Additional support for this conclusion comes from the results that were obtained when "mmm-hmm" was omitted. The frequency of plural responses declined to the point where the difference between the mean number of plural responses of the control group and Group I was not statistically significant.

The results obtained from the introduction of "huh-uh" following the plural response were significantly different from the results obtained when "huh-uh" was introduced following non-plural responses. The results were obtained, however, from only 6 Ss in Group II who did not verbalize the relationship between "huh-uh" and plural responses. This represents a rather small sample. The apparently diverse results in the case of "huh-uh" may clarify some of the thinking about reinforcing stimuli. It would appear from these results that one of the factors that may determine whether or not a particular stimulus will be a reinforcing stimulus is the response following which the stimulus is applied. An examination of the two responses used in this experiment reveals some differences. Plural responses are a smaller and more narrowly defined class in that all members of the class were plural nouns. The data from the control group indicate that approximately 11 per cent of the verbal responses were plural nouns. Non-plural responses form, therefore, a much larger class. They also presumably differ from the plural responses in being more heterogeneous. All parts of speech other than nouns, and also non-plural nouns, are included. Thus, either the relative size or the heterogeneity of the class, or both, may be factors in determining whether or not a particular stimulus will be a reinforcing stimulus.

It should be noted that there was little tendency for the Ss to repeat a particular word that had been followed by one of the contingent stimuli. It was possible for S to make responses which differed in many respects but were the same in that they were all plural nouns or were non-plural responses. Thus, the importance of the class is emphasized by this experiment. *E* limits the extent of the class by his use of the reinforcing stimulus; but, the extent of the class may in turn determine whether a stimulus has reinforcing effects.

The small differences in the number of non-plural responses between the control and experimental groups may be a function of the fact that the frequency of non-plural responses of the control group approaches a maximum. Any possible increase in frequency of non-plural responses is restricted when compared to the possible increase in the frequency of plural responses. This restriction in the size of the possible difference between the control and experimental groups may have reduced the statistical significance of the differences as well.

Summary

The purpose of this experiment was to determine the effect of two operations on two different verbal responses. The Ss were 75 undergraduate students at Indiana University. Each S served individually. Data from 10Ss who verbalized the relationship between the contingent stimulus and the response it followed were eliminated from further analyses. The operation performed was to present one of two stimuli, "mmm-hmm" or "huh-uh," after one of the two responses, plural nouns or any word not a plural noun. In a control group no stimulus was introduced following the response.

The S was instructed to say singly all the words, exclusive of sentences, phrases and numbers, that he could think of for 50 min. One of the contingent stimuli was introduced immediately following each response of a predetermined class during the first 25 min. and omitted during the second period of 25 min.

The results indicated that "mmm-hmm" increased the frequency of plural responses and "huh-uh" decreased the frequency of plural responses. Both stimuli tended to increase the frequency of non-plural responses. Thus, the contingent stimulus, "mmm-hmm," had the same effect on both responses. The stimulus, "huh-uh," had different effects on the two responses. This differential effect on the two responses suggested that the nature of the response is a determinant of the reinforcing character of the stimulus.

[2]
Blind Variation and Selective Retention in Creative Thought as in Other Knowledge Processes [1]

DONALD T. CAMPBELL

This paper proposes to examine creative thought within the framework of a comparative psychology of knowledge processes, and in particular with regard to one theme recurrent in most knowledge processes. This theme may be expressed as follows:

1. A blind-variation-and-selective-retention process is fundamental to all inductive achievements, to all genuine increases in knowledge, to all increases in fit of system to environment.
2. The many processes which shortcut a more full blind-variation-and-selective-retention process are in themselves inductive achievements, containing wisdom about the environment achieved originally by blind variation and selective retention.
3. In addition, such shortcut processes contain in their own operation a blind-variation-and-selective-retention process at some level, substituting for overt locomotor exploration or the life-and-death winnowing of organic evolution.

* * *

[1] A partially overlapping version of this paper was presented at the Inter-Disciplinary Conference on Self-Organizing Systems, sponsored by the Office of Naval Research and the Armour Research Foundation of the Illinois Institute of Technology, Chicago, May 5–6, 1959. The proceedings of the conference are to be published by Pergamon Press under the title *Self-Organizing Systems*. The author is indebted to Carl P. Duncan for contributing to the development of many of the points involved.

SOURCE: Donald T. Campbell, "Blind Variation and Selective Retention in Creative Thought as in Other Knowledge Processes," *Psychological Review*, 1960, **67**, 380–400. Reprinted by permission of the American Psychological Association and Donald T. Campbell.

Three conditions are necessary: a mechanism for introducing variation, a consistent selection process, and a mechanism for preserving and reproducing the selected variations.

Creative Thought

. . . At this level there is a *substitute* exploration of a *substitute* representation of the environment, the "solution" being selected from the multifarious exploratory thought trials according to a criterion which is in itself *substituting* for an external state of affairs. Insofar as the three substitutions are accurate, the solutions when put into overt locomotion are adaptive, leading to intelligent behavior which lacks overt blind floundering, and is thus a knowledge process. To include this process in the general plan of blind-variation-and-selective-retention, it must be emphasized that insofar as thought achieves innovation, the internal emitting of thought trials one by one is blind, lacking prescience or foresight. The process *as a whole* of course provides "foresight" for the overt level of behavior, once the process has blindly stumbled into a thought trial that "fits" the selection criterion, accompanied by the "something clicked," "Eureka," or "aha-erlebnis" that usually marks the successful termination of the process.

Today, we find the blind-variation-and-selective-retention model most plausibly applied at the levels of organic evolution and trial-and-error learning of animals, and least palatable as a description of creative thinking. Historically, however, the phrase "trial and error" was first used to describe thinking by Alexander Bain as early as 1855, two years before Darwin's publication of the doctrine of natural selection. Not only for historical interest, but also to further develop the psychology of creativity, the following quotations from him (Bain, 1874) are provided:

> Possessing thus the material of the construction and a clear sense of the fitness or unfitness of each new tentative, the operator proceeds to ply the third requisite of constructiveness—trial and error— . . . to attain the desired result. . . . The number of trials necessary to arrive at a new construction is commonly so great that without something of an affection or fascination for the subject one grows weary of the task. This is the *emotional* condition of originality of mind in any department.
>
> In the process of Deduction . . . the same constructive process has often to be introduced. The mind being prepared beforehand with the principles most likely for the purpose . . . incubates in patient thought

over the problem, trying and rejecting, until at last the proper elements come together in the view, and fall into their places in a fitting combination.

With reference to originality in all departments, whether science, practice, or fine art, there is a point of character that deserves notice. . . . I mean an Active turn, or a profuseness of energy, put forth in trials of all kinds on the chance of making lucky hits. . . . Nothing less than a fanaticism of experimentation could have given birth to some of our grandest practical combinations. The great discovery of Daguerre, for example, could not have been regularly worked out by any systematic and orderly research; there was no way but to stumble upon it. . . . The discovery is unaccountable, until we learn that the author . . . got deeply involved in trials and operations far removed from the beaten paths of inquiry.

* * *

Individual Differences and Genius

. . . What are the ways in which thinkers might be expected to differ, according to the trial-and-error model? First, they may differ in the accuracy and detail of their representations of the external world, of possible locomotions in it or manipulations of its elements, and of the selective criteria. Differences in this accuracy of representation correspond to differences in degree of information and intelligence. Second, thinkers can differ in the number and range of variations in thought trials produced. The more numerous and the more varied such trials, the greater the chance of success. Bain has emphasized the role of fanaticism or extreme dedication in producing large volumes of such explorations and . . . the role of advance preparation in assembling the elements whose blind permutation and combination make possible a wide range of trials. Many observers have emphasized the role of set and familiarity in reducing the range of variations, and have recommended ways of reducing trial-to-trial stereotypy, as by abandoning the problem for awhile, going on to other things. Devices abound which are designed to increase the likelihood that all permutations be considered and are used by most of us, as in going through the alphabet in finding rhymes or puzzle words. There are no doubt age differences in the rapidity and uninhibited range of thought-trial production. The sociology of knowledge makes an important contribution here: persons who have been uprooted from traditional cultures, or who have been thoroughly exposed to two or more cultures, seem to have the advantage in the range of hypotheses they are apt to consider, and through this means, in the frequency of creative innovation. . . . And more generally, it is the principle of variation which leads us to expect among innovators those of personal eccentricity and bizarre behavior. We can also see in this principle the value of those laboratories whose social atmospheres allow wide ranging exploration with great tolerance for blind alley entrances.

The value of wide ranging variation in thought trials is of course vitiated if there is not the precise application of a selective criterion which weeds out the overwhelming bulk of inadequate trials. This editing talent undoubtedly differs widely from person to person, as Poincaré (1913) has emphasized. With regard to selection criteria, one further point should be made. Much of creative thought is opportunistic in the sense of having a wide number of selective criteria available at all times, against which the thought trials are judged. The more creative thinker may be able to keep in mind more such criteria, and therefore increase his likelihood of achieving a serendipitous advance on a problem tangential to his initial main line of endeavor. Further areas of individual differences lie in the competence of the retention, cumulation, and transmission of the encountered solutions.

It need not be expected that these dimensions of talent all go together. In organic evolution, the variation process of mutation and the preservation of gains through genetic rigidity are at odds, with an increase in either being at the expense of the other, and with some degree of compromise being optimum. Just so we might expect that a very pure measure of innovative range in thought and a very pure measure of rote memory might be even negatively correlated, and similarly for innovative range and selective precision. Such considerations suggest complementary combinations of talent in creative teams, although the uninhibited idea-man and the compulsive edit-and-record type are notoriously incompatible office mates.

Notice regarding the individual differences thus described that while they do make creative innovation much more likely on the part of some individuals than others, they do not place the joys of creative innovation beyond the reach of the less gifted. Indeed, looking at large populations of thinkers, the principles make it likely that many important contributions will come from the relatively untalented, undiligent, and uneducated, even though on an average contribution per capita basis, they will contribute much less. The intricacy of the tradition to which innovation is being added of course places limitations in this regard.

The Enormous Domain of Possible Thought-Trials to Be Searched

A final type of objection to the blind-variation-and-selective-retention model of thought needs to be considered. This objection is to the effect that the domain of possible thought trials is so large that the solution of a given problem would take an impossibly long time were a search of all possibilities to be involved, either through a systematic scanning of all possibilities where these are enumerable, or through a random sampling of the universe of possibilities. Time and trial estimates thus based can be overwhelming. . . . Newell, Shaw, and Simon (1958) refer in this vein to what they call the "British Museum Algorithm," i.e., the possibility of a group of trained chimpanzees typing at random producing by chance in the course of a million years all of the books in the British Museum. Such parodies seem effectively to reject the blind-variation-and-selective-retention model though a *reductio ad absurdum.* Needless to say, such a rejection is not accepted in the present paper. As a matter of fact, it is judged to be in the same class as parallel objections to the theory of natural selection in evolution. Similar features in these two instances make the accidentalist interpretation more acceptable.

1. Neither in organic evolution nor in thought are all problems solved, nor all possible excellent solutions achieved. There is no guarantee of omniscience. The knowledge we do encounter is achieved against terrific odds. (Those advocating heuristically-programed problem-solving computers are careful not to guarantee solutions, and this modesty should be extended to all models of creative thought.)

2. The tremendous number of nonproductive thought trials on the part of the total intellectual community must not be underestimated. Think of what a small proportion of thought becomes conscious, and of conscious thought what a small proportion gets uttered, what a still smaller fragment gets published, and what a small proportion of what is published is used by the next intellectual generation. There is a tremendous wastefulness, slowness, and rarity of achievement.

3. In biological evolution and in thought, the number of variations explored is greatly reduced by having *selective criteria im-*

posed at every step. Thus mutant variations on nonadaptive variations of the previous generation are never tested—even though many wonderful combinations may be missed therefore. Some of the "heuristics" currently employed in logic and chess playing machines (Newell, Shaw, and Simon, 1958) have the similar effect of evaluating all next-possible moves in terms of immediate criteria, and then of exploring further variations upon only those stems passing the screening of each prior stage. It is this strategy of cumulating selected outcomes from a blind variation, and then exploring further blind variations only for this highly select stem, that makes the improbable inevitable in organic evolution. This strategy is unavoidable for organic evolution, but can obviously be relaxed in thought processes and in machine problem solving. However, the Pandora's box of permutations opened up by such relaxation can be used to infer that, in general, thought trials are selected or rejected within one or two removes of the established base from which they start. In constructing our "universal library" we stop work on any volume as soon as it is clear that it is gibberish.

4. When we make estimates of the number of permutations which would have to be called to obtain a given outcome, we often assume that problem solving was undertaken with that one fixed goal in mind. This overlooks the opportunistic, serendipitous course of organic evolution and of much of creative thinking. The likelihood of a productive thought increases with the wider variety of reasons one has for judging a given outcome "interesting." To neglect this opportunistic multipurposedness gives one a poor base for estimating the probability of encountering the one outcome hit upon and recorded. Thus when Newell, Shaw, and Simon's "Logic Theorist" (1958) sets out to prove the 60-odd theorems in a given chapter of Principia Mathematica, it may face a more formidable task than did Whitehead and Russell in generating them, if, except for the dozen classic theorems reproduced, Whitehead and Russell were otherwise free to record every deduction they encountered which seemed "interesting" or "nontrivial." Wigglesworth (1955) has noted this strategy on the part of "pure" scientists, in commenting on the relationship between pure and applied scientists in wartime:

In the pure science to which they were accustomed, if they were unable to solve problem *A* they could turn to problem *B*, and while studying this with perhaps small prospect of success they might suddenly come across a clue to the solution of problem *C*.

In presenting their case for adding "heuristics" to the program of the "Logic Theorist," Newell, Shaw, and Simon have emphasized the inadequacy of blind trial and error. So has Miller (1959) in advocating the heuristic of searching backward from the goal. There is, however, no essential disagreement between their point of view and the one offered here. By adding heuristics mechanical thought processes have indeed been made more like those of human beings, both in adequacy and type of errors. Such innovations have obviated the protests of those who, while conceding that machines could choose good moves at chess or solve logic problems, have found the machines failing to imitate life just in their orderly inspection of all possibilities. Newell, Shaw, and Simon recognize that a machine which would develop its own heuristics would have to do so by a trial and error of heuristic principles, with no guarantee that any would work. They further recognize that possession of an effective heuristic represents already achieved general knowledge about the domain under search, and that adding to this general knowledge will be a blind search process. (The devices of learning and vision and of coding environmental possibilities for thought-search all represent heuristics in this sense.) They might also agree that most heuristic devices will be limited to the specific domain of their discovery, and can only be extended to other domains on a trial basis. They would probably also agree that no problem solving process will be "direct." The disagreements I have . . . are thus minor matters of emphasis.

* * *

Another minor point of disagreement may be mentioned. In their efforts to consider how a "Logic Theorist" might be programed to learn a general heuristic from hindsight they propose that it keep a record of the outcomes of all past trials, successful and unsuccessful, in order to be able to scan its experience for general principles of strategy (1958). Implementing this would put a tremendous strain upon memory storage, and would introduce a scanning process as time consuming as the original search process which produced the record. The strategy of organic evolutions is to keep a record only of what works, even at the expense of repeating its errors. The general preponderance of wrong tries at every level, plus problems of memory glut and access, suggests a similar strategy for all knowledge processes. Heuristics can probably best be learned through a trial and error of heuristics, tried on new problem sets rather than old.

[3]

Experimental Studies in the Training of Originality [1]

IRVING MALTZMAN, SEYMORE SIMON, DAVID RASKIN, and LEONARD LICHT [2]

A basic difficulty in attempting to facilitate original thinking is that it may not occur at all or at such infrequent intervals that reinforcements cannot be administered with sufficient frequency to effect an increase in such behavior. Thus, a fundamental problem in the training of originality is to devise methods for increasing its occurrence in the first place, thereby permitting the operation of reinforcement. We are assuming that originality can be learned and that the same principles of conditioning hold as in other forms of operant behavior. Some of the problems attendant upon this assumption have been discussed elsewhere (Maltzman, 1960). For our present purposes we need indicate only that by originality, or original thinking, we mean behavior that occurs relatively infrequently, is uncommon under given conditions, and is relevant to those conditions. In order, then, to facilitate the occurrence of original behavior, techniques must be devised for evoking many un-

[1] This research was supported by Contract Nonr 233(50) between the Office of Naval Research and the University of California. Reproduction in whole or in part is permitted for any purpose of the United States Government.
[2] We are indebted to William Bogartz, Nira Kozak, and Bonnie Simon for their assistance in various stages of this research.

SOURCE: Irving Maltzman, Seymore Simon, David Raskin, and Leonard Licht, "Experimental Studies in the Training of Originality," *Psychological Monographs,* 1960, **74,** No. 493. Reprinted by permission of the American Psychological Association and Irving Maltzman.

common responses. Such training may then produce a disposition to give uncommon responses in other situations.

One procedure, used by Maltzman, Bogartz, and Breger (1958) is to repeatedly evoke different associations to the same stimulus words in a free association situation. This procedure prompts the subject to emit responses relatively low in the response hierarchy elicitable by each stimulus. They found that subjects receiving this training with intermittent reinforcement of uncommon responses were significantly more original on a new list of words than subjects without this training. A second experimental group which did not receive verbal reinforcement approached significance in comparison with the control group. When instructions to be original were added to the experimental and control treatments they showed a marked increase in the originality of their associations, and both experimental groups were now significantly more original than the control group. The Unusual Uses Test of originality devised by Guilford and his associates (1950) was administered following the free association test. Equivocal evidence for transfer of the association training effects to this situation was obtained in the form of a significant triple order interaction.

* * *

Conclusions

Each of the four experiments employing the standard experimental training procedure with free association materials produced a highly reliable increase in the uncommonness of responses on two different tests. The first two experiments suggest that the standard experimental training procedure of repeatedly evoking different responses to the same stimuli is the most successful of the three experimental procedures employed. It produced significantly greater facilitation of originality on one or both originality tests as compared with the method of evoking different responses by presenting different stimuli as in Exp. I, or evoking uncommon responses as textual responses as in Exp. II. Possible variables responsible for the efficacy of the standard training procedure have already been indicated earlier in this paper and elsewhere (Maltzman, 1960).

The results of Exp. IV and V lend some support to the hypothesis that originality is learned behavior and varies as a function of the same antecedent conditions as other forms of operant behavior.

Effects of originality training may persist for as long as two days, under the training and test conditions employed in Exp. V. Originality, at least, on the free association test, also varies as a function of the number of repetitions of the training list.

Although the standard training procedure has proved to be effective, there are many possible variations of the procedure that remain to be investigated. For example, instead of completing the entire training list of stimulus words before re-presenting it, successive responses to each stimulus might be evoked. Various combinations of these procedures may also be studied. Further experimental studies are also needed employing different types of test criteria, including the more traditional kinds of problem situations. Studies of this kind are currently in progress in the UCLA laboratory. Work of this sort may indicate the extent to which the kind of training procedure studied here might have practical applicability. In this connection, it should be noted that the behavior measured on the originality tests employed in these experiments and similar tests correlates reliably with ratings of original behavior (Drevdahl, 1956).

In conclusion, it should be noted that the term "originality" as employed in this paper refers to a particular kind of behavior measured by specified operations under given conditions. If it is objected that this is not genuine originality, then it should be incumbent upon the critic to specify the latter behavior in equally operational terms so that it too may be subjected to experimental study.

[4]
On the Training of Originality[1]

IRVING MALTZMAN

Scope of This Paper

The purpose of this paper is to review the experimental research that may be relevant to the problem of devising techniques for increasing originality and to indicate the behavioral principles possibly involved in the production of the desired effect.

For purposes of further discussion we shall distinguish between originality and creativity. Originality, or original thinking, as we shall use the term, refers to behavior which occurs relatively infrequently, is uncommon under given conditions, and is relevant to those conditions. Criteria of relevance and uncommonness, of course, must be established for any given situation. This is a problem more readily solvable within the laboratory than without. Creativity, according to the present usage, refers to products of such behavior and the reactions of other members of a society to those products. An invention is a creative product that may have an important effect upon society and is a consequence of original behavior. But considerably more variables enter into the determination of creative works than originality alone. Our distinction implies that an individual may be highly original but not creative. His brilliant theories are never published, or they are not implemented by the necessary research. Perhaps the original research is conducted, but the results are not published or patented. All this may be done, but the work may be overlooked or the implications disregarded by the appropriate com-

[1] This work was supported by Contract Nonr 233(50) between the Office of Naval Research and the University of California. Reproduction in whole or in part is permitted for any purpose of the United States Government.

SOURCE: Irving Maltzman, "On the Training of Originality," *Psychological Review,* 1960, **67**, 229–242. Reprinted by permission of the American Psychological Association and Irving Maltzman.

munity of scholars or society at large. Further common illustrations may be given, indicating that a great many more behavioral and societal variables influence creativity than originality, making the study of originality under simplified laboratory conditions more feasible than that of creativity. Many of these variables may affect original behavior as well, but they are not of such overwhelming importance when the training of originality is considered. Our subsequent discussion therefore will be concerned solely with originality as here defined. One further distinction in the experimental study of original behavior needs to be made. Such behavior is always relative, either to a given individual's past behavior or to the norms of a population of which he is a member. The two are no doubt correlated. But it is the latter which is related to creative works; and since all of the pertinent experimental research has been of this kind, we shall be concerned only with the study of originality relative to some group norm.

Guilford (1959) also distinguishes between originality and creativity. However, the basis for the distinction stems from his factor analytic approach. Originality, defined essentially in the same fashion as in the present paper, is one of several behavioral traits contributing to creativity. The latter is a more general behavioral trait including as components several forms of flexibility, fluency, and motivational and temperamental traits in addition to originality. Although this is a reasonable empirical classification of traits based upon factor analysis, it does not necessarily contradict the present one. We do not, however, accept Guilford's additional assertion that an S-R approach cannot deal adequately with creativity.

. . . Mearns (1958) in a book originally published in 1929 repeatedly emphasizes that in order to facilitate the originality of school children in the arts the teacher must reinforce, manifestly approve, his original efforts. He illustrates many techniques for inducing the child to make public his efforts, to gain the confidence of children so that communication will occur with their "secret unexpressed selves." Furthermore, the teacher is advised to approve of only the genuinely original effort. The teacher is further cautioned to wait patiently for the appearance of original behavior which is fostered by a "permissive atmosphere," the absence of "drill" and excessive discipline. According to Mearns, original behavior appears eventually because all normal children have an urge, energy, or impulse to be creative.

Aside from the romantic approach to a problem of behavior, we would agree that the way to foster originality is to reinforce such behavior when it occurs. A basic difficulty is that it may not occur at all or at such infrequent intervals that the reinforcements cannot shape up such behavior. Thus the fundamental problem in the training of originality is to devise methods for increasing its occurrence in diverse situations, is to get it to occur in the first place, thereby permitting the operation of reinforcement. If the operant level of originality is too low, conditioning will not be effective, training cannot occur. We are assuming, then, that originality can be learned and that the same principles of conditioning hold as in other forms of operant behavior. Once it occurs it can be reinforced, approved, recognized. It will then show an increased probability of occurrence. An apparent difficulty, however, is that originality is manifestly different from other behaviors. How can the reinforcement of one bit of uncommon behavior increase the frequency of other uncommon behaviors which by definition are different? Despite the apparent paradox, this sort of nonspecific transfer does occur, as we shall see.

* * *

"Productive" Thinking and Originality

Before turning to the current experimental research on originality training, however, note should be taken of several recent studies that have employed Maier's (1931) two-string or analogous problems as a test situation. The reason for commenting upon these studies is the assumption that there is no fundamental difference in the behavioral principles determining originality and problem solving behavior generally. Both involve the evocation of relatively uncommon responses, otherwise the situation would not be called a problem or the behavior original. This is especially apparent in connection with Maier's two-string problem. Maier (1931) considers the pendulum solution to be a consequence of productive thinking whereas other solutions represent reproductive thinking. As indicated elsewhere (Maltzman, 1955) these problem solving behaviors do not involve fundamentally different laws as demanded by Maier, but only a difference in the extent to which initial response hierarchies are modified. Furthermore, as far as can be determined this also is the basis that Maier used for distinguishing reproductive from productive solutions. The former solutions were given by his Ss upon the initial presentation of the problem. Only after these solutions were given and the Ss were told to find still another solution, which happened to be the pendulum solution, did Maier call it productive thinking. The empirical basis for the distinction between reproductive and productive thinking, then, was the probability of occurrence of the solution under his experimental conditions. The pendulum solution was relatively uncommon and is original in this sense.

Several studies have attempted to determine, with some success, whether verbal responses necessary for the solution of a subsequent problem are present in the initial response hierarchy of Ss. The determination is made by obtaining word associations to objects later found in the problem situation. Responses necessary for the solution of the problem are presumably uncommon, have a low probability of occurrence in the initial response hierarchy. An association procedure has also been used to determine the uncommonness of responses evoked in the initial response hierarchy and their relation to subsequent success in the two-string problem.

A series of experiments by Judson, Cofer, and Gelfand (1956) is a limiting case of the use of textual responses in facilitating "productive" problem solving or originality. They employed the two-string problem as the test and rote learning as the training situation. Instead of attempting to increase the occurrence of uncommon responses during training and determining their transfer effects in the test situation, they induced directly the response chain necessary for a pendulum solution to the problem. A group form of the two-string problem was employed, and the Ss were required to write as many solutions as possible to the problem of grasping both strings simultaneously. The design of the experiment was to prompt a pendulum solution to the problem by presenting an experimental group with different lists of words, one of which contained the relevant response chain "rope," "swing," "pendulum." Additional control groups were employed receiving word lists including none of these words, one or all three but each in a different list. In this study as well as in two replications, the experimental group was superior to the control groups, although the differences were not always statistically significant. A further qualification is that these results hold only for men. No reliable differences were obtained among women in the various conditions. An analogous experiment was conducted employing a group form of Maier's hat rack problem, and comparable results were obtained. These studies suggest that repeated evocation of the critical words during rote learning increased the probability of their occurrence in the problem situation which in turn led to an increased frequency of the desired problem solution.

* * *

If, as we have assumed, originality can be learned according to the principles of operant conditioning, then the effects of originality training should be of the same kind as those ordinarily obtained in experimental studies of learning. One of the gross characteristics of learning is that the behavioral changes produced by reinforcement persist for some time, are not relatively transistory. Increased originality induced by the training method previously described should therefore also persist. An experiment designed to investigate this property of originality training has been conducted, and positive results have been obtained (Maltzman et al., 1960). Using the standard control and experimental conditions of the previous experiments, a delay of approximately one hour was interposed between the training and test situations for a control and an experimental group, and a delay of two days for another control and experimental group. A significant training effect was obtained on the word association and the Unusual Uses Test of originality.

These results show that the effects of originality training persist to a significant degree for at least two days, under the given experimental conditions. We may conclude from these results and that of the previous experiment that the standard experimental procedure for training originality produces some kind of learning.

* * *

An Interpretation of Originality Training

Two basic problems, not unrelated, posed by the experiments on originality training by Maltzman and his associates (1958, 1960) demand an interpretation. First is the nature or source of the reinforcement for originality. In all of the experiments, successive training trials in the standard experimental conditions are accompanied by increases in the uncommonness of the responses. The originality induced in this manner transfers to different stimulus materials, and these effects tend to persist. Originality training thus produces behavioral changes that are characteristic of learning, yet they occur in the absence of differential reinforcement administered by *E*. Nevertheless, we believe that uncommon responses received differential reinforcement. Reinforcement was obtained, because the occurrence of any previously established intraverbal association is self-reinforcing. As Thorndike puts it: "The mere occurrence of a connection strengthens it." Thus, where there is an initial probability greater than zero that a given verbal stimulus will evoke a verbal response in an operant situation such as word association, the occurrence of that response will increase the probability of its occurrence on a subsequent presentation of that stimulus. Different initial conditions may only increase or decrease the amount of reinforcement affecting the stimulus-response connection. In the type of experimental situation with which we are concerned here, the uncommonness of the response evoked by the stimulus is one of these conditions. In other words, the amount of reinforcement is inversely related to the initial probability of a verbal stimulus evoking a verbal response. Originality is more reinforcing than commonplace responding.

An impression gained from observing Ss in the experimental situation is that repeated evocation of different responses to the same stimuli becomes quite frustrating: Ss are disturbed by what quickly becomes a surprisingly difficult task. This disturbed behavior indicates that the procedure may not be trivial and does approximate a nonlaboratory situation involving originality or inventiveness, with its frequent concomitant frustration. This impression of frustration accompanying the task of producing repeated uncommon responses would lend support to the notion that when such responses do occur they are self-reinforcing to a considerable degree. These speculations, however, are not essential to the investigation of the initial hypothesis of the self-reinforcing character of uncommon responses. However, these as well as other considerations suggest that the distribution and scheduling of the evocation of uncommon responses may be of great importance in determining the extent to which a transfer effect will be obtained.

It should be noted, however, that the role of self-reinforcement is probably less significant in producing an increase in originality during training, the successive repetitions of the same word list, than in the test situation. Since instructions to the standard experimental group prohibits the reoccurrence of the same response to a given stimulus word, successive responses to that word will be progressively lower in the related response hierarchy. This is sufficient to account for the increase in the uncommonness of responses with successive repetitions of the same stimulus words. However, we believe that a second variable contributes to the increase in originality during the training session, generalization of the reinforcement effects from the evoked response to still more uncommon responses in the same hierarchy. However, the role of self-reinforcement becomes significant when the transfer of originality to the test situations is considered. In this case the carrying out by S of previously administered instructions to give different responses will not account for the greater originality of the standard experimental condition in the test situations.

This leads to the second problem presented by the experimental data: the fact that the evocation of uncommon responses on one list of stimulus words facilitates the occurrence of original responses on a different list of words, and even more perplexing, on the rather different Unusual Uses Test. The problem is to account for the fact that reinforcement of one instance of original behavior increases the response tendency for other instances of such behavior under different stimulus conditions. A relatively nonspecific kind of transfer of training is induced. Without it, the facilitation of originality would not be possible.

We do not have any simple rigorous explanation of this phenomenon at the present time, but offer the following tentative suggestions. The intraverbal associations possessed by a normal educated adult are enormously extensive and complex. In all likelihood, almost every verbal response is associated to some extent with every other. Furthermore, the intraverbal associations among common verbal responses are stronger than between common and uncommon responses. Likewise, the intraverbal associations among uncommon responses are relatively stronger than between uncommon and common. The evocation and reinforcement of uncommon responses will, through complex kinds of mediated generalization, therefore increase differentially the probability of occurrence of other uncommon responses even though they do not ordinarily occur to the same stimuli as the original reinforced responses. In a similar fashion, the evocation of common responses would differentially increase the probability of occurrence of other common responses even though they may be members of different response hierarchies.

An additional characteristic of the standard experimental procedure used in originality training is that it provides for the inhibition of common responses as well as the facilitation of uncommon responses. Through mediated generalization the effects of inhibition will produce a decrement in the excitatory potential of other common responses. It is this characteristic which may be responsible for the more general transfer effects obtained with the standard experimental procedure than with the procedures that induce uncommon textual responses or employ uncommon stimulus situations for evoking, in turn, uncommon responses. None of these other procedures would involve the inhibition of common responses.

It should be clear that the foregoing hypotheses are speculative and their connection with the data presented is tenuous. Considerable careful experimentation tracing the intraverbal associations present in the experimental situation is needed as well as the development of laws of verbal compounding before a completely adequate explanation of the basis for originality training can be given. Whether or not such explanations can be given, the method of training originality described in this paper seems worthy of further study in its own right, and potentially may have considerable practical application. This again is a problem requiring sustained experimental research employing different kinds of test materials.

In conclusion, it should be emphasized that little is to be gained by disputing the usage of the term "originality" as it has been employed here, or whether the current experiments described are investigating the essence of originality. The important problem is the experimental one of determining the variables influencing the occurrence of uncommon responses in relatively simple situations and the functional relationships that obtain in these situations. Finally, the extent to which these effects hold for more complex behavioral situations must be determined. Such work is now in progress in the UCLA laboratory. But to designate only highly complex behavior of a given sort as original to the exclusion of simpler better controlled behaviors seems gratuitous, as well as an obstacle to the progress of research in this vital area.

[5]
The Associative Basis of the Creative Process

SARNOFF A. MEDNICK

The RAT was administered to a group of first year psychology graduate students at the University of Michigan whose native language was American English ($N = 35$). Faculty research supervisors (who had been directing the independent research efforts of the students), rated the eight highest and eight lowest RAT scorers either "high" or "low" in research creativity (no middle category allowed). Research creativity was defined as being demonstrated if the student developed new research methods and/or pulled together disparate theory or research areas in useful and original ways. Of the 16 research supervisors, one felt that he had not had enough contact with his student to make the judgment. His student was a low RAT scorer. Of the eight high RAT scorers, six were rated high on research creativity and two were rated low; of the seven low RAT scorers, only one was rated high, the other six being rated low. By Fisher's exact test the probability of these events occurring by chance is less than .05. Miller Analogies Test (MAT) scores were available for these students. Of the seven high MAT scorers, three were rated high on research creativity; of the eight low MAT scorers, four were rated high in research creativity.

* * *

Associative Behavior

In the discussion of illustrative predictions it was suggested that highly creative individuals would be characterized by a flat associative hierarchy rather than a steep associative hierarchy. Further,

---

SOURCE: Sarnoff A. Mednick, "The Associative Basis of the Creative Process," *Psychological Review*, 1962, **69**, 220–232. Reprinted by permisssion of the American Psychological Association and Sarnoff A. Mednick.

it was proposed that the greater the number of associations that an individual has to the requisite elements of a problem, the greater the probability of his reaching a creative solution. From these two independent statements it may be deduced that when required to display his reservoir of associations to single stimulus words, the highly creative individual will have greater access to less probable associates and therefore produce a greater number of associates. A study by Craig and Manis (1960 unpublished [1]) supports this deduction. Thirty-eight college students had the RAT and an associative task administered to them. In the associative task they were given 1 minute to write as many associates as they could to each of 20 words. The correlation of the number of such associates with RAT scores was .38 ($p < .01$).

In two related studies, Karp and Kowalski found RAT scores to be directly related to the originality and quantity of anagrams constructed using the test word "Generation." In the Karp study 40 undergraduates were given 5 minutes to produce as many four letter anagrams from the test word as they could. The productions were scored for quantity (number of acceptable answers) and originality (a weighted score for each response was developed from the frequency with which the response was given by the 40 subjects). The correlation of the RAT with the quantity scores was .44 ($p < .01$); the correlation of the RAT with the originality score was .37 ($p < .05$). Kowalski presented the anagrams task to 15 high RAT scorers and to 15 low RAT scorers, giving them 5 minutes to produce words of any length from the test word "Generation." In this study originality was measured by computing the percentage of responses given by an individual which had not been given by any other of the 30 subjects. The difference on this measure between high and low RAT scorers was significant ($U = 68$, $p < .04$). "Only four subjects in the low creative group gave *any* original responses at all while eleven subjects in the high creative group did."

[1] Craig, M., & Manis, M. Prediction of scores on the Remote Associates Test by size of response repertoire. Unpublished manuscript, 1960.

[6]
Creativity and the Need for Novelty [1]

JOHN P. HOUSTON and
SARNOFF A. MEDNICK

An experiment designed to demonstrate the reinforcing properties of associative novelty for creative Ss. Sixty undergraduates were separated into high (HC) and low (LC) creativity groups on the basis of their scores on the Remote Associates Test. Ss were then presented with a series of pairs of words (each pair containing a noun and a nonnoun) and asked to choose the word they preferred. The choice of a noun was followed by a novel association to that noun. Nonnoun choices were followed by common associations. The HC group significantly increased and the LC group significantly decreased the frequency of their noun choices over the series of pairs. The results support the need for novelty hypothesis.

A theory has been proposed which explains creative thinking in associative terms (Mednick, 1962). The theory concerns itself with the details of the thought process of the creative individual but does not deal explicitly with the motivational factors in creative behavior. This paper is an attempt to explore this aspect of the problem. In particular we shall be testing the hypothesis that the highly creative person has a strong *need* for associative novelty.

Positing a need for associative novelty in the highly creative person certainly seems a banal hypothesis until examined a bit more closely. There has been some considerable effort to assert and demonstrate that the creative individual has a preference for novelty

[1] This research was supported by the Office of Education, Cooperative Research Branch, United States Public Health Service, through Contract Number 1073 with Sarnoff A. Mednick and Martha T. Mednick. The authors wish to express their gratitude to Martha T. Mednick for her advice in all phases of this study.

SOURCE: John P. Houston and Sarnoff A. Mednick, "Creativity and the Need for Novelty," *Journal of Abnormal and Social Psychology*, 1963, **66**, 137–141. Reprinted by permission of the American Psychological Association and the authors.

(Barron, 1958; Glovin, 1959; Sprecher, 1959). However, demonstration of preference alone does not establish the existence of a need. There are several ways that the existence of a need as a drive state may be demonstrated. In this experiment we have attempted to satisfy the need and observe whether the consequent reinforcement would increase the probability of emittence of behavior which immediately preceded the reinforcement. Thus if there is a need for novel associative stimulation then supplying such stimulation should reduce the need (just as ingesting of food reduces hunger). If the need is reduced then this should produce reinforcement. To demonstrate the reinforcing properties of novel associative stimuli, a variation of the verbal operant conditioning technique was employed. Each time the subject chose the noun member of a pair of words he was answered with an improbable association to that noun; each time he chose the nonnoun member of a pair, a highly probable association was given. If the improbable, novel association has reinforcing properties the rate of the noun response would be expected to increase. We predicted that highly creative individuals would show the effect of such reinforcement while less creative individuals would not.

METHOD

Remote Associates Test

The theory of creative thinking which in part guided this research states that the creative process consists in the forming of associative elements into new combinations which meet specific requirements. The Remote Associates Test (RAT) is an operational statement of this definition. In RAT test items the subject is provided with words from mutually remote associative clusters and asked to find an *associative* link which combines these words in a specified manner. Here are some examples of the type of item found in the test. Evidence bearing on the usefulness of the test has been presented elsewhere (Mednick, 1962).

Example 1: surprise line Democratic

Example 2: rat blue cottage [2]

The test consists of 30 such items; the score is the number right.

Subjects

Subjects were chosen from a pool of University of Michigan undergraduates to whom the RAT had been administered several months prior

[2] Answers to sample RAT items: 1. party; 2. cheese.

to the onset of the present study. Thirty high RAT scorers composed the high creative (HC) group, and 30 low RAT scorers composed the low creative (LC) group. Mean HC score was 24.36, with a range of 22–29, and the LC mean score was 12.96, with a range of 4–19.

Materials

The materials consisted of a series of 180 3″ × 5″ index cards, on which a pair of words was centered and typed one above the other. All subjects received the series in the same order.

Free operant items. The first 40 items in the series of 180 were composed of pairs of nouns and nonnouns matched for frequency of occurrence by the Thorndike-Lorge (1944) lists. Half the nouns were randomly assigned to the top position on the cards. These 40 free operant items were introduced to obtain a baseline preference for choosing nouns. To each of the subject's 40 free operant choices the experimenter responded with its most common associate. Common associates were defined as one of the three associations most frequently given by a group of 25 Michigan undergraduates.

Filler items. Every ninth card in the series of 180 was printed with a pair of nonnouns. The experimenter always responded with a common associate to the two nonnouns. These 20 filler items, which are disregarded in the results, were introduced in the hope of preventing the subject from gaining insight into the experimental method. These word pairs were chosen in the same manner as the free operant items.

Critical items. The remaining 120 items were composed of pairs of nouns and nonnouns taken from the Minnesota Kent-Rosanoff norms (Russell & Jenkins, 1954) and from a set of word association norms prepared by Deese (1960 unpublished). Each pair was also matched for frequency of occurrence in the language by the use of the Thorndike-Lorge (1944) lists; half of the nouns were randomly assigned to the top position on the card. The common associations given by the experimenter to these words were the associations given most frequently in the Deese and Kent-Rosanoff norms. Novel associations were defined either as the associations occurring uniquely or not given at all in the norms. (In the latter case the experimenter supplied the association.)

Procedure

The HC and LC groups were each randomly divided into a control and experimental group of 15 subjects each. Table 1 presents the mean and range of RAT scores obtained by the four groups.

All subjects were seen individually; the experimenter read the following instructions:

> I am going to show you some cards, one at a time. On each card there are two words. I want you to look at both words and say aloud the one you like best. In response to each word you say aloud I will say a word, or give you an association. For example, if I show

TABLE 1

Mean and Range of RAT Scores

	Experimental Group		*Control Group*	
RAT Group	*M*	*Range*	*M*	*Range*
High	24.66	22–29	24.06	22–27
Low	13.26	4–18	12.66	6–16

you a card with the words *pencil* and *telephone* on it and you choose *pencil* I might say *paper*. If you said *telephone* I might say *call*. So, for each card you will choose one of the two words and say it out loud and I will give you a response word. Pay attention to the words and associations because I shall ask you to do something else later on. Any questions?

The experimenter then presented the 180-card series and recorded the number of nouns chosen by the subject.

Each time a member of the two Experimental groups (HC and LC) chose a noun on one of the 120 critical items, the experimenter responded with a novel association; each time he chose a nonnoun, the experimenter presented a common association. For example, if a pair of words were FATHER and WHITE and an experimental subject chose WHITE the experimenter would say *black*. If the subject chose FATHER, the experimenter might respond with *eggbeater*. The two Control groups (HC and LC) were given common associations to both nouns and nonnouns. For example, if a Control subject chose FATHER from the above example, the experimenter responded with *mother*. Pilot studies indicated that the HC subjects tended to choose the nonnoun before any experimental manipulations were introduced. Just as in **T** maze research the subject is trained away from his position preference, we attempted to operantly condition the high creatives to choose the nonpreferred noun.

After the completion of the series of 180 cards the experimenter asked the subject to try to recall all the words on the cards. An interview with the subject concerning the intent of the experiment followed the testing session.

RESULTS

The interview following the testing session revealed that none of the subjects had perceived or suspected the intent of the experimenter. The majority of the subjects reported an awareness of the difference between novel and common associations but none were conscious of their contingent relationship to the "nounness" of the stimulus words.

Conditioning Data

For purposes of analysis, the 180 items were divided into four trials of 40 items each. The 20 filler items were disregarded. Figure 1 presents the mean number of nouns chosen per trial by the High

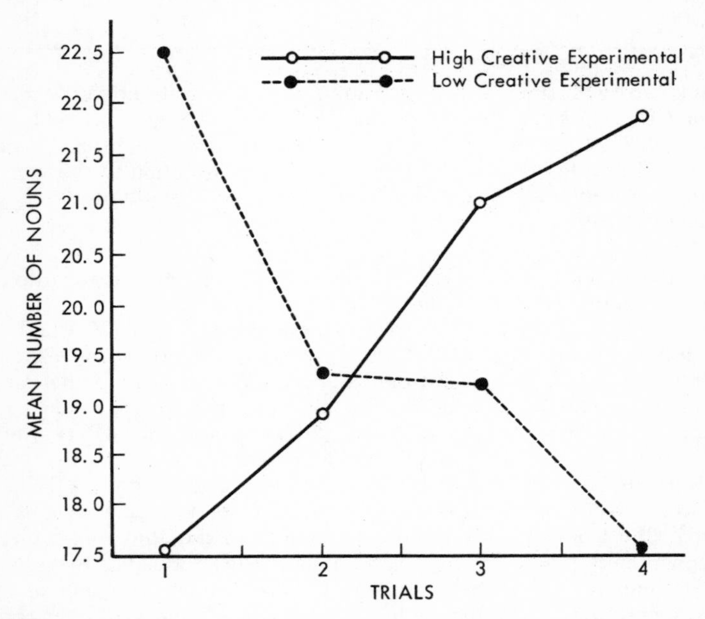

FIGURE 1. Mean number of nouns chosen per trial by the HCE and LCE groups.

Creative-Experimental (HCE) and the Low Creative-Experimental (LCE) groups. Table 2 contains the repeated measurements analysis of variance (Edwards, 1951) by which the HCE and LCE group performances were compared.

Neither of the main effects were significant. The Trials × Creativity interaction was significant at the .001 level. This interaction suggests that the novel associations had a differential effect on the performance of the HCE and LCE groups over trials.

The predictions that the HCE group would show an increase in the number of nouns they chose was supported by a significant corre-

TABLE 2

Repeated Measurements Analysis of Variance of HCE and LCE Groups

Source	*df*	*MS*	*F*
Creativity	1	.00	.00
Between subjects in same group	28	46.51	
Total between subjects	29		
Trials	3	7.36	.48
Creativity × Trials	3	96.61	6.44*
Interaction: Pooled subjects × Trials	84	15.27	
Total within subjects	90		

* $p < .001$.

lated t value obtained in comparing the HCE means on Trials 1 and 4 ($t = 2.37$, $df = 14$, $p < .05$). However, while the number of nouns chosen by the HCE group significantly *increased*, the number chosen by the LCE group significantly *decreased*.

The difference between the HCE and LCE means on Trial 1 was large enough to suggest that the number of nouns chosen on subsequent trials might have been affected in some way by this original difference. An analysis of variance comparing the performance of 10 subjects from each of the HCE and LCE groups matched in terms of the number of nouns chosen on Trial 1 yielded a Creativity × Trials interaction term significant at the .01 level. This significant interaction suggests that the effects observed in the HCE and LCE groups cannot be accounted for in terms of the large initial difference in group means on Trial 1. . . .

Table 3 contains the repeated measurements analysis of variance by which the HCC and LCC groups were compared. As can be seen none of these differences is significant. The lack of significance supports the interpretation that the differences observed in the experimental conditions were due to the manipulation of the associative novelty of the stimuli.

Recall Data

Table 4 contains a comparison of the percentage of nouns recalled by the four groups after the testing session. The t ratio for differences

TABLE 3

Repeated Measurements Analysis of Variance of HCC and LCC Groups

Source	*df*	*MS*	*F*
Creativity	1	1.01	.02
Between subjects in same group	28	51.66	
Total between subjects	29		
Trials	3	10.64	.86
Creativity × Trials	3	11.70	.95
Interaction: Pooled subjects × Trials	84	12.36	
Total within subjects	90		

in percentage of nouns recalled by the HCE and LCE groups was 3.41 ($df = 28$, $p < .01$). The t ratio obtained in comparing the LCC and HCC recall values was not significant ($t = .37$, $df = 28$). In view of the fact that the HCE group pronounced more nouns than the LCE group in the period of time immediately preceding the recall session this finding is not completely unexpected.

TABLE 4

Percentage of Nouns Recalled by the Four Groups

HCE	*LCE*	*HCC*	*LCC*
56.1	42.5	55.5	56.4

Discussion

We have apparently obtained results which are supportive to the hypothesis that the highly creative individual has a need for associative novelty. Let us examine this conclusion with some care. To begin with, while the results are most easily explained in terms of reinforcement brought about by reduction of the need for associative novelty, some other possibilities also suggest themselves. It could be argued that the highly creative subjects were not so much responding positively to novelty as they were responding negatively to banality. That is, with all due respect for our intentions, the behavior of these subjects may have been more controlled by the aversiveness of the highly probable association than by the novelty of the improbable association. This is almost analogous to saying that the rat does not approach the alley that has the food, but is actually avoiding the foodless alley. The analogy breaks down when we realize that in the case of the rat we can define the need relatively precisely in terms of antecedent conditions. In the case of the highly creative subject we cannot do so. This argument suggests that the next step in examining this question should consist of the institution of some antecedent conditions which would arouse the need for associative novelty. We could then test to see what are the effects of the interaction of varying levels of deprivation and levels of creativity. It would also be of interest to increase the number of trials so as to carry the performance to an asymptote and then note differential rates of extinction. The shortage of associational norms made this impossible in this study.

The noun choosing experimental subject was always presented with a novel associative stimulus. However, except for a statement of probability of S-R association we would be hard put to define precisely what we mean by novelty. Within a given level of probability the associative stimuli vary in complexity, humor, meaning, rhyme, incongruity, etc. Subsequent research might well be aimed at studying the dimension of associative novelty independently of the dimension of meaning, and vice versa.

Of considerable interest is the behavior of the low creative experimental group which shows a marked and significant tendency to avoid the improbable associations and/or approach the highly probable associations. Here again some further analytical research is needed to separate out the effect of these two variables. However, if we can for the moment argue in a mildly tautological fashion it is clear why low creative individuals become that way. The individual who eschews unusual ideas and/or prefers the highly probable is not likely to develop highly creative solutions to problems.

[7]
Reasoning in White Rats

NORMAN R. F. MAIER

Statement of Problem

The purpose of this investigation is to learn whether or not rats can solve problems without "trial and error." That is, can a rat, placed in a certain situation, adjust itself intelligently or adequately for its purpose, without previously having learned to respond in the situation concerned and without making a series of random responses that finally lead to an adjustment? Or further, can a rat be placed in a situation in which it can, by its solution, demonstrate insight? [1] Is the "puzzle-box" a valid measure of animal intelligence? Does it fully test an animal's capacity or can a rat behave in a manner that might be called reasoning? If it can reason, then (1) it must adequately adjust itself to a new situation, (2) it must be able to apply essential relations from other experiences to the new situation, and (3) the solution must be a continuous whole directed toward a definite end. This end need not be consciously appreciated.

Method and Results

The experiments were begun at the Psychological Institute of the University of Berlin in the winter of 1926 and were continued at the University of Michigan in the Fall of 1927. Three rats, A, B, and C, were used in Germany. At Michigan seven were available part of the time, but in most cases only six were used. They are nos. 44, 46,

[1] Insight is here used as Koehler uses it when describing it objectively, a connected or continuous or whole response which appears as a whole and may come suddenly, or may manifest itself as a sudden change in activity.

SOURCE: Norman R. F. Maier, "Reasoning in White Rats," *Comparative Psychology Monographs,* 1929, 6, No. 29. Reprinted by permission of The Johns Hopkins Press.

47, 48, 49, 50, and 51. All but 51 were experienced rats which had been used in maze work the year before. All of the ten rats were males, at least 7 months old.

The "set-ups" used vary from experiment to experiment and will be described in each case. Rats A, B, and C were put through a large number of "set-ups" and in some cases only enough results will be given to indicate training and qualitative results. The quantitative results were obtained largely with the rats used in the University of Michigan laboratory.

The problem for the rat was to obtain food which was so placed that it could not be reached directly. The normal or obvious route to food was blocked by a cage shaped like a triangle, one side being open, the other two sides and the top being made of wire. This cage was clamped to the table so that the open side extended about 15 cm. over the edge of the table. The pathways leading to food (that is, the indirect route) were made of strips of wood 2 cm. by 2 cm. in cross-section and were supported on tables and ringstands. . . . The units of these pathways are designated by numbers in the figures.

The starting point in the test was always on one side of the cage and the food on the other. The rats having been trained positively to a light, an electric light wrapped in paper was placed beside the food (unless otherwise indicated) and served as a food stimulus in case olfaction was not sufficient.

A general description of the situation is as follows: Point *A* is the starting position and *F* is the position of the food. *F* is separated from *A* by the wire cage. Let *b, c, d,* and *e* be points on the maze which leads from the table to food, and let *g, h, i, j,* and *k* be any points on the table except *b*. If the rat has previously been permitted to become familiar with all points except those lying on the maze (which has not been constructed at this time) then point *b* is no more favored than the points *g, h, i, j,* and *k*. After the situation has become familiar, the pathway is set up and the rat is taught to go from *b* to *F*. In the test the rat is placed at *A*, so that the only way to food is *A–b–F*. In order to reach the food the gap *A–b* must be filled in. The rat can do so, either by using the experience gained previously to learning *b–F* (that is, selecting the relation *A–b* rather than *A–g*, *a–h*, or some other) or it can wander away from A until by chance it comes to *b* which sets off the chain of associations that lead to *F*.

The first type of solution would be an "intelligent" solution, the second a "trial and error" solution. The rat does finally reach the food. It remains, therefore, for the results to show which of these solutions it uses.

The first type of solution, if described from behavior only, would show the animal trying to reach the food directly with considerable activity at point *A*, and then a direct and active running to point *b* and without hesitation continuing along the pathway. The second type would also show the rat trying to reach the food directly and then a gradual increase in activity at point *A*. This heightened activity would take the rat farther and farther from *A* until it carried the rat to far points on the table including point *b*. At *b* there would be sign of recognition (halting) followed by a taking of the path.

Rats not familiar with, or having no knowledge of, the pathway *b–F*, should come upon *b* (although they might not take the pathway) just as soon as the rats which know the path, if the latter did not apply their previous experience, but came upon it by random wandering around. If, however, they applied their experience of the table (points *b, g, h, i, j,* and *k*) to the situation, then there should be a considerable difference in time in going from *A* to *b*, for rats with and without the experience of running *b–F*. The same difference should hold also for rats familiar and not familiar with the immediate surroundings (points *b, g, h, i, j,* and *k*).

* * *

Experiment A

Results: Rat A. *A*—Around sides of cage—back and forth on table near the cage—at *p*—*A*—tries to get around cage—over wall at *p*—directly to box—at *b*—*F*.

Theoretical Discussion

The results show that chance and "trial and error" cannot explain the behavior of the rats in solving the type of problems presented in these experiments. Let us then turn to association, in the sense of mere stimulus-response connection, and see whether or not it can explain.

On the basis of associations, which depend on frequency, recency, and intensity, it might be assumed that the rat has associated point *A* with every other point in the known territory and every other point with all other points. Thus the associations *A–b, A–c, A–d, b–c, b–d,* etc. may have been formed. From *b* the rat then learns the pathway to *F*, forming the association *b–F*. In the test, the rat being placed at *A*, goes to *b* and then to *F*. Why, on the basis of association, should the rat go from *A* to *b* rather than to *c, d, e,* or some other point, all points being equally well associated with *A*? The experience of going from *b* to *F* must in some way make *b* stand out. On the basis of the present notion of association, the association *A–b* cannot be strengthened by the formation of the association *b–F*. Hence this notion of association is as unsatisfactory as chance and "trial and error" for explaining these results.

Instead of saying that a series of associations are formed it might be said that the rat has a pattern of the whole situation such as

c
A *b*
d e

. . . The above pattern is formed during the period that the rat is wandering about and investigating. In the learning of the pathway another pattern, *b*–1–3–5–*F*, is formed.

In the test the rat is placed in a situation which is different from the other two. Because of the food at *F*, point *A* has a new relation. The rat tries to get from *A* directly to *F*. This is a third pattern and dominates during the "trial and error" period when the rat tries to get through or around the cage.

The rat has now experienced three patterns:

(1) *A–F* (2) *A* *c* / *d e* *b* (3) *b*–1–3–5–*F*

"*A*" of patterns 1 and 2, *b* of patterns 2 and 3, and *F* of patterns 1 and 3 must become identical. When the solution comes, certain essential parts of patterns 2 and 3 must combine to form the new pattern *A–b–F*, which is the solution. This is a new combination, a new creation, and is made up of parts of two separate experiences. It is not a pattern that was formed by mere repetition as were patterns 2 and 3. The presence of pattern 1 gives the drive and a certain direction of energy. Patterns 2 and 3 then combine to take its place, *A* and *F* having an altogether different relation to each other than they had in pattern 1. The formation of the solution-pattern is the moment or flash of insight.

* * *

Because a certain pattern has frequently dominated does not make it most likely to dominate in a situation where such dominance does not lead to the goal. Placing the goal outside of the pattern necessitates the formation of a new pattern. The starting point and the end are the determining factors in the formation of a new pattern.

What causes a new pattern to form out of parts of two other patterns is another problem. It may be that the common elements have been made to stand out or become more intense, or it may be a matter of the recognition of essential likenesses and differences as Shepard holds. But that a new pattern, the solution, which is made up of essentials from two other patterns, has been formed seems to have been indicated. The end also seems to be a determining factor as to what the nature of the new pattern will be.

As the combination of two patterns in the solution of a problem is at the bottom of theories of reasoning that make reasoning more than "trial and error," it must be granted that white rats also reason.

The concept of patterns or *Gestalten* thus seems to be a necessary assumption to explain these complex types of behavior. The fact that a rat can choose the shorter means to an end without previously having reached this end by any of these means, seems to make a pattern concept almost a necessity. A temporal chain is not sufficient, it must be an immediate whole.

[8]
The Mechanism of the Assembly of Behavior Segments in Novel Combinations Suitable for Problem Solution [1]

CLARK L. HULL

The General Problem of Adaptive Novelty in Mammalian Behavior

Many persons have been puzzled by the paradox of the presumptive fertility and originality of the processes of reasoning on the one hand, as contrasted with the remarkable sterility of the syllogism on the other. It has been urged that if one already knows a major premise such as,

All men are mortal,

and that if an organism passing by the name of Socrates manifests traits generally characteristic of a man, it requires no particular originality or perspicacity to conclude that Socrates will himself prove ultimately to be mortal also. Fertility, originality, invention, insight, the spontaneous use of implements or tools—these things, clearly, do not lie in the syllogism. The fact that it has been found possible to construct a relatively simple mechanism of sliding disk segments of sheet metal which will solve automatically, that is, exhibit the conclusions logically flowing from, all of the known syl-

[1] The writer is indebted to the members of his seminar for a number of valuable criticisms and suggestions, notably, to Dr. T. L. McCulloch, Mr. S. D. S. Spragg, and Dr. J. B. Wolfe. Dr. N. R. F. Maier also read a preliminary draft of the manuscript.

SOURCE: Clark L. Hull, "The Mechanism of the Assembly of Behavior Segments in Novel Combinations Suitable for Problem Solution," *Psychological Review,* 1935, **42,** 219–245.

logisms and which will automatically detect all of the formal fallacies,[2] emphasizes the crudely mechanical characteristics of the syllogism.[3] The solution of the paradox is, of course, that the genuinely creative and novelty-producing portions of the reasoning processes take place in advance of the emergence of the substance or materials of the syllogism; that is, the solution consists in the *assembly*, from the considerable store of such materials presumably possessed by the more versatile and adaptive organisms, of the particular set of premises which are relevant to the problem situation in question. An understanding of the dynamics of the presumably numerous forms of intelligence, insight, thought, and reasoning must therefore be sought not in the mechanism and use of the syllogism as such, but in this period *antecedent* to the explicit emergence of the material which may be susceptible later of being arranged in the form of a syllogism.[4] It accordingly becomes our task to discover the principles by which, on the occasion of need, there emerge the habit segments or premises in the particular combination necessary for problem solution.

Something of the theoretical urgency of this problem is brought home to us when we consider the blind chaos which would result if, in problem situations, premises or habit segments should appear by pairs as if drawn by chance from a huge urn from the supply possessed by the organism. The probability that a particular pair of numbers would be drawn from a supply of 100 on any particular occasion is something like 1 in 10,000. Chance is evidently an element in intelligent behavior but, clearly, the dice of chance must be loaded in some way or problems would never get solved. In short, any adequate theory of higher adaptive behavior must show how the dice are loaded, that is, how the characteristics of the problem situation are able to evoke the particular combination of acts which alone will serve to extricate the organism from its difficulty.

[2] Such a mechanism has been designed and constructed by the author, but a description has not yet been published.

[3] So far as the writer is able to see, there is no *a priori* impossibility of constructing a mechanism which will display genuine thinking capacity. Indeed, it is expected with some confidence that such mechanisms will ultimately be constructed. But when, and if, this takes place the thinking mechanism will surely be of a far more subtle and complex character than a mere logic machine consisting of sliding disks.

[4] As a matter of fact, John Stuart Mill long ago pointed out that the syllogism is primarily a device for testing the accuracy of reasoning processes which have already taken place (20, Book II).

The Specific Problem of the Adaptive Assembly of Habit Segments in Novel Combinations

As a rule it is more economical and generally effective to attack difficult problems by investigating at the outset their simpler aspects and manifestations rather than their more complex ones. In accordance with this principle, we shall begin our analysis of the dynamics of novelty in mammalian behavior by the consideration of a concrete form of intelligent or insightful behavior to which attention has been directed by Norman Maier (1929). In this connection he has remarked significantly, ". . . the combination of two patterns in the solution of a problem is at the bottom of theories of reasoning that make reasoning more than 'trial-and-error.' . . ." As a result of ingenious experimental procedures, Dr. Maier believes that he has demonstrated the existence of such capacity in the albino rat.

In order to make the substance of Maier's fundamental bit of analysis explicit, let us consider a somewhat modified and conventionalized version of his experimental arrangement. This may be understood with the aid of Figure 1. Sections, *R*, *U*, *X*, and *H* repre-

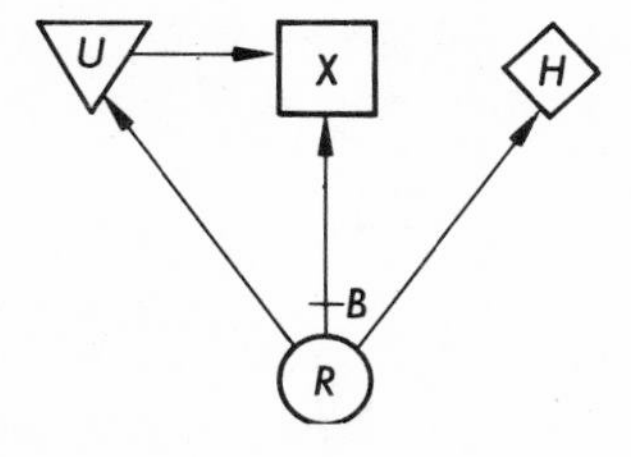

Figure 1. Diagrammatic representation of a series of locomotor paths representing a somewhat conventionalized form of Maier's "reasoning" experiment with rats. The pathways are enclosed, as are the areas *R*, *X*, *U*, and *H*. The floor of *X* would be of soft flossy silk, say; that of *U* of cold metal with rough, sharp points; that of *H*, of polished warm metal; that of *R*, of several layers of thin rubber dam. When training on one path is taking place, all others are closed.

sent enclosed boxes each of distinct shape. Distinctive cutaneous stimuli are provided for the animals' feet by the character of the floor of each box, on the assumption that a characteristic stimulus will lead to a distinct reaction while in each box, and so favor the arousal of partially distinct anticipatory reactions (Hull, 1931). For the same reason, additional special devices calculated to induce markedly characteristic and distinct postures in the animals whenever traversing the respective boxes, should probably be provided. The animal will be trained first to go from *R* to *X*, and from *U* to *X* as distinct habits, and will receive food. Next he will be trained to go from *R* to *U* and from *R* to *H* as distinct habits for the reward of water, say. Following this there should probably be given a few more forced runs on *UX* and *RX* with food reward, after which the animals should be given an opportunity to choose between *RU* and *RH* a number of times to determine objectively the relative strength of the tendency of each individual to enter the respective alleys. Then, with all the four paths open but with a barrier in *RX* at point *B* (Figure 1), the rat will be placed at *R*, very hungry but with the thirst drive thoroughly satiated. Insight in the sense here used will be shown by the animals' tending, in general, to choose path *RU* (and then *UX*) rather than path RH a significantly greater proportion of the trials than was the case on the control choices.

Let us now, for convenience and definiteness in exposition, represent schematically our conception of the essentials of the organization of the several habit segments generated by the foregoing procedure. We shall begin with that leading from *R* to *X*, Figure 1. We shall suppose that a mammalian organism in an external stimulus situation, S_R, and with an internal stimulus situation (drive), S_D, possesses at the end of some training the habit sequence,

$$\text{(Sequence I)} \qquad \begin{array}{c} S_R \\ \downarrow \\ R_P \rightarrow R_Q \rightarrow R_X \\ \uparrow \\ S_D \end{array}$$

Here S_R represents the visual, auditory, and other external stimuli coming to the organism from box *R*, and S_D represents proprioceptive stimuli such as result from hunger cramps of the digestive tract, say. R_X represents the final or consummatory reaction which abolishes S_D and thus naturally terminates the cycle. In this sense R_X may be said to be the solution of the problem jointly presented by S_R and S_D. R_P and R_Q represent the locomotor and other activity involved in traversing path $R \rightarrow X$.

Let us suppose, also, that in a different external stimulus situation, S_U, but one possessing the same drive as that of Sequence I, that is,

S_D, there has been formed a second behavior sequence which terminates in the same solution or goal reaction as Sequence I:

$$\text{(Sequence II)}\quad \begin{array}{c} S_U \\ \downarrow \\ R_U \rightarrow R_V \rightarrow R_W \rightarrow R_X \\ \uparrow \\ S_D \end{array}$$

This corresponds to the habit segment leading from *U* to *X*, Figure 1. Here S_U represents the visual, olfactory, and other external stimuli coming to the organism from box *U* (Figure 1). R_U, R_V, and R_W represent the activity of traversing the path from box *U* to box *X*, and R_X represents the final or consummatory response as in Sequence I.

In addition there are postulated two further sequences, both originating at S_R:

$$\text{(Sequence III)}\quad \begin{array}{c} S_R \\ \downarrow \\ R_R \rightarrow R_S \rightarrow R_T \rightarrow R_U \\ \uparrow \\ S_{D'} \end{array}$$

$$\text{(Sequence IV)}\quad \begin{array}{c} S_R \\ \downarrow \\ R_E \rightarrow R_F \rightarrow R_G \rightarrow R_H \\ \uparrow \\ S_{D'} \end{array}$$

Sequence III represents the path from *R* to *U*, and Sequence IV represents the path from *R* to *H* (Figure 1). It is to be noted, however, that Sequence III and Sequence IV are each supposed to have a drive (for example, thirst) which is different from that of Sequences I and II. We accordingly represent the drive of Sequences III and IV by $S_{D'}$. R_U and R_H represent that portion of the final or consummatory segments of the respective sequences which are characteristic and distinctive of each.

Now, suppose that Sequence I should be prevented from taking place by the barrier placed between S_R and R_P as indicated in Figure 2 and point *B*, Figure 1. How can the solution (reaction R_X) to the problem thus precipitated be brought about? In external stimulus situation S_R the organism now has but two choices, Sequence III or

Sequence IV. If Sequence IV is taken, this act leads only to R_H, which for the drive, S_D, is a mere blind alley and a failure, since it does not eliminate S_D. But if Sequence III is taken, this leads to Sequence II which, in turn, leads to R_X, the solution, thus:

$$\begin{array}{l} S_R \\ \downarrow \\ R_R \rightarrow R_S \rightarrow R_T \rightarrow R_U \rightarrow R_V \rightarrow R_W \rightarrow R_X \end{array}$$

In any realistic consideration of this problem it is important to note that there is always a possibility that the organism will find its way from S_R to S_U by mere chance (trial-and-error), in which case Sequence II would presumably follow at once and the problem would be solved for the organism but no insight would be involved. Since the trial-and-error type of behavior is almost certain to be present to a greater or less degree in situations such as the one here supposed, it is necessary to have in the experimental set-up some unambiguous opportunity for trial-and-error to operate relatively

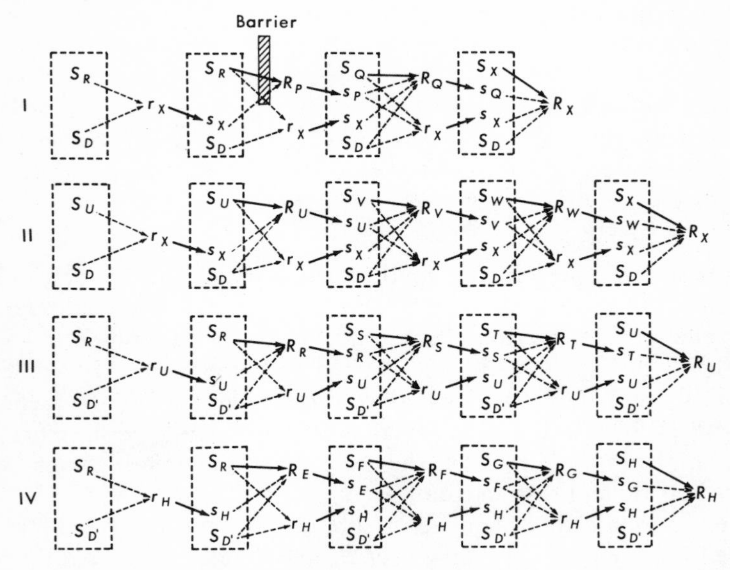

FIGURE 2. Diagrammatic representation of the major immediate excitatory tendencies in action sequences I, II, III, and IV, which correspond to Paths $R \rightarrow X$, $U \rightarrow X$, $R \rightarrow U$, and $R \rightarrow H$ respectively, of Figure 1. Remote excitatory tendencies are not represented. The barrier is assumed to have been placed before R_P after Sequence I had become fairly well practiced and was working smoothly.

uncomplicated by other factors in order to have a basis for comparison and possible contrast with a situation in which insight may be an appreciable additional element. It is to be noted that such an opportunity for the manifestation of pure trial-and-error behavior is provided for by the path from *R* to *H* of Figure 1 (and Sequence IV in Figure 2). Thus if upon the whole, after the frustration of Sequence I, Sequence IV is chosen as frequently by the organism as Sequence III, no insight is indicated. If, however, Sequence III is chosen a significantly greater proportion of the trials, this excess constitutes an indication of intelligence or insight and demands genuine explanation by any systematic theory of mammalian behavior.

Whatever may be the final conclusion regarding the abilities of albino rats in this respect, there can be little doubt that man and, presumably, some of the higher mammals show such a capacity.[5] Therefore we must face the question of why the organism should choose Sequence III, which will ultimately lead to success, rather than Seqeunce IV, which will not. How is the possession by the organism of the latent or implicit habit sequence (II) able to influence in any way the choice betwen III and IV in favor of III? If we can succeed in answering this question we shall probably not only have isolated one important and basic mechanism of intelligence and insight, but may possibly have made a step forward in the understanding of the more elaborate forms of reasoning proper where verbal symbolic reactions are primarily involved.

Maier's Gestalt Interpretation

Before proceeding to the consideration of our own interpretation of this fascinating problem, it will be well to glance briefly at that offered by Maier himself. He states that when he attempted to account for the animals' alleged preference for the path from *R* to *U* over that from *R* to *H*, by means of associative principles, he encountered difficulties. He argues, first, that since S_R has associations leading both to Sequences III and IV ($R \rightarrow U$ and $R \rightarrow H$, Figure 1), it should be expected that the animals would choose the one as readily as the other. But insightful behavior demands that some

[5] Recently Wolfe and Spragg have reported results which, taken in conjunction with certain characteristics of Maier's technique, lead them to question whether the albino rat can combine habit segments, as supposed by Maier.

preference should be shown to III over IV. Thus he concludes that association cannot account for the phenomenon (1929, p. 92).

He accordingly turns from association to *Gestalt* concepts as offering more promising possibilities. His remarks concerning a substantially similar situation appear also to be applicable to the one before us:

> The concept of patterns or *Gestalten* thus seems to be a necessary assumption to explain these complex types of behavior. The fact that a rat can choose the . . . means to an end without previously having reached this end by any of these means, seems to make a pattern concept almost a necessity. A temporal chain is not sufficient; it must be an immediate whole.

A little examination of the nature of our problem seems to show, however, that the concept of *Gestalten* leads to the same sterile issue as the naïve associative view which Maier quite properly rejected. It is to be observed that Maier does not claim to have demonstrated exactly how patterns lead in the above situation to correct rather than incorrect choices. One might say, of course, that under the stress created by the frustration of I, Sequences III and II become fused into a *Gestalt* or unity in the sense that together they somehow solve the problem, whereas Sequences IV and II do not so fuse. But such an interpretation of *Gestalten* as an explanatory principle would naïvely beg the question, since the deduction of this fusion from more basic principles is the essence of the problem before us. Such a utilization of the concept of *Gestalten* would be a mere tautological gesture; it would merely re-assert the fact of problem solution in a new terminology without in any sense deducing the outcome from any principles whatever. It is true that the history of science reveals many cases of such naïve procedures, though, so far as the writer is aware, no one has ever put forward this particular argument.

But if ordinary association and *Gestalt* principles have both failed, what other possibility remains? The writer is inclined to the view that the principles of association between stimuli and responses, particularly as revealed in modern conditioned-reaction experiments,[6] offer a possibility of explanation in a manner which Maier's

[6] In order to correct a frequent misunderstanding, due presumably to the wide dissemination of the views of J. B. Watson, the writer wishes to make it quite clear that neither here nor in any previous publications has he assumed that the more complex forms of behavior are synthesized from reflexes which

analysis failed to take into consideration. We shall now proceed to an examination of this possibility.

A Suggested Stimulus-Response Explanation of the Adaptive Assembly of Habit Segments

A somewhat detailed stimulus-response analysis of action Sequences I, II, III, and IV, as sketched above, is given in Figure 2. The S's at the top of each diagram represent typical stimuli as received from the external receptors. S_D and $S_{D'}$ represent persisting internal stimuli such as hunger, thirst, sex, etc., and the *s*'s represent proprioceptive stimulations. Broken arrows indicate acquired or learned tendencies, whereas solid lines indicate what are presumed to be innate or unacquired tendencies.

In this connection it is to be noted that an anticipatory goal reaction appears in the first segment of each of these sequences (Hull, 1931). For example, in the first sequence there appears r_X, which is supposed to be a relatively inconspicuous component of the goal reaction R_X, brought forward to the beginning of the series presumably through its association with S_D or through the action of trace reactions while in their early stages (or both), and which, once there, becomes associated with S_R. In the same way we find r_X at the beginning of Sequence II (having originally been a component of R_X),[7] r_U at the beginning of Sequence III (having originally been a component of R_U), and r_H at the beginning of Sequence IV (having originally been a component of R_H). It is assumed, further, that similar components of all reactions in any given series tend to come forward and become associated with the external stimulus component in the same manner, though because of the difficulty of representing them in detail only the anticipatory goal

play the rôle of building blocks. This may or may not be true. His working hypothesis is, rather, that the *principles of action* discovered in conditioned reaction experiments are also operative in the higher behavioral processes. The compound adjective in the expression, "conditioned-reflex principles," accordingly refers to the locus of *discovery* of the principles rather than to their locus of *operation*.

[7] That terminal or goal and near-goal reactions do come forward in behavior sequences is amply substantiated by a number of investigations. . . . In some of the investigations, the anticipatory (or antedating) reactions actually come forward in their entirety and supplant reactions properly belonging in the positions in question. . . .

reactions are shown in Figure 2. A complete set of anticipatory reactions, emanating from both goal and sub-goal reactions, are, however, shown in the first segment of Figure 3.

Figure 3 is designed to show the dynamics of the situation at point S_R after the barrier comes in to frustrate and extinguish Sequence I. This is regarded as the crucial point of the theoretical problem. A study of Figure 3, in conjunction with Figure 2 from which it was derived, shows that the ordinary principles of the association of stimuli and responses, when applied in a thoroughgoing fashion, actually lead in a logical and straightforward manner to the expectation that an organism capable of functional anticipatory reactions (for example, r_U) would be more likely to react with the sequence

$$R_R \rightarrow R_S \rightarrow R_T \rightarrow R_U \rightarrow R_V \rightarrow R_W \rightarrow R_X$$

and consequently with a successful solution, than by the reaction

$$R_E \rightarrow R_F \rightarrow R_G \rightarrow R_H$$

which is not a solution.

At bottom the decisive factor in this competition (Figure 3) is the presence of s_U, with its excitatory tendency to evoke R_R rather than R_E. But s_U, in turn, was necessarily dependent upon the presence of r_U, an anticipatory or antedating reaction. The details of the dominance of r_U over the other anticiptory reactions, and of R_R over R_E, are explained in the legend of Figure 3, which must be traced through in detail if the reader is to understand the deduction. It may be noted that r_U is a pure-stimulus or symbolic act, since the only function that it performs is to release by its action the proprioceptive stimulus s_U, which ultimately leads to an intelligent rather than to a stupid reaction.[8]

Here, then, we appear to have laid bare before us the mechanism of *one* type of intelligence or insight. It turns out, in fact, to be associative in nature, though distinctly not in the simple and direct

[8] It seems probable that when the animal meets the barrier (Sequence I, Fig. 1), R_p will be extinguished but r_X may largely escape extinction, and perseverate (see pp. 238 *ff.*) to the point where the choice is made between the two other paths. In that event s_X would appear in the first stimulus complex (and perhaps later ones) of Fig. 3. This would give r_U, as well as r_V and r_W (Sequence II, Fig. 1), an additional excitatory tendency at the outset. In the interest of simplicity of presentation this is left out of Fig. 3, since the deduction does not require it.

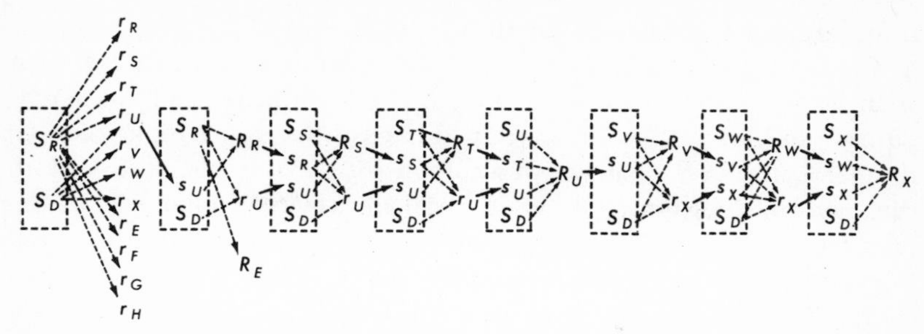

Figure 3. Diagrammatic representation of the dynamics of the situation at the problem point S_R after the frustration and extinction of the excitatory tendencies originally emanating from it to the sequence $R_P \rightarrow R_Q \rightarrow R_X$. Note that all of the excitatory tendencies here represented are taken from Figure 2. Thus the excitatory tendencies from S_R to r_R, r_S, r_T and r_U come from Sequence III, those from S_R to r_E, r_F, r_G, and r_H come from Sequence IV, and those from S_D to r_U, r_V, r_W, and r_X come from Sequence II. Referring, now, to the above figure, it may be seen that of the several anticipatory reactions just mentioned, r_U, only, has more than one excitatory tendency. The one from S_R comes from the beginning of Sequence III, whereas the one originating in S_D comes from the first reaction of Sequence II ($S_D \rightarrow R_U$). All the other r's are accordingly assumed to play minor rôles and are dismissed from further consideration.

At the next segment there appears another critical situation, the actual competition between R_R and R_E. It may be seen from the diagram that R_R has two excitatory tendencies, both originally functioning at the beginning of Sequence III, whereas R_E, its competitor, has only one excitatory tendency, that originating from the beginning of Sequence IV. Because of the advantage of the bond emanating from s_U to R_R, the latter reaction must have the advantage over R_E. Thus the presence of s_U raises the reaction from the status of trial-and-error into the realm of insight or intelligence without the intervention of any special psychic agent.

fashion conceived by Maier. Thus there has apparently evolved on a purely physical basis a type of reaction which has sometimes been supposed possible only by a kind of miraculous intervention of some non-physical (psychic) agent called mind or consciousness. To state the same thing in other words, we appear to have before us here a deduction of insight in terms such that it might conceivably be constructed by a clever engineer as a non-living—even an inorganic—mechanism.

* * *

The Problem of the Initial Spontaneous Use of Implements

Special interest attaches to the results of the preceding analysis because it rather looks as if the associative mechanisms there elaborated are also responsible for the spontaneous utilization of objects as implements or tools. An instance often cited as an example of such action is that described by Köhler, on the part of his chimpanzee, Sultan (1925, 132 *ff.*). In this case the ape had learned to drag in through the bars of his cage a bit of fruit placed a certain distance outside. On a particular trial, however, Köhler put in the cage two bamboo sticks, neither of which was long enough to reach the food. The animal first tried to obtain the fruit with one of the short sticks. After repeated failure he began playing with the two sticks. This (apparently) random manipulation finally resulted in the insertion of the end of the smaller stick into the hollow end of the larger. Soon after this took place, the animal reached through the bars with the combination stick and obtained the fruit. This union of action segments constituted the solution of the problem. Unfortunately it is not entirely clear whether the animal had ever before joined two objects in a somewhat similar manner, and there is no control in the plan of the experiment to show that the solution was not a mere accident. To be a clear case of insight in the sense of the term here employed, the joining of the sticks should have been performed a number of times in the recent past in random play, but should never have been used in the securing of food.

An experimental arrangement which promises less ambiguous evidence of insight in the field of implement or tool using might be set up on the analogy of the Maier experiment, somewhat as follows:

Sequence I. An ape is trained to press upward by means of a stick three feet long, against a toggle electric switch placed on the wall out of his reach; after which an electrically operated automatic machine close at hand will give him a grape.

Sequence II. A similar switch is placed three feet higher on the wall of another room, and the ape is trained to operate this with a six-foot stick which must be chosen from among two three-foot ones also available. After the pushing of the switch, a machine similar to that of Sequence I will give the animal a grape.

Sequence III. The animal is trained to put two sticks, each three feet long, together in such a way that one fits into a socket in the end of the other, making a stick six feet long. This training should be in still a different room. The reward in this case must be different from that of Sequences I and II, possibly the release from the room to return to the animal's living quarters.

Sequence IV. In a fourth room, the ape learns to place two sticks (other than those used in Sequence III) together so as to make a T, the reward in this case to be the same as that of Sequence III. One of the above sticks must have a socket in its middle instead of at its end, in order to permit the construction of the T.

The Problem. This would be set by placing the animal in the room with the high switch, as usual, but with two short sticks instead of the long one. This situation corresponds to the barrier placed in Path $R \rightarrow X$, in the rat experiment discussed above. The stick to be inserted into a socket would be like that in Sequences III and IV, but the other stick would have sockets both at one end and in the middle. *Insight would be shown by the animal tending to put the sticks together end to end rather than in the form of the T.*

A great variety of problems bearing on the nature of the presumably numerous mechanisms mediating intelligent behavior may be set up on this general pattern. In addition to the use of children at various ages, rich returns probably await the systematic utilization of such experimental approaches with the various intellectual levels of young adults in homes for the feebleminded. It is conceivable that, in addition to filling out the picture of intelligence as delineated by investigations concerned mainly with intelligence testing, a matter of pure science and of the greatest importance, the leads so obtained might yield valuable hints for increasing the validity of the tests in actual practice.

* * *

SUMMARY

Taking as a point of departure an analysis of intelligent behavior published by Norman Maier, the view is put forward that a basic mechanism mediating one great class of such behavior is that of the spontaneous assembly of habit segments never previously associated with each other. Behavior of this kind is deduced from stimulus-response principles. If this deduction should turn out to be sound, it would amount to a proof that at least one form of insightful behavior is not an ultimate, unanalyzable entity but is, instead, a special, though somewhat complicated, case of association between stimuli and reactions. Indeed, the principles of action which appear by this deduction are of such a nature that they might conceivably be incorporated into an inorganic machine which would automatically solve such problems. This is not to deny either the reality or the importance of such forms of behavior. On the contrary, it leads to the view, mainly on the grounds of the novel character and distinctiveness of the mechanism mediating it, that an adequate understanding of such behavior is of special importance, both theoretical and practical. The above analysis does lead, however, to the denial of the necessity of postulating any peculiarly experiential, psychic, or configurational factors in order to explain the existence of this particular form of intelligent action.

Whether the forms of behavior involving the spontaneous assembly of habit segments shall be called *reason* as Maier and Shepard are inclined to do, is not primarily a question of science, but, rather, one of taste and convenience. The present writer inclines to reserve the term *reason* for application to those problem situations in which the solution is mediated through the action of symbolic verbal reactions. There seems even less justification for applying the term *reasoning* to the behavior of animals on the *Y*-maze under the testing technique which we have explained on the basis of perseveration.

[9]
How We Think: The Analysis of a Complete Act of Thought

JOHN DEWEY

In this chapter we shall make an analysis of the process of thinking into its steps or elementary constituents, basing the analysis upon descriptions of a number of extremely simple, but genuine, cases of reflective experience.[1]

1. A Simple Case of Practical Deliberation. "The other day when I was down town on 16th Street a clock caught my eye. I saw that the hands pointed to 12:20. This suggested that I had an engagement at 124th Street, at one o'clock. I reasoned that as it had taken me an hour to come down on a surface car, I should probably be twenty minutes late if I returned the same way. I might save

[1] These are taken, almost verbatim, from the class papers of students.

twenty minutes by a subway express. But was there a station near? If not, I might lose more than twenty minutes in looking for one. Then I thought of the elevated, and I saw there was such a line within two blocks. But where was the station? If it were several blocks above or below the street I was on, I should lose time instead of gaining it. My mind went back to the subway express as quicker than the elevated; furthermore, I remembered that it went nearer than the elevated to the part of 124th Street I wished to reach, so that time would be saved at the end of the journey. I concluded in favor of the subway, and reached my destination by one o'clock."

2. A Simple Case of Reflection upon an Observation. "Projecting nearly horizontally from the upper deck of the ferryboat on which I daily cross the river, is a long white pole, bearing a gilded ball at its tip. It suggested a flagpole when I first saw it; its color, shape, and gilded ball agreed with this idea, and these reasons seemed to justify me in this belief. But soon difficulties presented themselves. The pole was nearly horizontal, an unusual position for a flagpole; in the next place, there was no pulley, ring, or cord by which to attach a flag; finally, there were elsewhere two vertical staffs from which flags were occasionally flown. It seemed probable that the pole was not there for flag-flying.

"I then tried to imagine all possible purposes of such a pole, and to consider for which of these it was best suited: (a) Possibly it was an ornament. But as all the ferryboats and even the tugboats carried like poles, this hypothesis was rejected. (b) Possibly it was the terminal of a wireless telegraph. But the same considerations made this improbable. Besides, the more natural place for such a terminal would be the highest part of the boat, on top of the pilot house. (c) Its purpose might be to point out the direction in which the boat is moving.

"In support of this conclusion, I discovered that the pole was lower than the pilot house, so that the steersman could easily see it. Moreover, the tip was enough higher than the base, so that, from the pilot's position, it must appear to project far out in front of the boat. Moreover, the pilot being near the front of the boat, he would need some such guide as to its direction. Tugboats would also need poles for such a purpose. This hypothesis was so much more probable than the others that I accepted it. I formed the conclusion that the pole was set up for the purpose of showing the pilot the direction in which the boat pointed, to enable him to steer correctly."

3. A Simple Case of Reflection Involving Experiment. "In washing tumblers in hot soapsuds and placing them mouth downward on a plate, bubbles appeared on the outside of the mouth of the tumblers and then went inside. Why? The presence of bubbles suggests air, which I note must come from inside the tumbler. I see that the soapy water on the plate prevents escape of the air save as it may be caught in bubbles. But why should air leave the tumbler? There was no substance entering to force it out. It must have expanded. It expands by increase of heat or by decrease of pressure, or by both. Could the air have become heated after the tumbler was taken from the hot suds? Clearly not the air that was already entangled in the water. If heated air was the cause, cold air must have entered in transferring the tumblers from the suds to the plate. I test to see if this supposition is true by taking several more tumblers out. Some I shake so as to make sure of entrapping cold air in them. Some I take out holding mouth downward in order to prevent cold air from entering. Bubbles appear on the outside of every one of the former and on none of the latter. I must be right in my inference. Air from the outside must have been expanded by the heat of the tumbler, which explains the appearance of the bubbles on the outside.

"But why do they then go inside? Cold contracts. The tumbler cooled and also the air inside it. Tension was removed, and hence bubbles appeared inside. To be sure of this, I test by placing a cup of ice on the tumbler while the bubbles are still forming outside. They soon reverse."

The Three Cases Form a Series

These three cases have been purposely selected so as to form a series from the more rudimentary to more complicated cases of reflection. The first illustrates the kind of thinking done by every one during the day's business, in which neither the data, nor the ways of dealing with them, take one outside the limits of everyday experience. The last furnishes a case in which neither problem nor mode of solution would have been likely to occur except to one with some prior scientific training. The second case forms a natural transition; its materials lie well within the bounds of everyday, unspecialized experience; but the problem, instead of being directly involved in the person's business, arises indirectly out of his activity, and accordingly appeals to a somewhat theoretic and impartial interest. We . . . are concerned only with the common elements found in all the types.

Five Distinct Steps in Reflection

Upon examination, each instance reveals, more or less clearly, five logically distinct steps: (*i*) a felt difficulty; (*ii*) its location and definition; (*iii*) suggestion of possible solution; (*iv*) development by reasoning of the bearings of the suggestion; (*v*) further observation and experiment leading to its acceptance or rejection; that is, the conclusion of belief or disbelief.

1. THE OCCURRENCE OF A DIFFICULTY. The first and second steps frequently fuse into one. The difficulty may be felt with sufficient definiteness as to set the mind at once speculating upon its probable solution, or an undefined uneasiness and shock may come first, leading only later to definite attempt to find out what is the matter. Whether the two steps are distinct or blended, there is the factor emphasized in our original account of reflection—*viz*. the perplexity or problem.

(*a*) *In the lack of adaptation of means to end.* In the first of the three cases cited, the difficulty resides in the conflict beween conditions at hand and a desired and intended result, between an end and the means for reaching it. The purpose of keeping an engagement at a certain time, and the existing hour taken in connection with the location, are not congruous. The object of thinking is to introduce congruity between the two. The given conditions cannot themselves be altered; time will not go backward nor will the distance between 16th Street and 124th Street shorten itself. The problem is *the discovery of intervening terms which when inserted between the remoter end and the given means will harmonize them with each other.*

(*b*) *In identifying the character of an object.* In the second case, the difficulty experienced is the incompatibility of a suggested and (temporarily) accepted belief that the pole is a flagpole, with certain other facts. Suppose we symbolize the qualities that suggest *flagpole* by the letters *a, b, c;* those that oppose this suggestion by the letters *p, q, r.* There is, of course, nothing inconsistent in the qualities themselves; but in pulling the mind to different and incongruous conclusions they conflict—hence the problem. Here the object is the discovery of some object (*O*), of which *a, b, c,* and *p, q, r,* may all be appropriate traits—just as, in our first case, it is to discover a course of action which will combine existing conditions and a remoter result in a single whole. The method of solution is also the same: discovery of intermediate qualities (the position of the pilot house, of the pole, the need of an index to the boat's direction) symbolized by *d, g, l, o,* which bind together otherwise incompatible traits.

(*c*) *In explaining an unexpected event.* In the third case, an observer trained to the idea of natural laws or uniformities finds something odd or exceptional in the behavior of the bubbles. The problem is to reduce the apparent anomalies to instances of well-established laws. Here the method of solution is also to seek for intermediary terms which will connect, by regular linkage, the seemingly extraordinary movements of the bubbles with the conditions known to follow from processes supposed to be operative.

2. Definition of the Difficulty. As already noted, the first two steps, the feeling of a discrepancy, or difficulty, and the acts of observation that serve to define the character of the difficulty may, in a given instance, telescope together. In cases of striking novelty or unusual perplexity, the difficulty, however, is likely to present itself at first as a shock, as emotional disturbance, as a more or less vague feeling of the unexpected, of something queer, strange, funny, or disconcerting. In such instances, there are necessary observations deliberately calculated to bring to light just what is the trouble, or to make clear the specific character of the problem. In large measure, the existence or non-existence of this step makes the difference between reflection proper, or safeguarded *critical* inference and uncontrolled thinking. Where sufficient pains to locate the difficulty are not taken, suggestions for its resolution must be more or less random. Imagine a doctor called in to prescribe for a patient. The patient tells him some things that are wrong; his experienced eye, at a glance, takes in other signs of a certain disease. But if he permits the suggestion of this special disease to take possession prematurely of his mind, to become an accepted conclusion, his scientific thinking is by that much cut short. A large part of his technique, as a skilled practitioner, is to prevent the acceptance of the first suggestions that arise; even, indeed, to postpone the occurrence of any very definite suggestion till the trouble—the nature of the problem—has been thoroughly explored. In the case of a physician this proceeding is known as diagnosis, but a similar inspection is required in every novel and complicated situation to prevent

rushing to a conclusion. The essence of critical thinking is suspended judgment; and the essence of this suspense is inquiry to determine the nature of the problem before proceeding to attempts at its solution. This, more than any other thing, transforms mere inference into tested inference, suggested conclusions into proof.

3. Occurrence of a Suggested Explanation or Possible Solution. The third factor is suggestion. The situation in which the perplexity occurs calls up something not present to the senses: the present location, the thought of subway or elevated train; the stick before the eyes, the idea of a flagpole, an ornament, an apparatus for wireless telegraphy; the soap bubbles, the law of expansion of bodies through heat and of their contraction through cold. (a) Suggestion is the very heart of inference; it involves going from what is present to something absent. Hence, it is more or less speculative, adventurous. Since inference goes beyond what is actually present, it involves a leap, a jump, the propriety of which cannot be absolutely warranted in advance, no matter what precautions be taken. Its control is indirect, on the one hand, involving the formation of habits of mind which are at once enterprising and cautious; and on the other hand, involving the selection and arrangement of the particular facts upon perception of which suggestion issues. (b) The suggested conclusion so far as it is not accepted but only tentatively entertained constitutes an idea. Synonyms for this are *supposition, conjecture, guess, hypothesis,* and (in elaborate cases) *theory.* Since suspended belief, or the postponement of a final conclusion pending further evidence, depends partly upon the presence of rival conjectures as to the best course to pursue or the probable explanation to favor, *cultivation of a variety of alternative suggestions* is an important factor in good thinking.

4. The Rational Elaboration of an Idea. The process of developing the bearings—or, as they are more technically termed, the *implications*—of any idea with respect to any problem, is termed *reasoning.*[1] As an idea is inferred from given facts, so reasoning sets out from an idea. The *idea* of elevated road is developed into the idea of difficulty of locating station, length of time occupied on

[1] This term is sometimes extended to denote the entire reflective process—just as *inference* (which in the sense of *test* is best reserved for the third step) is sometimes used in the same broad sense. But *reasoning* (or *ratiocination*) seems to be peculiarly adapted to express what the older writers called the "notional" or "dialectic" process of developing the meaning of a given idea.

the journey, distance of station at the other end from place to be reached. In the second case, the implication of a flagpole is seen to be a vertical position; of a wireless apparatus, location on a high part of the ship and, moreover, absence from every casual tugboat; while the idea of index to direction in which the boat moves, when developed, is found to cover all the details of the case.

Reasoning has the same effect upon a suggested solution as more intimate and extensive observation has upon the original problem. Acceptance of the suggestion in its first form is prevented by looking into it more thoroughly. Conjectures that seem plausible at first sight are often found unfit or even absurd when their full consequences are traced out. Even when reasoning out the bearings of a supposition does not lead to rejection, it develops the idea into a form in which it is more apposite to the problem. Only when, for example, the conjecture that a pole was an index-pole had been thought out into its bearings could its particular applicability to the case in hand be judged. Suggestions at first seemingly remote and wild are frequently so transformed by being elaborated into what follows from them as to become apt and fruitful. The development of an idea through reasoning helps at least to supply the intervening or intermediate terms that link together into a consistent whole apparently discrepant extremes.

5. CORROBORATION OF AN IDEA AND FORMATION OF A CONCLUDING BELIEF. The concluding and conclusive step is some kind of *experimental corroboration,* or verification, of the conjectural idea. Reasoning shows that *if* the idea be adopted, certain consequences follow. So far the conclusion is hypothetical or conditional. If we look and find present all the conditions demanded by the theory, and if we find the characteristic traits called for by rival alternatives to be lacking, the tendency to believe, to accept, is almost irresistible. Sometimes direct observation furnishes corroboration, as in the case of the pole on the boat. In other cases, as in that of the bubbles, experiment is required; that is, *conditions are deliberately arranged in accord with the requirements of an idea or hypothesis to see if the results theoretically indicated by the idea actually occur.* If it is found that the experimental results agree with the theoretical, or rationally deduced, results, and if there is reason to believe that *only* the conditions in question would yield such results, the confirmation is so strong as to induce a conclusion—at least until contrary facts shall indicate the advisability of its revision.

Thinking Comes Between Observations at the Beginning and at the End

Observation exists at the beginning and again at the end of the process: at the beginning, to determine more definitely and precisely the nature of the difficulty to be dealt with; at the end, to test the value of some hypothetically entertained conclusion. Between those two termini of observation, we find the more distinctively *mental* aspects of the entire thought-cycle: (*i*) inference, the suggestion of an explanation or solution; and (*ii*) reasoning, the development of the bearings and implications of the suggestion. Reasoning requires some experimental observation to confirm it, while experiment can be economically and fruitfully conducted only on the basis of an idea that has been tentatively developed by reasoning.

The Trained Mind Is One that Judges the Extent of Each Step Advisable in a Given Situation

The disciplined, or logically trained, mind—the aim of the educative process—is the mind able to judge how far each of these steps needs to be carried in any particular situation. No cast-iron rules can be laid down. Each case has to be dealt with as it arises, on on the basis of its importance and of the context in which it occurs. To take too much pains in one case is as foolish—as illogical—as to take too little in another. At one extreme, almost any conclusion that insures prompt and unified action may be better than any long delayed conclusion; while at the other, decision may have to be postponed for a long period—perhaps for a lifetime. The trained mind is the one that best grasps the degree of observation, forming of ideas, reasoning, and experimental testing required in any special case, and that profits the most, in future thinking, by mistakes made in the past. What is important is that the mind should be sensitive to problems and skilled in methods of attack and solution.

[10]
Thought and Choice in Chess

ADRIAAN D. de GROOT

In Chapter IV we came to find the alteration of elaborative and integrative phases as the basic structure of the thought process. In the light of the organization and methodology of the thought process this means that *the subject (player) periodically returns to more general problems, especially to the main problem.* The structure of all thought processes in which a difficult problem must be dealt with is characterized by this alternation. . . .

For chess thinking as well as thinking in general, the creative pauses and the principle of creative form-giving should be considered as mutually related.

In chess thinking we have found "pauses in the thought process," too. . . . They occurred typically in the *transitional phases.* These we have already come to know as phases in which the subject returns from the special subproblems of the prior elaborations to problems of higher order, in the most pronounced cases to the main problem. In the transitional phases the results already achieved are integrated, and it is here primarily that what we have called "problem tranformations" befall. After the first phase of problem formation it is by means of these *trans*formations that the problem develops—as discussed above. Therefore the interplay within the principle of creative form-giving . . . *corresponds with the alternation of phases* of active elaboration, on the one hand, and integration, "looking around," apparent pauses, on the other. During an elaborative phase the problem in its present state of development determines the course of the thought process via the schematic anticipation contained in the goal-awareness; conversely, in the

---

SOURCE: Adriaan D. de Groot, *Thought and Choice in Chess* (The Hague: Mouton & Co. n.v., 1965). Reprinted by permission of Mouton & Co. n.v. and Adriaan D. de Groot.

transitional phases the results of the elaborations cause a more or less drastic transformation of the problem.

The distinct pauses in a creative process or an ordinary thought process enjoy, in fact, to a very high degree, this character of a phase of integration, of returning to more general problems, of renewed receptivity in an enlarged field. It is often during these very pauses that the most important problem transformations appear: the subject takes a "fresh look" at the entire problem. The characteristic "looking around" in the situation—for the chessplayer: at the board; for the composer: in life—which is accompanied by a negative abstraction of all details of the situation in favor of the most general, but still influential, schematic anticipation, is a natural continuation and extension of the return to more general problems demanded by the preceding "integration of results." The distinct pauses must be viewed as special cases of the transitional phases which, of necessity, occur in complex thought processes.

[11]
Mathematical Creation

HENRI POINCARÉ

The genesis of mathematical creation is a problem which should intensely interest the psychologist. It is the activity in which the human mind seems to take least from the outside world, in which it acts or seems to act only of itself and on itself, so that in studying the procedure of geometric thought we may hope to reach what is most essential in man's mind.

This has long been appreciated, and some time back the journal called *L'Enseignement Mathématique*, edited by Laisant and Fehr, began an investigation of the mental habits and methods of work of different mathematicians. I had finished the main outlines of this article when the results of that inquiry were published, so I have

---

SOURCE: Henri Poincaré, *The Foundations of Science*, authorized translation by George Bruce Halsted (Lancaster, Pa.: The Science Press, 1913), pp. 383–394.

hardly been able to utilize them and shall confine myself to saying that the majority of witnesses confirm my conclusions; I do not say all, for when the appeal is to universal suffrage unanimity is not to be hoped.

A first fact should surprise us, or rather would surprise us if we were not so used to it. How does it happen there are people who do not understand mathematics? If mathematics invokes only the rules of logic, such as are accepted by all normal minds; if its evidence is based on principles common to all men, and that none could deny without being mad, how does it come about that so many persons are here refractory?

That not every one can invent is nowise mysterious. That not every one can retain a demonstration once learned may also pass. But that not every one can understand mathematical reasoning when explained appears very surprising when we think of it. And yet those who can follow this reasoning only with difficulty are in the majority: that is undeniable, and will surely not be gainsaid by the experience of secondary-school teachers.

And further: how is error possible in mathematics? A sane mind should not be guilty of a logical fallacy, and yet there are very fine minds who do not trip in brief reasoning such as occurs in the ordinary doings of life, and who are incapable of following or repeating without error the mathematical demonstrations which are longer, but which after all are only an accumulation of brief reasonings wholly analogous to those they make so easily. Need we add that mathematicians themselves are not infallible?

The answer seems to me evident. Imagine a long series of syllogisms, and that the conclusions of the first serve as premises of the following: we shall be able to catch each of these syllogisms, and it is not in passing from premises to conclusion that we are in danger of deceiving ourselves. But between the moment in which we first meet a proposition as conclusion of one syllogism, and that in which we reencounter it as premise of another syllogism occasionally some time will elapse, several links of the chain will have unrolled; so it may happen that we have forgotten it, or worse, that we have forgotten its meaning. So it may happen that we replace it by a slightly different proposition, or that, while retaining the same enunciation, we attribute to it a slightly different meaning, and thus it is that we are exposed to error.

Often the mathematician uses a rule. Naturally he begins by

demonstrating this rule; and at the time when this proof is fresh in his memory he understands perfectly its meaning and its bearing, and he is in no danger of changing it. But subsequently he trusts his memory and afterward only applies it in a mechanical way; and then if his memory fails him, he may apply it all wrong. Thus it is, to take a simple example, that we sometimes make slips in calculation because we have forgotten our multiplication table.

According to this, the special aptitude for mathematics would be due only to a very sure memory or to a prodigious force of attention. It would be a power like that of the whist-player who remembers the cards played; or, to go up a step, like that of the chess-player who can visualize a great number of combinations and hold them in his memory. Every good mathematician ought to be a good chess-player, and inversely; likewise he should be a good computer. Of course that sometimes happens; thus Gauss was at the same time a geometer of genius and a very precocious and accurate computer.

But there are exceptions; or rather I err; I can not call them exceptions without the exceptions being more than the rule. Gauss it is, on the contrary, who was an exception. As for myself, I must confess, I am absolutely incapable even of adding without mistakes. In the same way I should be but a poor chess-player; I would perceive that by a certain play I should expose myself to a certain danger; I would pass in review several other plays, rejecting them for other reasons, and then finally I should make the move first examined, having meantime forgotten the danger I had foreseen.

In a word, my memory is not bad, but it would be insufficient to make me a good chess-player. Why then does it not fail me in a difficult piece of mathematical reasoning where most chess-players would lose themselves? Evidently because it is guided by the general march of the reasoning. A mathematical demonstration is not a simple juxtaposition of syllogisms, it is syllogisms *placed in a certain order,* and the order in which these elements are placed is much more important than the elements themselves. If I have the feeling, the intuition, so to speak, of this order, so as to perceive at a glance the reasoning as a whole, I need no longer fear lest I forget one of the elements, for each of them will take its allotted place in the array, and that without any effort of memory on my part.

It seems to me then, in repeating a reasoning learned, that I could have invented it. This is often only an illusion; but even then, even if I am not so gifted as to create it by myself, I myself re-invent it in so far as I repeat it.

We know that this feeling, this intuition of mathematical order, that makes us divine hidden harmonies and relations, can not be possessed by every one. Some will not have either this delicate feeling so difficult to define, or a strength of memory and attention beyond the ordinary, and then they will be absolutely incapable of understanding higher mathematics. Such are the majority. Others will have this feeling only in a slight degree, but they will be gifted with an uncommon memory and a great power of attention. They will learn by heart the details one after another; they can understand mathematics and sometimes make applications, but they cannot create. Others, finally, will possess in a less or greater degree the special intuition referred to, and then not only can they understand mathematics even if their memory is nothing extraordinary, but they may become creators and try to invent with more or less success according as this intuition is more or less developed in them.

In fact, what is mathematical creation? It does not consist in making new combinations with mathematical entities already known. Any one could do that, but the combinations so made would be infinite in number and most of them absolutely without interest. To create consists precisely in not making useless combinations and in making those which are useful and which are only a small minority. Invention is discernment, choice.

How to make this choice I have before explained; the mathematical facts worthy of being studied are those which, by their analogy with other facts, are capable of leading us to the knowledge of a mathematical law just as experimental facts lead us to the knowledge of a physical law. They are those which reveal to us unsuspected kinship between other facts, long known, but wrongly believed to be strangers to one another.

Among chosen combinations the most fertile will often be those formed of elements drawn from domains which are far apart. Not that I mean as sufficing for invention the bringing together of objects as disparate as possible; most combinations so formed would be entirely sterile. But certain among them, very rare, are the most fruitful of all.

To invent, I have said, is to choose; but the word is perhaps not wholly exact. It makes one think of a purchaser before whom are displayed a large number of samples, and who examines them, one after the other, to make a choice. Here the samples would be so numerous that a whole lifetime would not suffice to examine them. This is not the actual state of things. The sterile combinations do not even present themselves to the mind of the inventor. Never in the field of his consciousness do combinations appear that are not really useful, except some that he rejects but which have to some extent the characteristics of useful combinations. All goes on as if the inventor were an examiner for the second degree who would only have to question the candidates who had passed a previous examination.

But what I have hitherto said is what may be observed or inferred in reading the writings of the geometers, reading reflectively.

It is time to penetrate deeper and to see what goes on in the very soul of the mathematician. For this, I believe, I can do best by recalling memories of my own. But I shall limit myself to telling how I wrote my first memoir on Fuchsian functions. I beg the reader's pardon; I am about to use some technical expressions, but they need not frighten him, for he is not obliged to understand them. I shall say, for example, that I have found the demonstration of such a theorem under such circumstances. This theorem will have a barbarous name, unfamiliar to many, but that is unimportant; what is of interest for the psychologist is not the theorem but the circumstances.

For fifteen days I strove to prove that there could not be any functions like those I have since called Fuchsian functions. I was then very ignorant; every day I seated myself at my work table, stayed an hour or two, tried a great number of combinations and reached no results. One evening, contrary to my custom, I drank black coffee and could not sleep. Ideas rose in crowds; I felt them collide until pairs interlocked, so to speak, making a stable combination. By the next morning I had established the existence of a class of Fuchsian functions, those which come from the hypergeometric series; I had only to write out the results, which took but a few hours.

Then I wanted to represent these functions by the quotient of two series; this idea was perfectly conscious and deliberate, the analogy with elliptic functions guided me. I asked myself what properties these series must have if they existed, and I succeeded without difficulty in forming the series I have called theta-Fuchsian.

Just at this time I left Caen, where I was then living, to go on a geologic excursion under the auspices of the school of mines. The changes of travel made me forget my mathematical work. Having reached Coutances, we entered an omnibus to go some place or other. At the moment when I put my foot on the step the idea came to me, without anything in my former thoughts seeming to have paved the way for it, that the transformations I had used to define the Fuchsian functions were identical with those of non-Euclidean geometry. I did not verify the idea; I should not have had time, as, upon taking my seat in the omnibus, I went on with a conversation already commenced, but I felt a perfect certainty. On my return to Caen, for conscience's sake I verified the result at my leisure.

Then I turned my attention to the study of some arithmetical questions apparently without much success and without a suspicion of any connection with my preceding researches. Disgusted with my failure, I went to spend a few days at the seaside, and thought of something else. One morning, walking on the bluff, the idea came to me, with just the same characteristics of brevity, suddenness and immediate certainty, that the arithmetic transformations of indeterminate ternary quadratic forms were identical with those of non-Euclidean geometry.

Returned to Caen, I meditated on this result and deduced the consequences. The example of quadratic forms showed me that there were Fuchsian groups other than those corresponding to the hypergeometric series; I saw that I could apply to them the theory of theta-Fuchsian series and that consequently there existed Fuchsian functions other than those from the hypergeometric series, the ones I then knew. Naturally I set myself to form all these functions. I made a systematic attack upon them and carried all the outworks, one after another. There was one however that still held out, whose fall would involve that of the whole place. But all my efforts only served at first the better to show me the difficulty, which indeed was something. All this work was perfectly conscious.

Thereupon I left for Mont-Valérien, where I was to go through my military service; so I was very differently occupied. One day, going along the street, the solution of the difficulty which had stopped me suddenly appeared to me. I did not try to go deep into it immediately, and only after my service did I again take up the question. I had all the elements and had only to arrange them and put them together. So I wrote out my final memoir at a single stroke and without difficulty.

I shall limit myself to this single example; it is useless to multiply them. In regard to my other researches I would have to say analogous things, and the observations of other mathematicians given in *L'Enseignement Mathématique* would only confirm them.

Most striking at first is this appearance of sudden illumination, a manifest sign of long, unconscious prior work. The role of this unconscious work in mathematical invention appears to me incontestable, and traces of it would be found in other cases where it is less evident. Often when one works at a hard question, nothing good is accomplished at the first attack. Then one takes a rest, longer or shorter, and sits down anew to the work. During the first half-hour, as before, nothing is found, and then all of a sudden the decisive idea presents itself to the mind. It might be said that the conscious work has been more fruitfult because it has been interrupted and the rest has given back to the mind its force and freshness. But it is more probable that this rest has been filled out with unconscious work and that the result of this work has afterward revealed iteslf to the geometer just as in the cases I have cited; only the revelation, instead of coming during a walk or a journey, has happened during a period of conscious work, but independently of this work which plays at most a role of excitant, as if it were the goad stimulating the results already reached during rest, but remaining unconscious, to assume the conscious form.

There is another remark to be made about the conditions of this unconscious work: it is possible, and of a certainty it is only fruitful, if it is on the one hand preceded and on the other hand followed by a period of conscious work. These sudden inspirations (and the examples already cited sufficiently prove this) never happen except after some days of voluntary effort which has appeared absolutely fruitless and whence nothing good seems to have come, where the way taken seems totally astray. These efforts then have not been as sterile as one thinks; they have set agoing the unconscious machine and without them it would not have moved and would have produced nothing.

The need for the second period of conscious work, after the inspiration, is still easier to understand. It is necessary to put in shape the results of this inspiration, to deduce from them the immediate consequences, to arrange them, to word the demonstrations, but above all is verification necessary. I have spoken of the feeling of absolute certitude accompanying the inspiration; in the cases cited this feeling was no deceiver, nor is it usually. But do not think this is a rule without exception; often this feeling deceives us without being any the less vivid, and we only find it out when we seek to put on foot the demonstration. I have especially noticed this fact in regard to ideas coming to me in the morning or evening in bed while in a semi-hypnagogic state.

Such are the realities; now for the thoughts they force upon us. The unconscious, or, as we say, the subliminal self plays an important role in mathematical creation; this follows from what we have said. But usually the subliminal self is considered as purely automatic. Now we have seen that mathematical work is not simply mechanical, that it could not be done by a machine, however perfect. It is not merely a question of applying rules, of making the most combinations possible according to certain fixed laws. The combinations so obtained would be exceedingly numerous, useless and cumbersome. The true work of the inventor consists in choosing among these combinations so as to eliminate the useless ones or rather to avoid the trouble of making them, and the rules which must guide this choice are extremely fine and delicate. It is almost impossible to state them precisely; they are felt rather than formulated. Under these conditions, how imagine a sieve capable of applying them mechanically?

A first hypothesis now presents itself: the subliminal self is in no way inferior to the conscious self; it is not purely automatic; it is capable of discernment; it has tact, delicacy; it knows how to choose, to divine. What do I say? It knows better how to divine than the conscious self, since it succeeds where that has failed. In a word, is not the subliminal self superior to the conscious self? You recognize the full importance of this question. Boutroux in a recent lecture has shown how it came up on a very different occasion, and what consequences would follow an affirmative answer.

Is this affirmative answer forced upon us by the facts I have just given? I confess that, for my part, I should hate to accept it. Reëxamine the facts then and see if they are not compatible with another explanation.

It is certain that the combinations which present themselves to the mind in a sort of sudden illumination, after an unconscious working somewhat prolonged, are generally useful and fertile combinations, which seem the result of a first impression. Does it follow that the subliminal self, having divined by a delicate intuition that these combinations would be useful, has formed only these, or has it rather formed many others which were lacking in interest and have remained unconscious?

In this second way of looking at it, all the combinations would be formed in consequence of the automatism of the subliminal self, but only the interesting ones would break into the domain of consciousness. And this is still very mysterious. What is the cause that, among the thousand products of our unconscious activity, some are called to pass the threshold, while others remain below? Is it a simple chance which confers this privilege? Evidently not; among all the stimuli of our senses, for example, only the most intense fix our attention, unless it has been drawn to them by other causes. More generally the privileged unconscious phenomena, those susceptible of becoming conscious, are those which, directly or indirectly, affect most profoundly our emotional sensibility.

It may be surprising to see emotional sensibility invoked *à propos* of mathematical demonstrations which, it would seem, can interest only the intellect. This would be to forget the feeling of mathematical beauty, of the harmony of numbers and forms, of geometric elegance. This is a true esthetic feeling that all real mathematicians know, and surely it belongs to emotional sensibility.

Now, what are the mathematic entities to which we attribute this character of beauty and elegance, and which are capable of developing in us a sort of esthetic emotion? They are those whose elements are harmoniously disposed so that the mind without effort can embrace their totality while realizing the details. This harmony is at once a satisfaction of our esthetic needs and an aid to the mind, sustaining and guiding. And at the same time, in putting under our eyes a well-ordered whole, it makes us foresee a mathematical law. Now, as we have said above, the only mathematical facts worthy of fixing our attention and capable of being useful are those which can teach us a mathematical law. So that we reach the following conclusion: The useful combinations are precisely the most beautiful, I mean those best able to charm this special sensibility that all mathematicians know, but of which the profane are so ignorant as often to be tempted to smile at it.

What happens then? Among the great numbers of combinations blindly formed by the subliminal self, almost all are without interest and without utility; but just for that reason they are also without effect upon the esthetic sensibility. Consciousness will never know them; only certain ones are harmonious, and, consequently, at once useful and beautiful. They will be capable of touching this special sensibility of the geometer of which I have just spoken, and which, once aroused, will call our attention to them, and thus give them occasion to become conscious.

This is only a hypothesis, and yet here is an observation which may confirm it: when a sudden illumination seizes upon the mind of the mathematician, it usually happens that it does not deceive him, but it also sometimes happens, as I have said, that it does not stand the test of verification; well, we almost always notice that this false idea, had it been true, would have gratified our natural feeling for mathematical elegance.

Thus it is this special esthetic sensibility which plays the role of the delicate sieve of which I spoke, and that sufficiently explains why the one lacking it will never be a real creator.

Yet all the difficulties have not disappeared. The conscious self is narrowly limited, and as for the subliminal self we know not its limitations, and this is why we are not too reluctant in supposing that it has been able in a short time to make more different combinations than the whole life of a conscious being could encompass. Yet these limitations exist. Is it likely that it is able to form all the possible combinations, whose number would frighten the imagination? Nevertheless that would seem necessary, because if it produces only a small part of these combinations, and if it makes them at random, there would be small chance that the *good*, the one we should choose, would be found among them.

Perhaps we ought to seek the explanation in that preliminary period of conscious work which always precedes all fruitful unconscious labor. Permit me a rough comparison. Figure the future elements of our combinations as something like the hooked atoms of Epicurus. During the complete repose of the mind, these atoms are motionless, they are, so to speak, hooked to the wall; so this complete rest may be indefinitely prolonged without the atoms meeting, and consequently without any combination between them.

On the other hand, during a period of apparent rest and unconscious work, certain of them are detached from the wall and put in motion. They flash in every direction through the space (I was about to say the room) where they are enclosed, as would, for example, a swarm of gnats or, if you prefer a more learned comparison, like the molecules of gas in the kinematic theory of gases. Then their mutual impacts may produce new combinations.

What is the role of the preliminary conscious work? It is evidently to mobilize certain of these atoms, to unhook them from the wall and put them in swing. We think we have done no good, because we have moved these elements a thousand different ways in seeking to assemble them, and have found no satisfactory aggregate. But, after this shaking up imposed upon them by our will, these atoms do not return to their primitive rest. They freely continue their dance.

Now, our will did not choose them at random; it pursued a perfectly determined aim. The mobilized atoms are therefore not any atoms whatsoever; they are those from which we might reasonably expect the desired solution. Then the mobilized atoms undergo impacts which make them enter into combinations among themselves or with other atoms at rest which they struck against in their course. Again I beg pardon, my comparison is very rough, but I scarcely know how otherwise to make my thought understood.

However it may be, the only combinations that have a chance of forming are those where at least one of the elements is one of those atoms freely chosen by our will. Now, it is evidently among these that is found what I called the *good combination.* Perhaps this is a way of lessening the paradoxical in the original hypothesis.

Another observation. It never happens that the unconscious work gives us the result of a somewhat long calculation *all made,* where we have only to apply fixed rules. We might think the wholly automatic subliminal self particularly apt for this sort of work, which is in a way exclusively mechanical. It seems that thinking in the evening upon the factors of a multiplication we might hope to find the product ready made upon our awakening, or again that an algebraic calculation, for example a verification, would be made unconsciously. Nothing of the sort, as observation proves. All one may hope from these inspirations, fruits of unconscious work, is a point of departure for such calculations. As for the calculations themselves, they must be made in the second period of conscious work, that which follows the inspiration, that in which one verifies the results of this inspiration and deduces their consequences. The rules of these calculations are strict and complicated. They require discipline, attention, will, and therefore consciousness. In the subliminal self, on the contrary, reigns what I should call liberty, if we might give this name to the simple absence of discipline and to the disorder born of chance. Only, this disorder itself permits unexpected combinations.

I shall make a last remark: when above I made certain personal observations, I spoke of a night of excitement when I worked in spite of myself. Such cases are frequent, and it is not necessary that the abnormal cerebral activity be caused by a physical excitant as in that I mentioned. It seems, in such cases, that one is present at his own unconscious work, made partially perceptible to the over-excited consciousness, yet without having changed its nature. Then we vaguely comprehend what distinguishes the two mechanisms or, if you wish, the working methods of the two egos. And the psychologic observations I have been able thus to make seem to me to confirm in their general outlines the views I have given.

Surely they have need of it, for they are and remain in spite of all very hypothetical: the interest of the questions is so great that I do not repent of having submitted them to the reader.

[12]
Experimental Psychology: Incubation

ROBERT S. WOODWORTH and
HAROLD SCHLOSBERG

"Incubation"—Laying Aside a Problem as a Step Toward Solution

The word *incubation* may serve as a useful catchword though it implies a theory which we do not accept, preferring as we do a theory suggested by the immediately preceding quotation from Ruger. Laying aside a problem is a means of getting rid of a false set or "direction" and so giving the true direction a chance to emerge.

Helmholtz, a brilliant inventor and discoverer in several scientific fields, including psychology as well as physiology and physics, took

---

SOURCE: Robert S. Woodworth and Harold Schlosberg, *Experimental Psychology,* Revised Edition, copyright 1938, 1954 by Holt, Rinehart and Winston, Inc. Used by permission.

occasion at a dinner in honor of his seventieth birthday to report something of his methods of work on original problems (1896).

> I must say that those fields of work have become ever more agreeable to me in which one need not depend on lucky accidents and "happy thoughts." But as I have found myself pretty often in the uncomfortable position of having to wait for happy thoughts, the experience I have gained on the question, when and where they came to me, may perhaps be useful to others. . . . So far as my experience goes, they never came to a fatigued brain and never at the writing desk. It was always necessary, first of all, that I should have turned my problem over on all sides to such an extent that I had all its angles and complexities "in my head" and could run through them freely without writing. To bring the matter to that point is usually impossible without long preliminary labor. Then, after the fatigue resulting from this labor had passed away, there must come an hour of complete physical freshness and quiet well-being, before the good ideas arrived. Often they were there in the morning when I awoke, just according to Goethe's oft-cited verses, and as Gauss also once noted. But they liked specially to make their appearance while I was taking an easy walk over wooded hills in sunny weather. The smallest amount of alcohol seemed to frighten them away.

So far as Helmholtz offers a theory, it is based on fatigue and the recovery from fatigue. The intensive preparatory work is an essential part of the story. An earlier psychologist (Carpenter, 1876) offered the theory of "unconscious cerebration" occurring during the interval of rest. He had gathered many instances from inventors, artists, and poets of their laying a problem aside and finding that after sleep or recreation just what they wanted "came into their heads," and he agreed with Oliver Wendell Holmes and other thinkers that the brain must have been working on the problem while conscious attention was otherwise occupied.

The theory of unconscious work was revived by the great mathematician Poincaré (1913) who had noticed in his own case that it was often safe to lay a problem aside and wait for the solution to emerge later. Fruitful unconscious work, however must be "first preceded and then followed by a period of conscious work. These sudden inspirations are never produced . . . except after some days of voluntary efforts which appeared absolutely fruitless. . . . The second period of conscious work . . . is necessary to work out the results of the inspiration . . . to verify them."

* * *

Theories of Incubation

The obvious theory—unconscious work, whether conceived as mental or as cerebral—should be left as a residual hypothesis for adoption only if other, more testable hypotheses break down (Skinner, 1953). Several other hypotheses have been suggested in what precedes.

Since the problem does *consciously recur* from time to time during the period of incubation, though without effortful work done upon it, partial solutions may be obtained.

If the illumination comes in a period, short or long, of *intense concentration* on the problem, the assumption of previous unconscious work is gratuitous.

The *freshness* or lack of brain fatigue which seems to be necessary for illumination may furnish a sufficient explanation.

The parallel but simpler case of the recall of a name, after futile attempts followed by dropping the matter, suggests that an essential factor in illumination is the *absence of interferences* which block progress during the preliminary stage. When the thinker makes a false start, he slides insensibly into a groove and may not be able to escape at the moment. He falls into certain assumptions which restrict his sector of exploratory activity, and as long as he continues actively at work, he does not escape from these assumptions, as he often does on coming back to the problem after giving it a rest. Several of the inventors noted a fact which favors this interpretation: the happy idea, when it came, amazed them by its simplicity. They had assumed a more complicated solution to be necessary. According to this line of evidence, the incubation period simply allows time for an erroneous set to die out and leave the thinker free to take a fresh look at his problem.

[13]
Mechanization in Problem Solving: The Effect of Einstellung

ABRAHAM S. LUCHINS

THE PROBLEMS

Several problems, all solvable by one somewhat complex procedure, are presented in succession. If afterwards a similar task is given which can be solved by a more direct and simple method, will the individual be blinded to this direct possibility?

If a blinding effect does result, will it be of characteristically different strength in groups that differ in educational level, age, etc.? Moreover, if we introduce means to save the subjects or to rescue them from such blindness, will these means readily work? Will they operate differently in various groups?

And what may be the real cause for the blinding effect? How are we to understand this phenomenon?

THE MAIN EXPERIMENTS

A. Introduction

The problem with which the present experiment is concerned was first investigated in the Berlin Institute of Psychology by Zener and Duncker. These experiments, which were preliminary in character, have not been published, the only published reference to them being the following passage in an article by N. R. F. Maier:

Zener, in some preliminary experiments at the Psychological Institute of the University of Berlin, in 1927, habituated his subjects to solve certain

---

SOURCE: Abraham S. Luchins. "Mechanization in Problem Solving: The Effect of *Einstellung*," *Psychological Monographs,* 1942, **54**, Whole Number 248. Reprinted by permission of the American Psychological Association and Abraham S. Luchins.

types of problems in the same way. A test problem was then given. He found that an obvious and simple solution of the test problem was usually overlooked because the characteristic method of solution, set up in the preceding problems, was used in the test problem. Control groups tended to solve the problem in the obvious and simple manner.[1]

It seemed important to conduct further experiments of this kind because the quoted findings of these preliminary experiments appeared to show clearly an interesting result: The successive, repetitious use of the same method mechanized many of the subjects —blinded them to the possibility of a more direct and simple procedure. We wished also to extend the scope of the method and to use various groups of subjects, children as well as adults. Furthermore, we wished to ascertain whether, if a tendency to repeat the habitually used method did develop, a change in response would be brought about if some factors to work against the habituation were employed.

Under the sponsorship of Professor Max Wertheimer,[2] the writer, in 1936, experimented with various sets of problems and finally

Problem		*Given the Following Empty Jars as Measures*			*Obtain the Required Amount of Water*
1		29	3		20
2	E_1*	21	127	3	100
3	E_2	14	163	25	99
4	E_3	18	43	10	5
5	E_4	9	42	6	21
6	E_5	20	59	4	31
7	C_1	23	49	3	20
8	C_2	15	39	3	18
9		28	76	3	25
10	C_3	18	48	4	22
11	C_4	14	36	8	6

* An explanation of these letters will be furnished later.

[1] N. R. F. Maier, *Reasoning in Humans,* Journal of Comparative Psychology, **2,** No. 1 (1936), 127.

[2] Professor Max Wertheimer furnished us with more specific information about the Berlin experiments mentioned in Maier's article.

selected the following, which are similar to those utilized by Zener and Duncker in Berlin; however, for theoretical and practical purposes, problems 9, 10, and 11 and a special "instructed group" were added. The problems selected may be shown in tabular form.

B. Our Basic Exploratory Experiment [3]

The problems were tried out in an exploratory experiment conducted, in 1936, in one of Professor Max Wertheimer's seminars at the Graduate Faculty of the New School for Social Research. Graduate students, college instructors, and research workers composed this select group of 15 people, of whom many possessed the Ph.D. or M.D. degree.

The experimenter told the class that its task was to figure out on paper how to obtain a required volume of water, given certain empty jars for measures. To illustrate this principle we presented Problem One. The subjects were asked for the solution, and the method of solving the problem was then written on the blackboard. After this, Problem Two was put on the blackboard, 21, 127, 3, get 100! After 2½ minutes the subjects were asked for their solutions. The answer was then illustrated in both a written and verbal form; verbally, "One fills the 127-quart jar and from it fills the 21-quart jar once and the 3-quart jar twice. In the 127-quart jar there then remain the 100 quarts of water."

Without any further interruptions the other problems, in succession, were presented one at a time on the blackboard, at intervals of 2½ minutes—or oftener, if the students had required less time for the problem.

The method which solves Problem Two also solves Problems Three through Six; the solution which is applicable to these five problems may be described as: "Fill the middle jar, and from it fill the jar to the right twice and the jar to the left once, leaving the required amount of water in the center jar." Or we may state the method as $B - A - 2C$, if we designate the jars, in the order written, as *A*, *B*, and *C*, respectively.

This $B - A - 2C$ method may also be used in Problems Seven and Eight. But Problem Seven may be solved more simply by subtracting 3 from 23 ($A - C$), and Problem Eight by adding 3 to 15

[3] Unless otherwise stated in the text, it should be understood that all experiments reported herein were conducted by the writer himself.

$(A+C)$. Of eleven New School subjects (we shall speak first of those eleven who received only the instructions given above) all employed the circuitous method—$B-A-2C$. Not one subject used the more direct method in Problems Seven and Eight. Having become habituated to the mode of solution $(B-A-2C)$, they used it in the succeeding similar problems. Later, when they were shown the more direct method after the whole experiment was completed, the subjects spontaneously said more or less passionately, "How dumb I was;" "How stupid of me;" "How blind I was;" or made other similar comments. A few of the subjects saw the light themselves—after the experiment.

Before any problems were presented, four other members had been taken outside of the classroom and had been told, in the absence of the eleven subjects whose results were reported above, "After returning to the classroom you will get a number of problems. After you will have completed Problem Six, write on your papers the words, '*Don't be blind!*' " In some cases this warning appeared to be effective: 5 of their 8 answers to Problems Seven and Eight showed the direct method of solution. Three of their answers, in spite of the warning, showed only the tedious $B-A-2C$ procedure.

Problems Ten and Eleven possessed the same ambiguity as Problems Seven and Eight. Before Problem Ten, we had introduced the ninth problem which could not be solved in the $B-A-2C$ manner but could easily be solved by $A-C$, taking 3 away from 28. Would it disrupt the tendency to repeat blindly the $B-A-2C$ method and bring about the more direct solution of Problems Ten and Eleven? A comparison of the per cent of solutions of Problems Ten and Eleven with the per cent of solutions of Problems Seven and Eight yielded an increase of 15 per cent direct solutions in the former for the 11 subjects who had not received the warning, "Don't be blind," and an increase of 12 per cent for the "Don't be blind" subjects. To this degree Problem Nine seemed effective.

[14]

On Functional Fixedness of Real Solution Objects [1]

KARL DUNCKER

1. Setting of the Problem. The Concept of Heterogeneous Functional Fixedness

In Chapter II, 6 and 7, it was pointed out that the different parts of the situation, whose (appropriate) variations represent solutions of the problem, or which enter into solutions as "material," may display very different degrees of "disposability" (looseness). For the psychology of thinking, there hardly exist more fundamental differences among the various relevant elements of a problem-situation than those which determine how easily or with what difficulty they may be recognized as conflict-elements or as solution material. These differences are independent of possible "knowledge" by which *post festum*—the elements concerned could be evaluated with respect to their conflict character or their suitability as material.

A few of the factors which determine disposability, specifically that of conflict elements, have already been worked out in Chapter II. Now we shall examine more closely the *disposability of solution material,* in the more specific form of "real solution objects sought."

Whether a sought "object" is found more easily or with more difficulty depends, among other things, on the degree of *"fixedness"* of the object. A chimpanzee who stands in need of a stick (something long, firm . . .) sometimes has difficulties in recognizing the stick in a branch still growing on the tree, in seeing it as a percept apart. On the tree it is a "branch," a part of the visual figural unit

[1] The minuteness of detail in the following treatment of a special problem is somewhat out of proportion to its theoretical importance in the framework of the present investigation.

SOURCE: Karl Duncker, "On Problem Solving," *Psychological Monographs,* 1945, 58, Whole Number 270, 85–95. Reprinted by permission of the American Psychological Association.

"tree," and this part-character—more generally, this "*fixedness*"—is clearly responsible for the fact that to a search for something like a stick, the branch on the tree is less "within reach" than the branch on the ground.

What we just named "fixedness" may, however, be conditioned *functionally* as well as by such factors of visual organization. For instance, a stick that has just been used as a ruler is less likely to appear as a tool for other purposes than it would normally be. In the following, the discussion will be chiefly of such functional fixedness ("bias"), more particularly, of *heterogeneous* functional fixedness, i.e., fixedness as the result of a function *dissimilar* to that demanded. The question is: *What determines whether, and to what degree, heterogeneous functional fixedness of an object hinders the finding of this object?*

On this question I undertook a series of experiments.[2] The principle was as follows: For a particular purpose, a certain function, a suitable object is needed. *This object has already been used in the same problem-context, but in another way, in another function.* Question: what effect has this pre-utilization? When does it hinder the selection of the object for the new function, the "*recentering*" of the object?

Be it expressly noted that what, in the present chapter, is stated for thing-objects (specifically tools) is valid, in principle, for thought-material in general.

2. Experimental Procedure, Method of Evaluation, and Problems

We experimented with all sorts of objects in daily use (for example, boxes, pliers, etc.), which were first claimed in their usual function (F_1) and then, within the same problem-situation, for a new, unusual function (F_2). The crucial object was each time to be selected as the suitable tool out of a great number of objects which lay in confusion on a table.

In our problems, the pre-utilization of the crucial object was chosen in such a way as not to give it a special prominence in the problem situation. In other words, in F_1 no new centering took place, but solely a freshening, an "actualization" of the usual cen-

[2] For the conscientious carrying out of these experiments, I am greatly indebted to Miss Rosenbusch, cand, phil.

tering of the object concerned. For F_2, on the contrary, the object concerned was "unprepared," although by no means inappropriate.

In order to observe the effect of fixedness on recentering, each problem was given in two settings, once without and once after pre-utilization of the crucial object. The setting without pre-utilization we shall briefly designate *w.p.*, that after pre-utilization, *a.p.* The most important experiments were carried out on five different problems. One-half of the Ss received the problems in the settings: 1) w.p.; 2) a.p.; 3) w.p.; 4) a.p.; 5) w.p.; the other half of the Ss, in the opposite settings. In this way, differences of results in the w.p. and the a.p. experiments were made independent of individual differences among the Ss and among the problems.

The following is a short description of the five problems and of the experimental technique.

The "gimlet problem": Three cords are to be hung side by side from a wooden ledge ("for experiments on space perception"). On the table lie, among many other objects, two short screw-hooks and the crucial object: a gimlet. *Solution:* for hanging the third cord, the gimlet is used. In the setting a.p., the holes for the screws had yet to be bored; in w.p., the holes were already there. Thus, F_1: "gimlet"; F_2: "thing from which to hang a cord."

The "box problem": On the door, at the height of the eyes, three small candles are to be put side by side ("for visual experiments"). On the table lie, among many other objects, a few tacks and the crucial objects: three little pasteboard boxes (about the size of an ordinary matchbox, differing somewhat in form and color and put in different places). *Solution:* with a tack apiece, the three boxes are fastened to the door, each to serve as platform for a candle. In the setting a.p., the three boxes were filled with experimental material: in one there were several thin little candles, tacks in another, and matches in the third. In w.p., the three boxes were empty. Thus F_1: "container"; F_2: "platform" (on which to set things).

The "pliers problem": A board (perhaps 8 inches broad) is to be made firm on two supports (as "flower stand or the like"). On the table lie, among other things, two iron joints (for fastening bars and the like on stands), a wooden bar perhaps 8 inches long (as the one "support") and the crucial object: the pliers. *Solution:* this pair of pliers is utilized as the second support of the board. In the setting a.p., the bar was nailed to the board and had to be freed with the help of the pliers; in w.p., it was only tied to the board. Thus F_1: "pliers"; F_2: "support."

The "weight problem": A pendulum, consisting of a cord and a weight, is to be hung from a nail ("for experiments on motion"). To this end, the nail must be driven into the wall. On the table lies, among other things, the crucial object: a weight. *Solution:* with this weight (as "hammer"), the nail is driven into the wall. In the setting a.p., the weight is given expressly as pendulum-weight (with the string already tied to it); in w.p., a joint serves as pendulum-weight. Thus F_1: "pendulum-weight"; F_2: "hammer."

The "paperclip problem": A piece of white cardboard with four black squares fastened to it is to be hung on an eyelet screwed into the low ceiling ("for visual experiments"). On the table lie paperclips, among other things. *Solution:* a paperclip is unbent, one end is fastened to the eyelet, and the other put through the cardboard. In the setting a.p., the four black squares must previously be attached to the cardboard with paperclips; in w.p., on the other hand, they must be glued to it. Thus F_1: "something for affixing"; F_2: (unbent) "hook."

The general *instruction* for all the problems ran as follows: "You will receive several little technical tasks. For solution, certain objects are needed which you will find among the objects here on the table. Everything which lies on the table is completely at your disposal. You may use what you like in any fashion you wish. Please think aloud during the experiment, so that I may hear as many of your ideas as possible, including those which you take less seriously."

With each problem there lay on the table—aside from the objects already mentioned—all kinds of material, partly less suitable and partly completely unsuitable for the solution, such as paperclips, pieces of paper, string, pencils, tinfoil, old parts of apparatus, ashtrays, joints, pieces of wood, etc. Each problem had its own inventory. (No object was put at the subject's disposal which might be better suited to the solution than the object then crucial.) The objects lay in apparent confusion, but in definite places. The crucial object never occupied a prominent place.

The experiments were *evaluated* in two ways: (1) The solved and the unsolved problems were counted. Of course, a problem counted as "correctly" solved only when it was solved by use of the crucial object, which, as stated, was always the best and simplest of the possible solutions. A problem was broken off as unsolved if for two to three minutes the S produced no more proposals, and if at the same time his attitude had become so negative that no more sensible ideas seemed forthcoming. (2) The proposals preceding the solution and different from it, the "pre-solutions," were counted (but only with those experiments in which the correct solution was finally found, as otherwise measurements 1 and 2 would not have been independent of each other). As "pre-solutions" counted not only those actually carried out, but also proposals merely formulated, also such as the S rejected as unsuitable. If, however, an object was only "grazed," that is, just touched or picked up quite briefly and silently laid aside again, the fact did not count as a pre-solution.

Of the two methods of evaluation just described, the first is naturally the more adequate and by far the more important, while the second is rather superficial and dependent on chance influences. We shall find, however, that both methods yield results which are essentially in agreement.

3. Principal Experiments and Principal Results

The principal result of the experiments is immediately evident from Table 1.

We see that the results of the a.p. experiments clearly deviate from those of the w.p. experiments in the expected direction. This holds in both measurements, which are independent of each other, and not only for the average of all five problems, but also within

TABLE 1

	Problems	*No. of Ss*	*No. of Problems Solved*	*No. of Problems Solved in %*	*Average No. of Pre-solutions Per Problem*
w.p.	Gimlet	10	10	100	0.3
	Box	7	7	100	1.3
	Pliers	15	15	100	1.9
	Weight	12	12	100	0.8
	Paperclip	7	6	85.7	0.8
Arith. Mean		—	—	97.1	1.0
a.p.	Gimlet	14*	10	71.4	1.6
	Box	7	3	42.9	2.3
	Pliers	9*	4	44.4	2.3
	Weight	12	9	75.0	0.8
	Paperclip	7	4	57.1	1.5
Arith. Mean		—	—	58.2	1.7

* The inequalities in the number of Ss in w.p. and a.p. are due to the fact that certain Ss transformed the problem-setting intended for them into the opposite setting. In the gimlet problem, for instance, three Ss assigned to the w.p. group actually had to be counted in the a.p. group: one attempted, using the gimlet, to stuff the cords into the holes which were already there; the other two bored holes with it because they did not quite trust the holes which were there. On the other hand, one *S* assigned to the a.p. group immediately picked up the gimlet as "thing with which to hang up. . . ." Thus he did not use it in F_1, and had therefore to be counted with the w.p. group.—In the pliers problem, three Ss did not utilize the pliers for freeing the bar which was nailed to the board, and therefore had to be counted in the w.p. group.

each single problem. Only in the weight problem are the two averages of pre-solutions equal.

Therefore we can say: *Under our experimental conditions, the object which is not fixed is almost twice as easily found as the object which is fixed.*

The quantitative results were supported and clarified through qualitative findings. When, at the close of an a.p. experiment, the S was asked: "Why have you not used this object" (the crucial one) or, "Why have you used it only so late?," the answer was frequently: "But that is a tool," or, "Such a use would not be suited to the material," or, "I thought it was there simply for . . . (F_1)."

The last observation might suggest the following objection: It is not the effect of a "bias" of the crucial object which is measured in the experiments but rather the effect of a bias of the subject. The S may be of the opinion that the experimenter has put the crucial object on the table especially as a tool for F_1, that it does not belong to the actual experimental material. (Such false "self-instructions" are not infrequent in the relatively artificial situations of the laboratory.) This objection, however, hardly holds water. In the first place, little significance should be ascribed to statements after the fact, such as "I thought. . . ." They often express only "rationalizations." Secondly, there were many among our Ss for whom it was as if "the scales had fallen from their eyes" when the crucial object was afterwards pointed out. They did not have the feeling of having been victims of a false interpretation of the experimental conditions. In the third place, certain [other] experiments . . . also refute this objection.

4. On Fixedness "Relevant to the Situation" and on "Contact"

With the box problem and one not mentioned till now, the cork problem, we undertook a few more specific experiments on the possible influence of certain differences in the way the crucial object was pre-utilized.

The cork problem consisted of the following: A triangle was to be drawn on a piece of cardboard which was in turn to be fastened to a wooden bar. The wooden bar was then to be fixed in a doorframe without the help of nails. But the bar was about 2 cm. shorter than the distance between the two sides of the frame. On the table lay, among other things, the crucial object: a cork. Solution: With the help of the cork, the bar is wedged between the sides of the frame. In the a.p. setting, the cork stuck as a stopper in an ink bottle, from which the ink for drawing the triangle was to be taken. In w.p., the cork lay free on the table, at some distance from the ink bottle. Thus, F_1: "stopper"; F_2: "thing for wedging something."

The cork problem is clearly related to the box problem even by external appearance. Here, as there, F_1 is given not by an action but "statically." Here, as there, the crucial object is fixed by F_1 not only functionally, but visually as well. The cork problem, incidentally, proved to be the most difficult of our six problems.

These two problems were also given in the following variation (a.p.′): The crucial object was burdened with a *function* F_1 *"peripheral to the situation,"* not with one *"relevant"* or *"central to the situation."* That is, in the box problem, the three boxes were filled not with material relevant to the problem (candles, matches, tacks), but with neutral material (buttons and the like). In the cork problem, analogously, the cork was not stuck in a full ink bottle necessary to the drawing, but in a superfluous empty one (the triangle was here to be drawn with pencil). The crucial objects, therefore, had a function F_1, it is true (therefore the designation a.p.′), but a relatively peripheral, irrelevant function F_1. We expected that in this situation the recentering would succeed more easily, in the belief that an irrelevant ("dead") function comes nearer to absence of function than does a "living" one. The experimental results (see Table 2), and above all certain qualitative remarks of the Ss, soon made us aware, however, that in this reasoning we had obviously overlooked an important factor.

TABLE 2

Problems		*No. of Ss*	*No. of Problems Solved*	*No. of Problems Solved in %*	*Average No. of Pre-solutions Per Problem Solved*
a.p.	Box	7	3	42.9	2.3
	Cork	7	1	14.3	2
a.p.′	Box	7	1	14.3	4
	Cork	7	0	0	—

Eleven of the 13 Ss who had not solved the cork problem in the a.p. and the a.p.′ settings subsequently received this same problem in the w.p. setting. Under these circumstances 8 of the 11 Ss, i.e.,

72.7% solved the problem. Of course, the fact has here been of some influence that the Ss were especially directed to the stopper by the difference: "formerly stopper in full ink bottle, now stopper near empty ink bottle" (although we tried to counteract this suggestive difference by other differences introduced *ad hoc*). The suggestive effect of such differences is considerable.

Table 2 shows—and similar experiments undertaken in a seminar furnished corroboration—that, far from facilitating the solution, the a.p.′ setting actually makes it more difficult in comparison with the a.p. setting. For this reversal of the expected results, a factor is responsible which was also met elsewhere: *the more central to the situation is F_1, the greater the "contact" between the S and the crucial object.* For example, the candles, as the most important objects in the box problem, are undeniably in the center of the material offered, one might almost say: in the fixation point. And the box holding the candles profits from this. For, it is mostly emptied first, i.e., before the two other, less central boxes. The box of buttons, on the other hand, is a quite peripheral part of the problem. In the cork problem, the situation is to some degree similar. The same factor of "contact" was expressed in the remarks of two Ss when they solved the a.p. setting of the paperclip problem: "in handling the paperclips" (in affixing the square, thus in F_1), "I became aware of them."

TABLE 3

	Box	*Pliers*	*Paperclip*	*Gimlet*	*Weight*
$\frac{S(w.p.)}{S(a.p.)}$	2.3	2.3	1.5	1.4	1.3

"Contact" between S and object probably played a role also in the following proposal from the pliers experiment: "Break off a piece of the board and use it as the second support." The board stands, of course, in the center of the situation—the S even had it in his hand—just as did the candles in the box experiment. (Of course, the fact also has an influence here that the board can "give up parts"; further that, like the first support, it is wooden.)

Everything indicates that this factor of "contact" has sometimes an effect of facilitating the solution. "Contact" might well be able to overcome the necessarily accompanying fact that a F, which is relevant to the situation causes strong fixation.

5. Correlation of Quantitative and Qualitative Findings

Until now, the experimental results have been considered only in reference to the general difference between the w.p. and the a.p. settings. However, it is obvious that the different problems exhibit the hindering effect of heterogeneous fixedness of the crucial object in different degrees. The box problem shows the greatest difference between the w.p. and the a.p. settings, the weight problem the least.

If one orders the five problems according to the size of this difference, measured by its most important indicator, namely, the size of the quotient:

$$\frac{\text{no. of solutions with w.p.}}{\text{no. of solutions with a.p.}},$$

abbreviated:

$$\frac{S(\text{w.p.})}{S(\text{a.p.})},$$

the rank order in Table 3 results.

In the following discussion, we shall include the cork problem as well. This problem was surprisingly seldom solved in the a.p. setting; see Table 2. The w.p. setting of this problem was given only subsequently, it is true, i.e., after the a.p. or the a.p.′ setting. Therefore the uncommonly large quotient

$$\frac{S(\text{w.p.})}{S(\text{a.p.})} = \frac{72.7}{14.3} = 5.1$$

is not fully analogous to the quotients of Table 3, and probably too large in comparison with them. Yet an entirely analogous quotient would probably still be among the largest.

Let us now examine these characteristic differences of the quotients in their relation to the psychological nature of the problems concerned. To this end we shall investigate each one of the six a.p. problems as to all the factors which might be supposed to hinder the required recentering. In Table 4, in the left-hand column, is a list of ten such factors, beginning with those which are probably

TABLE 4*

	Cork	*Box*	*Pliers*	*Paper-clips*	*Gimlet*	*Weight*
1. No signalling of the perceptual properties of the crucial object	+	+	—	—	—	—
2. F_1 still quite real	+	+	—	+?	—	+
3. F_1 habitual for the crucial object	+	+	+	+	+	—
4. The crucial object not familiar as "differently applicable"	—	—	—	+	+	—
5. F_2 not familiar as realizable by different objects	+	—	+?	+	+?	—
6. The crucial object must first be altered for F_2	+?	+?	—	+	—	—
7. F_1 given really (not merely "in thought")	+	+	+	+	+	—
8. The crucial object individually identical in F_1 and F_2	+	+	+	—	+	+
9. The crucial object not very suitable for F_2	+	—	+?	—	—	—?
10. The crucial object not ready for F_2 as a result of F_1	+	+	+	+	—?	+

* Explanations: + means that the hindering factor is present.
— means that it is not present.
+? means that it is probably to some degree present.
—? means that it is hardly present.

the most effective. (The more precise explanation and analysis of these factors will follow in the next paragraph.) The six problems are given side by side above, ordered from left to right according to diminishing quotients

$$\frac{S(\text{w.p.})}{S(\text{a.p.})}.$$

If one of the six problems contains one of the ten hindering factors, this is indicated by a plus sign at the proper place in the table. A positive correlation between the quotients of the different problems on the one hand and the number and probable weight of the hindering factors on the other hand should therefore be noticeable in an increase of plus signs from right to left.

6. Analysis of the Factors Which Hinder Recentering

For the understanding of Table 4, an analysis of the ten hindering factors is required. We shall treat them in order.

1. "No signalling of the perceptual properties of the crucial object." In all six problems, an application or function of the object sought is originally anticipated, "something to. . . ." But for a search in the perceptual field—in our problems, the table is searched with the eyes—such a functional and topical signal is too vague, too *unprägnant.* Visual search concerns visual properties. *The functional and topical anticipation must therefore be transformed into an anticipation in terms of perceptual content, into a signalling of visual contents, in order to be prägnant, to "hit."*

Example: Something is sought "with which to drive a nail into the wall" (see the weight problem). This topical anticipation forthwith arouses the visual image of a hammer or of an object like a hammer, i.e., hard and heavy (transformation into signal in terms of content). And not until there is such a visual model is the visual search begun.

How promptly the original topical anticipation may lead to an (approximate) anticipation in terms of content follows from these remarks of Ss in the weight problem: "I am accustomed to use as a hammer whatever is at all solid and heavy," or: "Often enough I take a stone, if I have no hammer." It is generally true that, the more typical the function F_2 is for the crucial object or its like, the more easily the original signal by function is transformed into a signal by content appropriate to the crucial object.

Analogously in the pliers problem, the functional and topical anticipation: "a support for the board," immediately calls forth the anticipation by content: "something long, solid. . . ." Just so, the anticipation: "something from which to hang a cord," suggests something in the form of a hook or of an eyelet.

Two of our problems—the cork and the box problem—are in this respect worse off than the rest. Here, as a rule, the original functional and topical signal did not succeed in arousing an adequate model of search in terms of content. It could be seen quite clearly how in these two problems the visual search frequently took place under the original function-signal as such ("something to fix the bar which is a bit too short," or, "something to fasten the candles to the door"). But that means that here—*faute de mieux*—the search is with an *unprägnant* signal.

To such anticipations of function, not defined by content, quite different objects may correspond. The candles could simply be fastened to the door somehow or other with tacks or with the help of a cord or of a plug—solutions which were often actually tried. In other words, the anticipation was not specifically directed to something like boxes. It was interesting to see, both from reports and from observed behavior, that, with the box problem, two of the three successful Ss in the a.p. group arrived at the solution in this way: they started from tacks and looked for a "platform to be fastened to the door with tacks." To these Ss, therefore, the tacks suggested a signal already fairly concrete, which in turn could not fail to suggest immediately the visually represented properties: "light material," "supporting surface"—perhaps, as immediately as in the pliers problem the support-function suggests the visual properties: "something long, stable . . ."

Now, if the general function alone is anticipated, there is a "gap" between signal and object. The filling in of this "gap" has to start from "below," from the object.[3] *And it is really this emergence of the new centering* (F_2) *from the object itself which is hindered by functional fixedness of this object.*

This statement will find corroboration in further experimental results to be cited below. There we shall see that a heterogeneous functional fixedness of the crucial object is unable to resist a sufficiently "pointed" (*prägnant*) property-signal. For the time being, the statement will suffice that the condition: "no signalling of perceptual properties of the crucial object," radically hinders a recentering.

2. "F_1 still quite real" means that at the time in which F_2 becomes real the function F_1 is still psychologically real, still "lives" as function. The boxes, e.g., persist in their ("static") function of con-

[3] See related material on "suggestion from below" in Chapter I.

tainers. On the other hand, the ("dynamic") pliers-function of the pliers actually ceases along with its use as pliers. Here, therefore, no more than after-effects of the function F_1 exist at the time when F_2 becomes real. In a more general sense of the word (if we include after-effects in "reality"), F_1 is of course in both cases "still real."

This general factor, the "overlapping of the spheres of reality of F_1 and F_2," will also be subjected to closer examination in the report on further experiments. Here its immediate plausibility may suffice: if something like functional fixedness exists at all, it must be the greater, the more real F_1 still is.

A few examples from other experiments and observations: A child builds a tower. This collapses. A block remaining upright promptly becomes a "soldier," and when the "soldier" falls, it at once becomes a "sword." This chain of recenterings is made possible, *inter alia,* through the fact that every time a structure is destroyed from without (cf. the collapse of the tower), the old function vanishes, so that the object becomes once more relatively *neutral.*—This same reduction of "reality" can be caused by "satiation." The recentering of playthings to be observed so often with children typically appears after they have played with a given object for some time and after satiation has therefore set in. According to Karsten, satiation finds its clearest expression in striving for variation. On the other hand, often it is indubitably the unfolding of the F_2-situation which destroys the "reality" of the old situation and of the function F_1 indigenous to it. In reference to this, an observation of my own: I lay the pencil as bookmark between two pages, while I read something at another place in the book. I wish to make a note on what I have read here, and unhesitatingly take for the writing (F_2) the pencil, whose function as a bookmark then naturally becomes illusory. This is facilitated by the further fact that the function "for writing" is the habitual function of the pencil.

3. "F_1 habitual for the crucial object" means that the function F_1 has really passed into the "flesh and blood" of the crucial object, and can now be called its "quasi-property." Now this is not the case with the weight problem. A weight is for weighing, but it is by no means familiar as pendulum weight. To be sure, a weight may originally have about as much affinity to a pendulum weight (F_1) as to a hammer (F_2). An object is of course especially easy to recenter when F_2 represents its original function which is only temporarily supplanted by F_1. (Example: a large log of firewood,

still to be chopped, which has served as chopping block for its like, is itself eventually chopped up.)

4. "The crucial object not familiar as 'differently applicable.'" It is clear that a heterogeneous pre-utilization will "fix" the object the less, the more this object already has the character: "variously applicable." A box, a pair of pliers, e.g., are probably less specialized in function than a paperclip or a gimlet. Thus, pliers are often used as substitute for a hammer, a box frequently as support.

A parallel from Köhler's experiments: "Besides, the blanket is seen and used daily, and is thus unique and in a different category from other objects." This is given as partial explanation of the fact that the blanket was relatively promptly used as substitute for a stick. The effect of the daily handling can hardly be conceived otherwise than in the sense of our factor of variable applicability—in connection with the factor of "contact."

5. "F_2 not familiar as realizable by different objects." Some functions are "fixed" from the start to quite definite objects; other functions may be realized by rather heterogeneous objects. The statement of a subject: "I am accustomed to use anything suitable as a hammer," points directly to the fact that the hammer function does not tend to be very fastidious in the selection of its objects. In the same way, the function F_2 in the box problem: "something on which to put . . ." has, of course, countless possibilities of realization in objects. In the course of time one does put almost everything on about everything else.

6. "The crucial object must first be altered for F_2." This factor is unambiguously present in the paperclip problem. A paperclip which is unbent and a proper paperclip have not much more in common than their material. To be sure, in the box problem, and similarly in the cork problem, the necessary alteration does not happen to the crucial objects *per se;* but it does happen to the visual whole of which the crucial object is a part. An empty box is visually something other than a filled one, an isolated stopper something other than one "sticking in" a bottle. An alteration (in our case, a rupture) of a whole alters the phenomenal character of the part.

7. "F_1 given really (not merely 'in thought') means that F_1 was or is an actual 'fact,' that it is not merely ideally ('merely psychologically') given"—as is the function of the weight as a pendulum weight in the weight problem. (Despite the string fastened to it,

the pendulum weight would be fully realized only if the pendulum were hung up.)

8. "The crucial object individually identical in F_1 and F_2." Only in the paperclip problem does F_2 not take place with the identical object of F_1, but merely with a representative of the same *genus proximum*. A whole genus may be functionally "fixed."

9. "The crucial object not very suitable for F_2." This factor is related to Factor 1. The less adequate F_2 is for the object, the more difficult is the recentering into F_2. Pliers and cork were sometimes perceived as not especially suitable for F_2, and once this happened with the weight.

10. "The crucial object not ready for F_2 as a result of F_1." This factor is just about the rule in our problems. Yet it happened in the gimlet problem that the gimlet used for boring (F_1) obtruded itself as a thing on which to hang the cord because it was already sticking in place.

By this discussion, the ten hindering factors in Table 4 ought to have become concrete. Now if we look at Table 4, at least one thing must strike us immediately: the great difference between the first two problems and the sixth, in respect to the number and weight of the hindering factors. We have here all the correlation with our quantitative results which one can wish for. Also in respect to the difference between the first two and the last four problems, the correlation is fairly good—as good as one can expect with factors considered merely in a qualitative, not in a quantitative sense.

[15]
Mild Stress and Problem Solving

WILBERT S. RAY

This paper reports experiments to test the assumption that stress interferes with problem-solving. The experiments supported the

---

SOURCE: Wilbert S. Ray, "Mild Stress and Problem Solving," *The American Journal of Psychology*, 1965, **78**, 227–234. Reprinted by permission of *The American Journal of Psychology*.

hypothesis. The stress used in each case was rather mild. It was an experimentally-induced drive rather than the generalized drive inferred from manifest-anxiety scales.

Problems exist only in situations in which the correct response is not the first to appear, is not the dominant response. It has been pointed out, *e.g.* by Maltzman and Taylor, that Hull's multiplicative drive-theory implies that an increase in drive-strength will increase the reaction-potential of the already dominant response more than the reaction-potential of the correct but weaker response. It will therefore be more difficult for the organism to produce the correct response as drive-strength increases. The effect will be greater with more complex problems with their greater difference between the dominant and non-dominant responses. Hull has applied this hypothesis, that increasing drive will increase the differential, to one specific sort of problem-solving—the *Umweg* problem.

* * *

Set for Speed as an Inhibitor of Problem-Solving

This is a repetition of an experiment on inhibition accompanying a set for speed performed by the writer's classes, in experimental psychology in 1957.

There is an experimental basis for set for speed as an independent variable in the work of Weiss, who found an inhibitory effect from a set for speed in a situation that is at least much like problem-solving. The problem employed was a simplified form of the puzzle, "The Tower of Hanoi" —also known as the "Tower of Brahma"—in which S transfers a tower of disks from one peg to a vacant peg, moving one disk at a time without placing a larger disk on top of a smaller, and using a third peg as a way-station. The shortest solution of the problem in number of moves being 2^n-1 disks, an n of only four disks was used. S made the transfer only once each.

Conditions. In the experimental condition the Ss were requested to work as fast as possible, the request being emphasized by ostentatiously starting a stopwatch with the signal to begin. The control group did not receive these instructions, or see the stopwatch.

Subjects. The Ss were 32 students from a class in general psychology who participated in the experiment as part of their assigned course work.

Results. All Ss solved the problem. Figures for the dependent variables are shown in Table 1. The speed-group made more moves, at a statistically significant level, but showed no difference in the total amount of time needed for the problem. They worked faster in the sense of using less time per move.

Heterogeneity of variance was unexpectedly found in the previous experiment (May), and since it was found there it was predicted here. The size of the variance in the control groups of the two experiments was about the same, but in the experimental groups the amount decreased markedly, presumably because of more careful control of the experimental conditions. This decreased the difference between the two groups in this present experiment, but the difference is still significant. Since differences in number of moves and of variance were predicted, one-tailed tests are used.

TABLE 1

The Effects of a Set for Speed
(16 Ss in each group)

	Speed Group	*Non-speed Group*		*P**
Mean no. of moves	37.75	24.56	$t = 2.37$	.02
Mean no. of sec.	172.06	173.31		
Variance of moves	347.19	116.00	$F = 2.99$	.03

* Tests are one-tailed.

The minimal number of moves necessary to re-stack four disks is 15. If we subtract 15 from each of the means for moves in Table 1, we have 22.75 errors in the experimental and 9.56 errors in the control condition.

Discussion. An increase in variance in an experimental group has also been reported by Anderson, who found it when Ss were required to shift back and forth between two problems at 3-min. intervals. She describes it by saying that "the shift-procedure enhanced differences between individuals." A similar statement applies to our results.

Weiss' report of impairment due to a set for speed has been mentioned above. Bruner, Goodnow, and Austin give somewhat similar results in a concept-attainment task, "time pressure has a relatively small deleterious effect on the success of focusing, but a major (deleterious) effect on the success of scanning."

Our major hypothesis is that stress will show an inhibitory effect on problem-solving, but the results reported and quoted here cannot be interpreted to mean that asking an individual to hurry will necessarily interfere with his work. The heterogeneity of variance suggests that the effect may occur only in some persons. The Bruner,

Goodnow, and Austin study suggests that the inhibition appears in some conditions and not in others. We may, then, assume that a set for speed perhaps produces stress in some persons under some conditions, and suggest that the impairment of the problem-solving appears only when the stress appears.

Inhibition Produced by Failure on a Preceding Problem

A third sort of stress which may be easily produced in mild degrees in the laboratory is frustration. It was assumed that failure to solve a problem would produce frustration which would inhibit a following problem, especially if the problems were very similar to each other. The failure was produced very simply by giving S an insoluble problem.

Conditions. The experimental task was a row of 46 digits mimeographed across a sheet of paper, containing 10 examples of sequences of three consecutive digits (*e.g.*, 3, 4, 5 or 5, 6, 7), with an *X* below the third digit in each of these sequences. This task was used in a previous study. S is requested to discover "What is it in the digits that tells where to put an *X*?" and then to put *X*s in the proper places in a "test" set of 14 digits at the bottom of the page. Time allowed was 12 min.

TABLE 2

Number Successful in Solving Numerical Problem after Frustration and No-Frustration Conditions

	Problem first (*No frustration*)	*Problem second* (*Frustration*)
N successful	34	23
N unsuccessful	35	48
Chi-squared = 4.13; *P* = .02		

The frustrating (failure) task was a similar set of digits and *X*s, but with no patterns among them. S spent 12 min. on this task also.

The two problems were assembled under a cover sheet, with the insoluble task as the second sheet and the real task as the third sheet for half the booklets, and with the two task-sheets reversed for the other half. These booklets were alternated in a pile and passed out to the Ss, who were assembled in one room. It was assumed that this would insure a random assignment of treatments to S.

Subjects. The Ss were the members of the three sections of a course in elementary psychology given in an evening college.

Results. The results of the treatments are shown in Table 2. Forty-nine per cent of the Ss in the control group were successful, but when the insoluble problem was presented first, the number successful fell to 32%. Chi-square was 4.13. Since it was predicted on the basis of the hypothesis about the effects of increased drive, and on the basis of the set-for-speed experiment, that the frustration would inhibit problem-solving, a one-tailed test is applicable, and thus we get a probability of approximately 0.02.

Discussion. This same experiment was tried with a class in elementary psychology at Bethany College some seven months previous to the trial described here. With 110 students divided equally between the treatments, 51% were successful in the control condition, and 38% succeeded in the frustration condition. This gave a non-significant Chi-square of 1.80. The difference between the two experiments was that in the Bethany situation the frustration- and work-periods were 7, rather than 12 min. in duration. After the first trial of the hypothesis we assumed that a longer failure period would produce more frustration and the change from 7 to 12 min. of failure did produce more failures in the succeeding experiments.

Roberts reports results which agree with those reported here. His task was a modification of the "Twenty Questions" task which has previously been used in problem-solving research. Roberts counted the number of clues each *S* received before identifying an object. In one condition the Ss had more failures in a preceding task than in the other condition, and the mean numbers of clues necessary were, respectively, 18.88 and 16.93. . . . The analysis of variance showed an *F*-ratio of 3.50, which provides a one-tailed significance level of 0.05.

General Discussion

The hypothesis offered above says that increase in drive strength will produce increasing inhibition of problem-solving, and that the inhibition will be greater with more complex problems. The inhibition will not start with zero drive strength, since there must be some minimal amount of motivation present to produce any work on the problem. That latter statement is reminiscent of analogous statements about the relation of drive strength to degree of learning. Deese concludes that associative factors in learning are not influenced by level of motivation, but "If an animal is to learn, it must be motivated at least enough to be goaded into activity."

The most popular current hypothesis concerning the relation of motivation level to problem-solving proficiency is that given, for example, by Krech and Crutchfield. They say, "As the degree of motivation increases from zero, the problem solving efficiency first increases and then decreases." In support of this function, they quote Birch,

> When motivation is very low the animals are easily diverted from the problem. . . . Under conditions of very intense motivation, the animals concentrated upon the goal to the relative exclusion of other features of the situation which were essential to the solution of the problem. . . . Those animals who worked . . . under intermediate conditions of motivational intensity . . . were not . . . incapable of responding to other relevant features of the problem situation.

Birch's statement can be recast into the form of ours without losing its applicability to his observations. Animals who were not motivated toward the problem did not work on it. Of the animals who were motivated, and who did work on it, those who were the most strongly motivated were the ones who showed the interference.

It is possible to say that the Krech and Crutchfield hypothesis is somewhat similar to ours if their inverted-bow-shaped curve is so distorted that the rising-facilitation half becomes our stipulation that there must be enough motivation present to produce work at the problem.

It is impossible to tell exactly what is meant by "high" and "low" drive, and it may be suggested that in the discussion of the interference of high drive with performance and learning "high" merely means the highest level used in some particular experiment, which gives no information as to the position of the drive level on any general scale of intensity. French's pseudo-fire, and Patrick's shock, cold water, and loud noise seem to be of a nature to produce high degrees of motivation, but Köhler's change of valence with increasing proximity of food is probably not classifiable as "very intense." The set-for-speed and frustration reported herein may be assumed to produce fairly mild intensities. Available evidence, then, supports the position that low degrees of motivation also inhibit problem-solving, and permits the hypothesis that any increase in motivation will interfere with problem-solving processes.

Comparison of the specific drives and the specific experimental tasks reported in the literature suggests that the inhibiting motivation is not necessarily directly related to the task. The hypothesis under discussion refers to the intensive dimension of the motivation rather than to its directional aspect.

Kendler and his associates assume that drive interferes with problem-solving responses that are low in the hierarchy, and not with those higher. This could be restated to say that drive interferes more with responses low in the hierarchies than with those higher, and their results can be interpreted to support this position. Such a statement would correspond to the section of ours that speaks of greater interference with more complex problems. Spence, Farber, and McFann's report on competitional and non-competitional paired-associates learning also supports this position on complex tasks.

If the hypothesis that increase in drive is accompanied by increasing inhibition of problem-solving, and that the increase is greater as problem complexity grows, is accepted, then it becomes desirable to attempt to explain the mechanism of such interference. Kendler and Kendler say, "It would be expected that a strong drive would retard problem-solving because it would retard the extinction of the dominant incorrect response." This would apply to both parts of our present hypothesis.

A further, and not incompatible, hypothesis is the generalization that an increase in drive will restrict the range of cue-utilization and thus interfere with at least some sorts of learning and perception, which may easily be extended to problem-solving on the assumption that ignoring of cues will prevent solutions of at least some problems. This would describe the work of the chimpanzees in the quotation from Birch above, and the behavior of Köhler's bitch in an *Umweg* problem of which he says, "When . . . the food . . . was dropped just outside the fence . . . she stood seemingly helpless, as if the very nearness of the object and her concentration upon it . . . blocked the 'idea' of the wide circle around the fence."

Summary

. . . It was suggested that, above a minimal level necessary to produce work at the problem, further increase of drive-level would produce increasing inhibition of problem-solving, the effect being greater with complex problems. Our experiments contradict the first half of the inverted-bow-shaped relation between motivation and problem-solving which has been postulated by previous theorists.

Bibliography

Ach, N. *Über die Willenstätigkeit und das Denken.* Göttingen: Vardenhoeck, 1905.

Adamson, R. Inhibitory set in problem solving as related to reinforcement learning. *J. exp. Psychol.*, 1950, **58**, 280–282.

Adamson, R. E. Functional fixedness as related to problem solving: A repetition of three experiments. *J. exp. Psychol.*, 1952, **44**, 288–291.

Adamson, R. E. & Taylor, D. W. Functional fixedness as related to elapsed time and to set. *J. exp. Psychol.*, 1954, **47**, 122–126.

Andreas, B. G. *Experimental psychology.* New York: Wiley, 1960.

Ashby, W. R. *Design for a brain.* (2nd ed.) New York: Wiley, 1960.

Bacon, F. *Advancement of learning and Novum organum.* New York: Willey Book Co., 1944.

Baernstein, H. D. & Hull, C. L. A mechanical model of the conditioned reflex. *J. gen. Psychol.*, 1931, **5**, 99–106.

Bain, A. *The senses and the intellect.* New York: Appleton, 1855.

Barron, F. The psychology of imagination. *Scient. Amer.*, 1958, **199**, 150–166.

Bartlett, F. *Thinking.* New York: Basic Books, 1958.

Benedetti, D. T. A situational determiner of the *Einstellung*-effect. *J. gen. Psychol.*, 1956, **54**, 271–278.

Berkeley, E. C. *Giant brains or machines that think.* New York: Wiley, 1949.

Bernstein, A. & Rubin, H. Artificial evolution of problem solvers. *Amer. behav. Sci.*, 1965, **8**, 19–23.

Birch, H. G. The role of motivational factors in insightful problem solving. *J. comp. Psychol.*, 1945, **38**, 295–317.

Birch, H. G. & Rabinowitz, H. S. The negative effect of previous experience on productive thinking. *J. exp. Psychol.*, 1951, **41**, 121–125.

Boring, E. G. *A history of experimental psychology.* (2nd ed.) New York: Appleton-Century-Crofts, 1957.

Bugelski, B. R. & Huff, E. M. A note on increasing the efficiency of Luchins' mental sets. *Amer. J. Psychol.*, 1962, **75**, 665–667.

Buss, A. H. Some determinants of rigidity in discrimination-learning. *J. exp. Psychol.*, 1952, **44**, 222–227.

Campbell, D. T. Adaptive behavior from random response. *Behav. Sci.*, 1956, **1**, 105–110. (a)

Campbell, D. T. Perception as substitute trial and error. *Psychol. Rev.*, 1956, **63**, 330–342. (b)

Campbell, D. T. Blind variation and selective retention in creative thought as in other knowledge processes. *Psychol. Rev.*, 1960, **67**, 380–400.

Carpenter, W. B. *Principles of mental physiology.* New York: Appleton, 1876.

Chown, S. M. Rigidity—a flexible concept. *Psychol. Bull.*, 1959, **56**, 195–223.

Claparède E. La psychologie de l'intelligence. *Scientia*, 1917, **22**, 353–368.

Cohen, M. R. & Nagel, E. *An introduction to logic and scientific method.* New York: Harcourt, Brace, 1934.

Cowen, E. L. The influence of varying degrees of psychological stress on problem-solving rigidity. *J. abnorm. soc. Psychol.*, 1952, **47**, 512–519.

Deese, J. Influence of inter-item associative strength upon immediate free recall. *Psychol. Rep.*, 1959, **5**, 305–312.

de Groot, Adriaan D. *Thought and choice in chess.* The Hague: Mouton & Co., n.v., 1965.

de Solla Price, D. J. Networks of scientific papers. *Science*, 1965, **149**, 510–515.

Dewey, J. *How we think.* Boston: Heath, 1910.

Drevdahl, J. E. Factors of importance for creativity. *J. clin. Psychol.*, 1956, **12**, 21–26.

Duncan, C. P. Recent research on human problem solving. *Psychol. Bull.*, 1959, **56**, 397–429.

Duncker, K. On problem solving. *Psychol. Monogr.*, 1945, **58**, No. 270.

Duvall, A. N. Functional fixedness: A replication study. *Psychol. Rec.*, 1965, **15**, 497–499.

Ebbinghaus, H. *Abriss der Psychologie.* 1908.

English, H. B. & English, A. V. *A comprehensive dictionary of psychological and psychoanalytic terms.* New York: Longmans, Green, 1958.

Flavell, J. H., Cooper, A., & Loiselle, R. H. Effect of the number of pre-utilization functions on functional fixedness in problem solving. *Psychol. Rep.*, 1958, **4**, 343–350.

Forster, N. C., Vinacke, W. E., & Digman, J. M. Flexibility and rigidity in a variety of problem situations. *J. abnorm. soc. Psychol.*, 1955, **50**, 211–216.

Frick, J. W. & Guilford, J. P. An analysis of a form of the water jar test. *Amer. J. Psychol.*, 1957, **70**, 427–431.

Gallup, H. F. Originality in free association responses. Paper read to Eastern Psychological Association, Atlantic City, April 1962.

Gardner, R. A. & Runquist, W. N. Acquisition and extinction of problem-solving set. *J. exp. Psychol.*, 1958, **55**, 274–277.

Gelfand, S. Effects of prior associations and task complexity upon the identification of concepts. *Psychol. Rep.*, 1958, **4**, 567–574.

Ghiselin, B. (Ed.) *The creative process.* Berkeley: Univer. of Cal. Press, 1952.

Gibson, J. J. A critical review of the concept of set in contemporary experimental psychology. *Psychol. Bull.*, 1941, **38**, 781–817.

Glucksberg, S. The influence of strength of drive on functional fixedness and perceptual recognition. *J. exp. Psychol.*, 1962, **63**, 36–41.

Glucksberg, S. Effects of verbal behavior on problem solving: Labeling the functionally fixed object. *Amer. Psychol.*, 1964, **19**, 575. (Abstract) (a)

Glucksberg, S. Functional fixedness: Problem solution as a function of observing responses. *Psychon. Sci.*, 1964, **1**, 117–118. (b)

Glucksberg, S. Personal communication. 1964. (c)

Golovin, N. F. The creative person in science. In C. W. Taylor (Ed.), *The 1959 University of Utah conference on the identification of creative scientific talent.* Salt Lake City: Univer. of Utah Press, 1959. Pp. 268–281.

Goodnow, J. J. Personal communication. 1965.

Gordon, W. J. J. *Synectics: The development of creative capacity.* New York: Harper, 1961.

Grant, D. A. & Berg, E. A. A behavioral analysis of degree of reinforcement and ease of shifting to new responses in a Weigl-type card-sorting problem. *J. exp. Psychol.*, 1948, **38**, 404–411.

Greenspoon, J. The reinforcing effect of two spoken sounds on the frequency of two responses. *Amer. J. Psychol.*, 1955, **68**, 409–416.

Guetzkow, H. An analysis of the operation of set in problem-solving behavior. *J. gen. Psychol.*, 1951, **45**, 219–244.

Guilford, J. P. Creativity. *Amer. Psychol.*, 1950, **5**, 444–454.

Guilford, J. P. The structure of intellect. *Psychol. Bull.*, 1956, **53**, 267–293.

Guilford, J. P. Intelligence: 1965 model. *Amer. Psychol.*, 1966, **21**, 20–26.

Guilford, J. P. Traits of creativity. In H. H. Anderson (Ed.), *Creativity and its cultivation.* New York: Harper, 1959.

Guilford, J. P., Wilson, R. C., Christensen, P. R., & Lewis, D. J. A factor-analytic study of creative thinking: I. Hypotheses and description of tests. *Reports from the Psychological Laboratory, No. 4.* Los Angeles: Univer. of Sth. Cal. Press., 1951.

Harlow, H. F. The formation of learning sets. *Psychol. Rev.*, 1949, **56**, 51–65.

Helmholtz, H. *Vorträge und Reden.* Vol. 1. Braunschweig: Vieweg, 1896.

Herrick, C. J. *Brains of rats and men.* Chicago: Univer. of Chicago Press, 1926.

Hoffman, H. S. The analogue lab: A new kind of teaching device. *Amer. Psychol.*, 1962, **17,** 684–694.

Houston, J. P. & Mednick, S. A. Creativity and the need for novelty. *J. abnorm. soc. Psychol.*, 1963, **66,** 137–141.

Hull, C. L. The mechanism of the assembly of behavior segments in novel combinations suitable for problem solution. *Psychol. Rev.*, 1935, **42,** 219–245.

Hull, C. L. Goal attraction and directing ideas conceived as habit phenomena. *Psychol. Rev.*, 1931, **38,** 487–506.

Hull, C. L. The problem of stimulus equivalence in behavior theory. *Psychol. Rev.*, 1939, **46,** 9–30.

Humphrey, G. *Thinking: An introduction to its experimental psychology.* New York: Wiley, 1951.

Hurlock, E. B. The evaluation of certain incentives used in school work. *J. educ. Psychol.*, 1925, **16,** 1–49.

James, W. *Principles of psychology.* New York: Holt, 1890.

Jenkins, J. J. Mediated associations: Paradigms and situations. In C. N. Cofer and B. S. Musgrave (Eds.), *Verbal behavior and learning: Problems and processes.* New York: McGraw-Hill, 1963.

Judson, A. J., Cofer, C. N., & Gelfand, S. Reasoning as an associative process: II. "Direction" in problem solving as a function of prior reinforcement of relevant responses. *Psychol. Rep.*, 1956, **2,** 501–507.

Karp, S. A validity study of a measure of creativity. Senior honors thesis, Univer. of Mich., 1960.

Kendler, H. H., Greenberg, A., & Richman, H. The influence of massed and distributed practice on the development of mental set. *J. exp. Psychol.*, 1952, **43,** 21–25.

Kendler, H. H. & Karasik, A. D. Concept formation as a function of competition between response-produced cues. *J. exp. Psychol.*, 1958, **55,** 278–283.

Kendler, H. H. & Kendler, T. S. Vertical and horizontal processes in problem solving. *Psychol. Rev.*, 1962, **69,** 1–16.

Köhler, W. *The mentality of apes.* New York: Harcourt, Brace, 1925.

Kowalski, J. Attitudes and occupational interests of creative individuals. Senior honors thesis, Univer. of Mich., 1960.

Krech, D. & Crutchfield, R. S. *Elements of psychology.* New York: Knopf, 1958.

Krechevsky, I. "Hypotheses" in rats. *Psychol. Rev.*, 1932, **39,** 516–532.

Leeper, R. Cognitive processes. In S. S. Stevens (Ed.), *Handbook of experimental psychology*. New York: Wiley, 1951.

Long, L. & Welch, L. Reasoning ability in young children. *J. Psychol.*, 1941, **12**, 21–44.

Luchins, A. S. Mechanization in problem solving: The effect of *Einstellung. Psychol. Monogr.*, 1942, **54,** No. 248.

Luchins, A. S. & Luchins, E. H. New experimental attempts at preventing mechanization in problem solving. *J. gen. Psychol.*, 1950, **42,** 279–297.

Maier, N. R. F. Reasoning in white rats. *Comp. Psychol. Monogr.*, 1929, **6,** No. 29.

Maier, N. R. F. Reasoning in humans: I. On direction. *J. comp. Psychol.*, 1930, **10,** 115–143.

Maier, N. R. F. Reasoning in humans: II. The solution of a problem and its appearance in consciousness. *J. comp. Psychol.*, 1931, **12,** 181–194.

Maier, N. R. F. An aspect of human reasoning. *Brit. J. Psychol.*, 1933, **24,** 144–155.

Maltzman, I. Thinking: From a behavioristic point of view. *Psychol. Rev.*, 1955, **62,** 275–286.

Maltzman, I. On the training of originality. *Psychol. Rev.*, 1960, **67,** 229–242.

Maltzman, I., Belloni, M., & Fishbein, M. Experimental studies of associative variables in originality. *Psychol. Monogr.*, 1964, **78,** No. 580.

Maltzman, I., Bogartz, W., & Breger, L. A procedure for increasing word association originality and its transfer effects. *J. exp. Psychol.*, 1958, **56,** 392–398.

Maltzman, I. & Morrisett, L., Jr. Different strengths of set in the solution of anagrams. *J. exp. Psychol.*, 1952, **44,** 242–246.

Maltzman, I. & Morrisett, L., Jr. The effects of single and compound classes of anagrams on set solutions. *J. exp. Psychol.*, 1953, **45,** 345–350. (a)

Maltzman, I. & Morrisett, L., Jr. Effects of task instructions on solution of different classes of anagrams. *J. exp. Psychol.*, 1953, **45,** 351–354. (b)

Maltzman, I., Simon, S., Raskin, D., & Licht, L. Experimental studies in the training of originality. *Psychol. Monogr.*, 1960, **74,** No. 493.

Mearns, H. *Creative power: The education of youth in the creative arts.* New York: Dover, 1958.

Mednick, S. A. The associative basis of the creative process. *Psychol. Rev.*, 1962, **69,** 220–232.

Miller, N. E. Liberalization of basic S-R concepts: Extensions to conflict behavior, motivation, and social learning. In S. Koch (Ed.), *Psychology: A study of a science*. Vol. 2. *General systematic formulations, learning, and special processes*. New York: McGraw-Hill, 1959.

Moore, O. K. & Anderson, S.B. Modern logic and tasks for experiments on problem-solving behavior. *J. Psychol.*, 1954, **38**, 151–160.

Newell, A., Shaw, J. C., & Simon, H. A. Elements of a theory of human problem solving. *Psychol. Rev.*, 1958, **65**, 151–166.

Osborn, A. F. *Applied imagination.* (Rev. ed.) New York: Scribner's, 1957.

Osgood, C. E. *Method and theory in experimental psychology.* New York: Oxford Univer. Press, 1953.

Patrick, C. *What is creative thinking?* New York: Philosophical Library, 1955.

Peterson, G. M. An empirical study of the ability to generalize. *J. gen. Psychol.*, 1932, **6**, 90–114.

Poe, E. A. Maelzel's chess-player. See any of various collections of Poe's works.

Poincaré, H. *The foundations of science.* Lancaster, Pa.: The Science Press, 1913, 383–394.

Popper, K. R. *The logic of scientific discovery.* New York: Science Editions, 1961.

Ray, Wilbert S. Complex tasks for use in human problem solving research. *Psychol. Bull.*, 1955, **52**, 134–149.

Ray, Wilbert S. A framework for problem solving. In G. Finch and F. Cameron (Eds.), *Symposium on Air Force human engineering, personnel, and training research.* Washington: National Academy of Sciences-National Research Council Publication 455, 1956.

Ray, Wilbert S. Generalization among meaningful relations in problem solving. *Amer. J. Psychol.*, 1958, **71**, 737–741.

Ray, Wilbert S. On the encouragement of original thinking among college students. *Liberal Educ.*, 1962, **48**, 396–404.

Ray, Wilbert S. Mild stress and problem solving. *Amer. J. Psychol.*, 1965, **78**, 227–234. (a)

Ray, Wilbert S. Three experiments on functional fixedness. *Pyschol. Rec.*, 1965, **15**, 489–495. (b)

Ray, Wilbert S. Problem-solving set as a function of number of reinforcements. *Psychon. Sci.*, 1965, **3**, 567. (c)

Ray, William S. *An introduction to experimental design.* New York: Macmillan, 1960.

Rees, H. J. & Israel, H. E. An investigation of the establishment and operation of mental sets. *Psychol. Monogr.*, 1935, **46**, No. 210.

Rignano, E. *Psychology of reasoning.* New York: Harcourt, Brace, 1923.

Rosenbaum, M. E., Arenson, S. J., & Panman, R. A. Training and instructions in the facilitation of originality. *J. verb. Learn, verb. Beh.*, 1964, **3**, 50–56.

Runquist, W. N. & Sexton, B. Supplementary report: Spontaneous recovery of problem-solving set. *J. exp Psychol.*, 1961, **61**, 351–352.

Russell, W. A. & Jenkins, J. J. The complete Minnesota norms for responses to 100 words from the Kent-Rosanoff Word Association Test. *Technical Report No. 11.* Minneapolis: Univer. of Minn. Contract N8 onr 66216, 1954.

Safren, M. A. Associations, sets, and the solution of word problems. *J. exp. Psychol.*, 1962, **64**, 40–45.

Scheerer, M. & Huling, M. D. Cognitive embeddedness in problem solving. In B. Kaplan and S. Wapner (Eds.), *Perspectives in psychological theory.* New York: International Univer. Press, 1960.

Schroder, H. M. & Rotter, J. B. Rigidity as learned behavior. *J. exp. Psychol.*, 1952, **44**, 141–150.

Selz, O. *Die Gesetze der produktiven und reproduktiven Geistestätigkeit, Kurzgefasste Darstellung.* Bonn: 1924.

Simon, H. A. & Newell, A. The uses and limitations of models. In M. H. Marx (Ed.), *Theories in contemporary psychology.* New York: Macmillan, 1963.

Skinner, B. F. *Science and human behavior.* New York: Macmillan, 1953.

Sprecher, T. B. A proposal for identifying the meaning of creativity. In C. W. Taylor (Ed.), *The 1959 University of Utah conference on the identification of creative scientific talent.* Salt Lake City: Univer. of Utah Press, 1959. Pp. 29–45.

Storms, L. H. Apparent backward association: A situational effect. *J. exp. Psychol.*, 1958, **55**, 390–395.

Székely, L. Knowledge and thinking. *Acta Psychol.*, 1950, **7**, 1–24.

Taylor, D. W., Berry, P. C., & Block, C. H. Does group participation when using brainstorming facilitate or inhibit creative thinking? *Technical Report No. 1.* New Haven: Yale Univer., Dep. of Industr. Admin., NR 150–166, 1957.

Terman, L. M. Genius and stupidity. *Ped. Sem.*, 1906, **13**, 307–373.

Thorndike, E. L. *The psychology of wants, interests and attitudes.* New York: Appleton-Century, 1935.

Thorndike, E. L. & Lorge, I. *The teachers word book of 30,000 words.* New York: Teachers Coll., Columbia Univer., Bur. of Publs., 1944.

Tresselt, M. E. and Leeds, D. S. The *Einstellung* effect in immediate and delayed problem solving. *J. gen. Psychol.*, 1953, **49**, 87–95.

Underwood, B. J. *Experimental psychology.* New York: Appleton-Century-Crofts, 1949.

Underwood, B. J. An orientation for research on thinking. *Psychol. Rev.* 1952, **59**, 209–220.

Uttley, A. M. The design of conditional probability computers. *Information and Control,* 1959, **2**, 1–24.

van de Geer, J. P. *A psychological study of problem solving.* Haarlem: Uitgeverij de Toorts, 1957.

Wallas, G. *The art of thought.* New York: Harcourt, Brace, 1926.

Walter, W. G. *The Living Brain.* New York: Norton, 1953.

Watt, H. J. Experimentelle Beiträge zu einer Theorie des Denkens. *Arch. ges. Psychol.,* 1905, **4,** 289–436. Published also as Experimental contribution to a theory of thinking. *J. anat. Physiol.,* 1905–1906, **40,** 257–266.

Whitehead, A. N. & Russell, B. *Principia mathematica.* (2nd ed.) Cambridge: Cambridge Univer. Press, 1925.

Wigglesworth, V. B. The contribution of pure science to applied biology. *Ann. appl. Biol.,* 1955, **42,** 34–44.

Wilson, R. C., Guilford, J. P. & Christensen, P. R. The measurement of individual differences in originality. *Psychol. Bull.,* 1953, **50,** 362–370.

Wolfe, J. B. & Spragg, S. D. S. Some experimental tests of "reasoning" in white rats. *J. comp. Psychol.,* 1934, **18,** 455–469.

Woodworth, R. S. *Experimental psychology.* New York: Holt, 1938.

Woodworth, R. S. & Schlosberg, H. *Experimental psychology.* New York: Holt, 1954.

Youtz, R. P. The relation between number of confirmations of one hypothesis and the speed of accepting a new and incompatible hypothesis. *Amer. Psychol.,* 1948, **3,** 248–249. (Abstract)

Index

Artificial intelligence, 89–93
Association, 122, 124, 134, 146, 147; *see also* mediation processes
  flat associative hierarchy, 122
  steep associative hierarchy, 23, 122

Brainstorming, 36–38

Characteristics of functional fixedness problems, Duncker's, 65–82, 178, 187

Definitions
  cognition, 5, 48–49
  cognitive operations, 49, 87
  creativity, 4, 22, 29, 114
  original thinking, 3, 4, 8, 22, 29, 114, 137
  problem solving, 5
  pure stimulus act, 146
  representational mediation processes, 5
  response hypothesis, 49, 85, 89
  thinking, 5
Desirable characteristics of tasks
  difficulty level, correct, 67, 75, 85
  overt behavior, 85, 89
  preference ratings known in functional fixedness, 78
  reliability, 50, 79, 84
  score continuum, 85
  validity, 84
Directing tendency, 47, 49

Discrepancies and other difficulties in data, 55, 58, 59, 61, 62, 69, 74, 75, 79, 81

Functional fixedness, 12, 24, 64, 177
  heterogeneous, 65, 177
  homogeneous, 65
  of thought material, 65
  relation to set, 76

Gimmicks for improvement of original thinking, 38, 45

Habit-family hierarchy, 19, 29, 31

Incubation, *see* unconscious
Intelligence level and originality, 52, 62

Massed and distributed practice, 56, 57, 62
Mediation processes, 5–8, 31, 32, 35, 53, 121; *see also* association
Spoken thought, method of, 69, 88–89
Motivation, effect on problem solving, 46, 51, 56, 62, 190–197

Operant behavior, 8, 21, 40, 97, 118, 126

Problem solving and thinking as part of learning, 35, 62–63

Problems; *see* tasks
Psychology vacuum effect, 35

Reinforcement, 118
- number of reinforcements, 56, 57
- partial reinforcement, 60, 62
- self reinforcement, 40, 57, 60, 119

Set, 12, 24, 47, 87
- *Einstellung*, 49, 173
- extinction, 51, 52, 56, 61, 88
- facilitation, 55–57
- inhibition, 57–59
- recovery from, 54
- recovery, spontaneous, 61
- susceptibility (susceptivity), 54, 76

Simulation of human problem solving, 89–93; *see also* trial and error
- criteria of genuine thinking capacity, 138
- intelligent machines, specific examples of, 89, 90, 92, 93
- Logic Theorist, 90, 91, 92, 109, 110

Synectics, 36–38

Tasks, experimental
- anagrams, 52, 53
- book, 65
- box, 65, 77, 87, 179, 186
- brick uses, 28, 29
- candle problem; *see* box problem
- concept-formation task, 53
- cork, 65, 182, 186
- digit patterns, 194
- Einstellung; *see* water jars
- gimlet, 65, 179, 186
- hat rack, 87, 117
- inclined plane, 86
- insight, 28
- making the last draw, 85, 89
- moments of levers, 84
- object naming, 28
- paperclip, 65, 180, 186
- picture, 9
- pliers, 65, 179, 186
- remote associates test (RAT), 11, 21, 22, 24, 25, 85, 89, 125
- Schroder-Rotter, 59
- standard experimental condition (Maltzman's), 17, 19, 89
- symbolic logic, 85
- tower of Hanoi, 192
- two-string, 13, 22, 86, 87, 116
- unusual uses, 20, 21, 28, 29, 84, 85, 112, 118, 120
- van de Geer's block, 76
- water jar, 12, 49, 50, 54, 55, 87
- weight, 65, 79, 179, 186
- Wisconsin Card Sorting Tests, 9, 55, 60–61, 85
- word association, 10, 17, 21, 53, 118
- yardstick, 65

Trial and error in thinking, 14–17, 105, 110, 132, 134, 142
- British Museum algorithm, 16, 108
- Twenty chimpanzees, 16, 108

Unconscious thinking, 45–46, 165, 166, 168, 170, 171

Würzburg, University of, 47, 50, 55